ETHNIC MINORITIES IN THE NATION STATE

MIGRATION, MINORITIES AND CITIZENSHIP
General Editors: Zig Layton-Henry, *Professor of Politics and Head, Centre for Research in Ethnic Relations, University of Warwick* and Danièle Joly, *Lecturer in Politics, Centre for Research in Ethnic Relations, University of Warwick*

This new series has been developed to promote books on a wide range of topics concerned with migration and settlement, immigration policy, refugees, the integration and engagement of minorities, dimensions of social exclusion, racism and xenophobia, ethnic mobilisation, ethnicity and nationalism. The focus of the series is multidisciplinary and international, and both theoretical and empirical works based on original research are included.

Ethnic Minorities in the Modern Nation State

Working Papers in the Theory of Multiculturalism and Political Integration

John Rex
Professor Emeritus
University of Warwick
Coventry

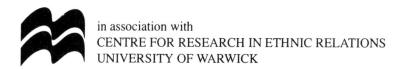
in association with
CENTRE FOR RESEARCH IN ETHNIC RELATIONS
UNIVERSITY OF WARWICK

First published in Great Britain 1996 by
MACMILLAN PRESS LTD
Houndmills, Basingstoke, Hampshire RG21 6XS
and London
Companies and representatives
throughout the world

A catalogue record for this book is available
from the British Library.

ISBN 0–333–65019–0 hardcover
ISBN 0–333–65020–4 paperback

First published in the United States of America 1996 by
ST. MARTIN'S PRESS, INC.,
Scholarly and Reference Division,
175 Fifth Avenue,
New York, N.Y. 10010
ISBN 0–312–12923–8

Library of Congress Cataloging-in-Publication Data
Rex, John.
Ethnic minorities in the modern nation state : working papers in the
theory of multiculturalism and political integration / John Rex.
  p.   cm. — (Migration, minorities and citizenship)
Includes bibliographical references and index.
ISBN 0–312–12923–8 (cloth)
1. Minorities—Political activity.   2. Ethnic groups—Political
activity.   3. Multiculturalism.   4. Pluralism (Social sciences)
5. Nationalism.   6. Ethnic relations.   7. Race relations.
I. Title.   II. Series.
JF1061.R49   1996
305.8—dc20   95–35009
                                                    CIP

10   9   8   7   6   5   4   3   2   1
05   04   03   02   01   00   99   98   97   96

Printed and bound in Great Britain by
Antony Rowe Ltd, Chippenham, Wiltshire

In honour of the late
Reverend Michael Scott
and of all he did in South Africa and the world
at large to promote the ideal and the reality of
ethnic and racial justice

Contents

Acknowledgements

The chapters of this book have arisen out of papers which I have given during the last few years of my Research Professorship and since my retirement. They are, however, very far from being the 'pipe and slippers' reflections of an old man. Rather they have arisen in sharp engagement with colleagues over some of the most difficult political issues facing Britain and Europe today and represent some of my own central political concerns.

These were not the issues which preoccupied so-called race relations research in Britain and they formed no part of the research programme of the Centre for Research in Ethnic Relations between 1984 and 1994. In these circumstances I owe a special debt to the University of Warwick for giving me a room and facilities in the Centre, and for allowing these privileges to continue in the five years since my retirement, and to the Economic and Social Research Council for two personal grants under the small grants scheme. Amongst colleagues in the Centre the closest to me in terms of my interests was Beatrice Drury and I am very grateful to her for the intellectual stimulation and personal support she offered me. Cathie Lloyd kept me in touch with the theorisation of ethnic relations by the French Left and I should also like to thank Danièle Joly without whose passionate opposition to racism, inequality and injustice the Centre would be a drearier place. My grateful thanks also to the two assistants who worked with me under my grants, John King and Yunus Samad. The so-called support staff were also important to me and by no means only for the technical assistance which they offered. Anne Shaw not only ran a fine Resource Centre but also on occasions helped me with skilled advice on my English. Liz Doyle-Saul was for a while my personal secretary, and someone whom I miss greatly since she left for another post. Rose Goodwin has handled this and many other typescripts for me with care and patience and Sam Hundal and Claudette Brennan have also given me help whenever I have asked for it.

Much of the stimulation and provocation which led to these papers, however, has been provided by my European and American colleagues, of whom I would especially like to mention the following: Alexandra Alund, Albert Bastenier, Rainer Baubock, Jochen Blaschke, Felice Dasetto, Catherine Delcroix, Liana Giorgi, Tomas Hammar, Friederich Heckmann, Jan Hjarno, Sev Isajiw, Magdalena Jaakola, Danielle Juteau, Riva Kastoryano, Giles Keppel, Didier Lapeyronnie, Remy Leveau, Karmella Liebkind, Albert Martens. Marco Martiniello, George Muskens, Jurgen Nielsen, Rinus Penninx, Ronald Pohoryles, Bente Puntervold Bo, Frank-Olaf Radtke, Jan Rath, Ben Ringer, Ake Sandar, Eva Sandis, Carl-Ulrich Schierup, Angela Sellner, Stephen Steinberg, Ed Tiryakian, and Michel Wieviorka. I know there are also many others and hope that they will accept my thanks collectively.

Finally, while I do not want in any way to undervalue the importance of intellectual stimulation as such, another dimension has always been added for me by many quite humble people from ethnic minorities who have explained the condition of their lives to me, as well as those from all groups who take part in the struggle for racial and ethnic justice. Outstanding amongst the latter during my lifetime was the Rev Michael Scott who, when he saw the injustice of White supremacy in South Africa, identified with and gave his life to working with and for the oppressed. I dedicate this book and the thinking and work which went into the making of it to his memory.

JOHN REX

Introduction

The study of ethnic relations in Britain in the 1950s and the 1960s was primarily concerned with the quantitative study of discrimination on grounds of colour and the degree of disadvantage to which such discrimination gave rise. In many ways it reproduced in a new sphere the kind of sociology which had previously been dominant in Britain in relation to the study of inequalities based upon class or occupational position. Whereas that sociology had been concerned with the relative life chances of manual and non-manual workers' children, the sociology of ethnic relations concentrated on the differences in these life-chances as between people of different skin colour.

In an early text on the nature of sociological theory (Rex, 1961), I had suggested that sociology should be about the relations between individuals in groups and between groups, and what passed as sociology was really nothing more than the book-keeping of social reform. What it did not deal with was the way in which those in the same income and other categories related to one another and to those in other categories and what they were likely to do about their condition. The assumption seemed to be that inequality existed primarily because of an absence of information and that, given this information, benevolent governments would put matters right. In what were perhaps rather simplistic Marxist terms it seemed to me that what British sociology lacked was any conception of class struggle, and that it was necessary to go beyond the facts of inequality to understand the forms of consciousness to be found in the various classes.

Very similar issues arose in relation to the study of what were commonly referred to as race relations in the late 1950s and 1960s. Despite the fact that successive governments had discriminated against dark-skinned people in immigration policy, the assumption underlying much academic, as well as political, discussion was that there was a government opposed to racial discrimination which only required the facts in order to put matters right. This was the assumption behind the successive surveys carried out by Political

1

and Economic Planning and the Policy Studies Institute (Daniel, 1968; Smith, D., 1977; Brown, 1984) as well as behind the various ameliorative policies adopted. Here again little, if any, attention was given to the nature of the groups involved and the strategies they pursued. Black people were seen primarily as victims and the amelioration of their condition was regarded as a routine task of government.

There was, however, also a rather different problem involved in the study of ethnic relations, for here it was not merely the case that those in a similar situation as a result of discrimination were forced by their condition to act together; the fact of the matter was that they were discriminated against, *inter alia*, because of their cultural characteristics, and that when they acted together they drew on pre-existing cultural resources. An additional question to that of equality and inequality, therefore, was that of how far policy would allow for the sustaining of these resources and how far it would seek to destroy them.

These questions were posed especially sharply in the schools in Britain. Much early research was focused on the differential educational chances of Black children and a major enquiry into the position of the children of immigrants in schools was focused on the relatively poor performance of Afro-Caribbean children in schools. This problem was compounded by the fact that many of the children of immigrants, especially those from South Asia, differed from their indigenous peers in their language, religion and home culture. Even if equality were to be achieved, therefore, there was the question of how far other cultures should be respected, sustained or encouraged in the schools.

One of the problems about the espousal of a multicultural policy which recognised different cultures was that such a policy did not necessarily go along with an insistence on equality. The danger was that the cultures of immigrant groups would be accorded recognition, but that members of these groups and their children would be treated as inferior, and that, worse than this, the use of cultural markers would actually aid the promotion of inequality. The problem therefore was to develop a democratic or egalitarian form of multiculturalism which coupled the recognition of cultural diversity with the promotion of equality between individuals. This was the main aim of the early papers in this volume. What they do is to shift the focus of research from studying minority members merely as victims to trying to look at their problems in terms of their own goals and values.

The first three chapters which follow deal with these questions. The first picks up the definition of 'integration' offered by the British Home Secretary, Roy Jenkins, in 1968 and uses it as the charter of egalitarian multiculturalism. It argues that such a concept rests on the recognition of two cultural or value domains, one a shared political culture of the public domain based on the idea of equality, the other a private or communal one based upon differences of language, religion and family customs. The sociology underlying this, however, is shown to be complex, particularly in the educational sphere, where schools as social institutions are seen to have dealings with both domains.

The second paper in this group looks not simply at the structural spelling-out of the ideal but at the actual institutional patterns which stand in the way of its realisation in Britain and other European societies. The implication of this seemed to be that the ideal of egalitarian multiculturalism had to be fought for and many existing institutional patterns swept away. By contrast the third paper appears more realistic. While it does not abandon the notion that it is essential for an acceptable form of multiculturalism that all institutions should foster the ideal of equality, it nonetheless recognises that it is inevitable that immigrants should accept an institutional framework imposed by the host society. While some gradual change could be envisaged in these institutions, it was not argued that there was likely to be a change from monoculturalism to multiculturalism in the indigenous society. Indeed the problem of multiculturalism is seen there as asking how, given the inevitability of some continuity in indigenous culture, there could still be a place for separate communal cultures.

By the time these papers were written, it had become obvious that the ideal of multiculturalism which I was thought to have been advocating was not acceptable to many European colleagues and some of their objections are spelt out in the papers that follow as well as in a book of carefully considered conference papers edited by Beatrice Drury and myself (Rex and Drury, 1994). Amongst the more important of these objections are: those which place such emphasis upon equal citizenship that they can see no place for the recognition of difference; those which see the creation of separate cultural institutions for liaison with minorities as undermining the unity of the working class or the institutions of a social democratic welfare state; those which see multiculturalism as simply a way of controlling inferior minorities; those which see Western European societies as based upon a precarious balance between class and status cultures, which is likely to be upset if it is called upon to assimilate more alien and distant cultures; and those which emphasise the diversity of response by minority members. Cross-cutting most of these criticisms is another one which suggests that the advocates of multiculturalism adopt what is called an 'essentialist' view of cultures, that is to say that they think of these cultures as having some kind of philosophical essence rather than as existing within and modifying social structures which can be studied empirically.

A number of the subsequent essays are concerned with clarifying what is meant by ethnic minority cultures and, more generally, 'ethnicity'. This leads to the repetition in several essays of the argument between what are commonly called the primordialist and the instrumental or situational views of ethnicity. These arguments were often developed within the framework of social anthropology and dealt originally with small-scale societies and structures. Even here there is need for the concepts which they use to be spelt out and sometimes supplemented, but these difficulties become even more acute when an attempt is made to extend the notion of the small-scale ethnic group to a much larger one called an 'ethnie', something which is inevitable with the spread of literacy and the improvement of means of communication. Here one finds a tendency towards polarisation amongst scholars as between those who still regard ethnicity as some sort of primordial and mysterious force and others who see it as an invention of elites seeking to control the masses in support of their projects. The view which is taken here is that there is some truth in both the primordialist position (at least when it is stated in a demystified form) and in the situationist one in that elites do call upon the resource of ethnicity primarily in order to mobilise the masses in support of their projects. What is necessary is a systematic sociology which looks at all the kinds of bonding which exist in human communities and societies. This would include kinship, neighbourhood and territorial relations, shared economic activities, shared beliefs and religion, shared language, and shared history, myth, or narrative regarding the group's origin. Some of these factors cut the group off from other groups; others like language, religion and the economy have the potentiality to establish connections with larger groups and precisely for this reason may come to be controlled because they threaten the group's autonomy.

Much of this sociological discussion has gone on in connection with the theory of nations, nationalism and the state and there is an important argument about whether the modern state, and the nationalist ideologies which support it, are a wholly new phenomenon quite distinct from that discussed in the theory of ethnies and ethnicity. Again the suggestion made in these papers is that the historical and political realities with which we have to deal involve both the development of political projects drawing on the resource of ethnicity and the creation of new social formations in accordance with the ideology of nationalism. It is unfortunate that a somewhat Eurocentric set of concerns seems to have directed the theorists of nationalism towards studying a pure type of nation state represented most clearly in post-revolutionary France. In the view taken here this is seen as one ideal type only and one which has to be used in conjunction with others in the analysis of concrete historical cases.

In the several papers which discuss the nation, the nation state and nationalism some attempt is made not merely to give due weight to the interaction between ethnicity and the modernising nation state, but also to point to the more complex problems which arise when nations conquer nations and establish empires or multinational states, and the even more complex problems which occur when imperial power collapses. It is this complex reality with which political sociology has had to deal since 1989 and a theory of nationalism worked out to deal with the problems of nineteenth-century Europe is hardly adequate to the task. Most important, the theory of nationalism today has to address itself to the problems posed by the emerging or re-emerging nations which came into being after the collapse of the Russian Communist Empire.

In any case, however, the theory of nations and nationalism by no means exhausts the study of ethnicity and ethnically based structures in the modern world. Most particularly it leaves out the study of migration. The only way in which the theory of nations and nationalism can deal with this problem is to represent such groups as diasporas and to understand their ideologies in terms of some kind of return to a lost Zion. One of the main aims of this set of papers is to draw attention to what is called, in the title of one of them, the 'second project of ethnicity'. This second project is migration and it is argued that the migrant ethnic communities which form across national boundaries cannot be understood in terms of the concept of diaspora.

One early essay contained here suggests that the study of migrant ethnic minorities must inevitably focus on people's differential relation to the means of production, a theme surprisingly lacking in arguments about nationalism, as well as in the sociology of post-modernism which seems to be arguing that relations to the means of production and, indeed, the simple question of earning a living, are no longer important, and that today group formation rests primarily on the quest for 'identity'. The position taken in these papers is by contrast, at least in a loose sense, a Marxist one. It sees the theory of nationalism as failing to deal adequately with class conflict, and post-modernist sociology, however relevant it may be to intellectuals in late-twentieth-century Paris, is out of touch with the problems facing migrant workers.

With this said, however, it is clear that the position of migrant ethnic minorities cannot be understood in terms of classical sociological class theory. Clearly this is true of any attempt to see them simply as an undifferentiated part of the working class. There is more to be said for treating them as a differentiated part of that class, recognising that the discrimination they suffer in the employment market gives them a distinct relation to the means of production and distinct interests. Even here, however, there are additional dimensions to the migrant's situation. He or she is related not merely to national society in the land of settlement, but to a global society, and the place of transnational migrant communities within it. Moreover it would be wrong to ignore the fact of cultural differentiation in itself. This cultural differentiation is, of course, a source of solidarity in pursuing shared interests, and that gives it continuing strength, but there may also be cultural values as well as material interests which migrant ethnic minority groups continue to defend.

If one wished to point to a single central theme in this book as a whole it is that of the relation between transnational migrant ethnic groups and nation states. In the present state of the world following the post-war migrations, the nation state is forced to deal with groups which have a transnational structure going far beyond national boundaries. It may seek to undermine these groups and to seduce its younger members into accepting a new purely national affiliation and identity, but present evidence would suggest that the migrant groups have sufficient strength to continue to exist despite some loss of members.

The ethnic minority group, however, does have, apart from its relation to the world economy, a particular problem of negotiating its position within the nation states where at any moment it is settled, and it is in terms of this problem that the notion of the multicultural society with which we started has to be understood. What all the papers here are attempting to do is to describe the structure of that encounter and to ask which minority interests can be accommodated in a democratic society. The argument is that, far from threatening such a society, the arrangements which are negotiated with minorities actually give its strength. Indeed it could be argued that what is necessary now in these societies is that the welfare state deal, through which problems of conflict of class interests were previously resolved, has to be supplemented by an additional compromise for dealing with migrant minorities, though these two deals cannot and should not be regarded as entirely separate.

A further complication is hinted at in these papers. Since the immigration stop in Europe in the early 1970s and, more particularly, since 1989, many of the foreigners arriving in European countries are not simply immigrants at all, but refugees or others fleeing from intolerable political or ecological conditions. The situation of these groups will mostly be considerably different from that of transnational migrant communities and will depend both on the strength of the moral legal and political commitment of host nations to recognising different kinds of refugee community, and on the differing degrees of interest in possible return among different refugee communities. Given the numbers now involved in these groups it would seem necessary not so much to abandon the theory of multiculturalism based upon the problems of immigrants, as to supplement it with another theory, or perhaps other theories relevant to refugees.

There is no doubt that since the outbreak of the Yugoslavian war, ethnicity is in ill repute. To speak up for the recognition of ethnicity is to be suspected of supporting 'ethnic cleansing'. One should, however, ask who it is in Western European societies who is embarking on such a policy. Immigrant ethnic minority groups wish to preserve their own culture to protect themselves, but they do not seek to impose it on anyone else. What really represent ethnic cleansing are the policies advocated by those in the host community who call for the exclusion of aliens or for the abandonment of their culture by those outsiders who settle.

The general ideas developed in the main papers here are also developed in several ways. On the one hand they come to be concerned with the way in which ethnicity is structured by particular features such as religion. On the other, they take up the problems of multiculturalism as they are presented in regions outside Western Europe.

Religion looms large as an element in ethnic conflict in many parts of the world. Two cases in which it does are discussed here, namely the conflict in Northern Ireland and that between Muslim immigrants and Christian/secular societies in Western Europe. What is suggested in both these cases is that although it may reinforce national, political and economic conflicts and the contending parties may assume religious labels, religion alone is not the source of the conflict, and any negotiated end to the conflict must deal with the underlying political and economic conflicts.

So far as Muslims in Europe are concerned, however, it must be admitted that at the moment they are feared by their hosts and they fear their hosts. So much is this the case that it can be argued that Islam is now a focus of 'racist' hostility at least as important as colour. This is usually expressed by describing Muslims almost indiscriminately as 'fundamentalists', a term which is taken to imply that those concerned are unchangeably beyond reason. Unfortunately such attitudes are shared not merely by minorities of racists but by commentators in the quality media and many social scientists. The position taken here is that it is necessary to look at the varieties of social, cultural and political stances taken by Muslims of various sectarian persuasions, and the compatibility of these positions with the normal processes of democratic societies. A consideration of these empirical facts would, I believe, show that it is possible to envisage a European society which recognises Muslim minorities and gives them a legitimate political place.

In terms of regional problems one area in which the theory of multiculturalism has to be developed is in the post-Communist and newly independent societies of Eastern Europe. Their new national governments now have the problem of deciding what recognition they should give to neighbouring nations also aspiring to independence as well as to the large minorities of settlers from Russia who have remained after the collapse of external Russian imperial domination. It would seem that Yugoslavia has broken up, and that separate ethnicities have been reinforced there leading to a state of ethnic civil war. None the less, in the future, as the economy recovers there will be a need for migration and there will still be within the separate nations problems of dealing with their own ethnic regions (as in the case of the Albanians of Kossovo). These problems are not dealt with here except in the most abstract terms and the only paper which deals with an East European society is that which discusses the possibilities of a multicultural society in Latvia. What it shows is that it is by no means easy to apply the general principles of multiculturalism to a formerly privileged and dominant minority.

The other regional extension of the theory of multiculturalism which is suggested here is to North America. The paper argues that what is being discussed under the heading of multiculturalism in the United States in the 1990s is rather different from what is being discussed in Europe. There the problem was that in the 1960s and early 1970s the Civil Rights programme and Affirmative Action had raised hopes of achieving the goal of racial equality, but that, when disillusion with this process began to set in, in many complex ways there was a move away from the notion of unity to one of separatism, and it was often this which went under the name of multiculturalism. It remains to be seen whether such separatism will lead to the negotiation of a new compromise involving equality for all, or whether there is, as Schlesinger suggests (Schlesinger, 1992), a move towards the 'disuniting' of America. This situation is also shown to be very different from that of Canada where the problems of race and the visible minorities has not until recently loomed as large, where the principal ethnic debate has been about the possible independence of Quebec, and where multiculturalism has been largely focused on the preservation of the heritage of other minority groups, mostly of European origin.

The papers in this book are papers which the author has been challenged to give in dealing *ad hoc* with a number of European political situations. They are strictly working papers. Nonetheless it becomes increasingly clear that they hang together in terms of an overall sociological and political theory the main lines of which are now beginning to emerge. They are published here in the belief that theory which arises in this way will give us a better grip on the political realities of the present than would a mere recapitulation or modification of mainstream theory. There is no reason why we should be theoretically philistine about this, however. What is being attempted here is the understanding of contemporary realities with the same clarity as was attained by Weber, Durkheim, or Marx, in dealing with the problems of their times.

What one would hope this book will achieve is to promote the discussion amongst social scientists as well as the general public of the kinds of problems which all modern societies are likely to have in dealing with ethnic difference, whether between geographically located national groups or between migrant minorities and national societies. From the point of view of social science these problems are arguably now of central importance, in the way in which those relating to class conflict were fifty years ago. From the point of view of the ordinary citizen they are, along with economic growth or survival, the central problem of politics today.

1 The Concept of a Multicultural Society[*]

INTRODUCTION

The establishment of the Centre for Research in Ethnic Relations in the University of Warwick marked the third stage of the initiative of the Social Science Research Council (now the Economic and Social Research Council) in the sphere of race and ethnic relations research. The Council originally established a Unit in the University of Bristol under the direction of Michael Banton in 1970. This Unit moved to the University of Aston under my own Directorship in 1979. Finally the Unit was transformed into a Centre which has now become fully part of the University of Warwick.

Although these changes have not prevented continuity in the Unit and Centre's work, it is of some importance to notice that at different stages the task of Units and Centres was envisaged differently by the Council. At first it was thought that they should do fundamental research, leaving short-term policy issues to be dealt with by government departments. Later, however, they were pressed more and more towards research with practical policy applications. Within the latter option, moreover, there was pressure to do research on commission for government departments.

In these circumstances it was necessary that the Unit should be clear about the principles of academic research. On the one hand its staff felt that they should perform more than a technical role, gathering facts which might be useful to government in the pursuit of undisclosed policy objectives. On the other if the *ends* of such policies were to be subject to criticism, some way had to be found of

---

[*] A lecture to mark the establishment of the Centre for Research in Ethnic Relations in the University of Warwick (Rex, 1986b).

distinguishing the value standards used by researchers from those of political partisans.

VALUE ORIENTATIONS IN SOCIAL SCIENCE

Fortunately these were not new problems. They had been discussed in 1939 by the great Swedish social scientist Gunnar Myrdal (1944), when he was invited to make a definitive study of race relations in the United States and the Unit was able to respond to the pressure to do policy-oriented research by reaffirming his fundamental principles. These were as follows:

(1) Social science always involves something more than the mere description of facts.

(2) It claims not merely that such-and-such is the case but that it is necessarily the case. That is to say, it not merely describes but explains.

(3) The concept of something being necessarily the case, however, has a special meaning in sociology. What is necessary from the point of view of one value standpoint is not necessary from another. What is necessary from the point of view of one interest is not necessary from the point of view of another.

(4) Sociology cannot of itself declare one value standpoint to be morally preferable to another. All it can do and what it certainly should do is to make its value standpoint or the state of affairs which it is taking as desirable, clear and explicit.

Myrdal, himself, in studying American race relations, chose to ask the question, 'what structures, institutions and policies are necessary to achieve the ends set out in the American constitution, as interpreted?'

The key to any honest approach to policy-oriented research is to be found in Myrdal's fourth principle. If asked what conditions are necessary for the successful implementation of policy, the researcher should ask for a clear and explicit declaration of policy goals. Unfortunately, all too often, when policy questions are posed there is no such explicitness or clarity. The honest researcher must therefore begin with a critical review of policy goals, making clear what states of affairs are being held to be desirable and claiming 'necessity' for any policy, institution or structure only relative to the stated goals.

What I am going to suggest in this chapter is that a new goal has become widely accepted in British race relations, namely that of the multicultural society, but that the meaning of this term remains remarkably obscure. One of the first and central tasks of a Centre for Research in Ethnic Relations must be to clarify its meaning, because it is in relation to the meaning given to the concept that our various specific researches fall into place.

Multiculturalism is a new goal for British race relations. It was not discussed much before 1968 and even today much research is directed by another and quite different value-standpoint, namely that which emphasises equality of individual opportunity. In theory, if not in practice, this other ideal is shared across a wide political spectrum and is certainly the basis of much discourse in the social service departments about social policy.

In the first fifteen years of its existence the Unit and Centre has concentrated very largely on the study of inequality and racial discrimination in the spheres of housing, employment, education and urban planning, and most of its work served to confirm in special institutional contexts the conclusion reached in successive Policy Studies Institute studies of national samples, that in all these spheres immigrant minorities from Asia, Africa, and the West Indies have suffered disadvantage due to racial discrimination (Daniel, 1968; Smith, 1977).

There is, of course, a need to continue such studies and to locate and publicise the origins of and responsibility for discrimination. But more and more of the problems posed to us are not about equality and how it can be promoted, but about the multicultural society, which, *prima facie* at least, must mean a society in which people are not equally but differently treated. If in fact we pretend that multiculturalism and equality are the same goal under different names we are creating precisely that kind of fuzziness which Myrdalian principles would suggest we should avoid. The issues which arise here originally arose for me in a sharp form when participating in the UNESCO experts' meeting on the nature of racism and race prejudice in 1967 (Montagu, 1972). The main theme of the statement that we drew up was about racial discrimination and inequality and how they could be overcome. Some Black American on the committee then argued that the statement should begin with an affirmation of 'the right to be different'. Our decision, however, was to exclude such a reference, because, as one member of the Steering committee put it, 'every racially oppressive and segregationist government would seize on the statement as a justification of inequality'.

It was surprising perhaps that the desire to include a reference to difference came from Black Americans. After all, the whole history of the Civil Rights movement had turned upon a rejection of the *Plessey* v. *Ferguson* decision of 1896 that facilities which were separate and segregated could nonetheless be equal. What was evident now, however, was that Black politics included another theme. Assimilation was rejected as a sign of equality. The goal of the Black Movement was to attain *equality of respect* for separate Black culture.

In Britain today there are many egalitarians who take a similar view. They believe that anti-racism and the goal of equality requires that all minority cultures should enjoy equal respect. But the unfortunate thing is that because of the fuzziness of the ideal of multiculturalism, they gain apparent support from many whose aim, far from being equality, is precisely that minorities should receive something different and inferior. This is particularly true in the sphere of education.

PLURAL AND MULTICULTURAL SOCIETIES

One good way of clarifying these issues is to look at the theories which sociologists and anthropologists have developed in studying plural multicultural and multiracial societies. It can be seen from these studies that such societies are far from providing us with an ideal and it must therefore be in some very special sense that we speak of such an ideal in contemporary conditions.

Most sociological theory had dealt with unitary societies or with conflict within society. Furnivall broke new ground, however, with his study of the plural society in Indonesia (Furnivall, 1939). There he found different ethnic groups living side by side but interacting with each other only in the market place. The result of this was that while the separate ethnic communities were governed by the morality and the religion and the kinship order, the market place was subject to no kind of moral control. While European capitalism had grown slowly out of the past and was constrained by some kind of common will, capitalism in Indonesia involved a market place in which one group simply oppressed or resisted another. The plural society was plural in two senses. One was that each ethnic community existed separately and had its own communal morality. The other was that the private and communal world was separated from that of the market place. The question which this raises for us is whether what we will achieve if we have a multicultural society is the encouragement of tight-knit communal morality within groups and a world of total exploitation between groups.

M. G. Smith argues along similar lines (Smith, 1965). Whereas, as he sees it, unitary social systems have a single and complete set of institutions covering the spheres of domestic life, religion, law, politics, economics, education and so on, it is characteristic of plural societies in the British West Indies that there is no such overall institutional set. Rather what we have is a number of ethnic segments each of which has its own nearly complete institutional set. These segments would in fact be separate societies were they not bound together by the political institution, i.e. the state. Putting this in another way Smith says that such societies are held together only because one group dominates the others. The various groups are differentially incorporated, if not *de jure* at least *de facto*. Here again it would seem the plural society model is a model of racial domination.

If we are to maintain the model of the multicultural society it must clearly be distinguished from that suggested by Furnivall and Smith. This can best be done by drawing a distinction between the public and the private domain. There appears then to be four possibilities:

(a) One might envisage a society which is unitary in the public domain but which encourages diversity in what are thought of as private or communal matters.

(b) A society might be unitary in the public domain and also enforce or at least encourage unity of cultural practice in private or communal matters.

(c) A society might allow diversity and differential rights for groups in the public domain and also encourage or insist upon diversity of cultural practice by different groups.

(d) A society might have diversity and differential rights in the public domain even though there is considerable unity of cultural practice between groups.

The ideal of multiculturalism, in which multiculturalism is held to be compatible with equality of opportunity, is represented by (a); (b) is possibly represented by the French ideal of assimilation of minority groups; (c) is common under all forms of colonialism and is represented above all by the South African apartheid system; (d) is the state of affairs which existed in the Deep South of the United States before the Civil Rights programme took effect. The crucial point about our multicultural ideal is that it should not be confused with (c). All too often it is, and those who support (c) are likely to accept the slogan of multiculturalism and bend it in that direction.

Let us now be more precise about what we mean by the public and private domain. In fact the notion of the two domains seems at first to be at odds with mainstream sociological theory, since most sociologists see all institutions as being interconnected with one another in a single system. This seems to me to be equally true of the functionalist paradigm as developed by Malinowski (1952) and Radcliffe Brown (1952), of the structural functionalism of Talcott Parsons (1952) and the structuralism of recent French Marxism (Althusser, 1969). In all of these the private domain is not an optional extra but plays a part in socialising individuals for participation in the public sphere. *Per contra* the public domain is seen as shaped by the morality which is inculcated in the family and through religious institutions.

The actual history of European social institutions, however, belies functionalist theory. The polity, the economy and the legal system have been liberated from control by traditional values and have been based on new values of an abstract kind. On the other hand it has seemed possible to permit the continuance of folk values and folk religions as long as these do not interfere with the functioning of the main political economic and legal institutions of society.

In fact a great deal of classical sociological theory deals principally with the evolution of the new abstract value systems which a large-scale society requires. Ferdinand Tonnies saw that folk community must give way historically to association and society, the first being based on the natural or real will, the second on the deliberate artificial and rational will (Tonnies, 1955). Durkheim wrote about 'organic solidarity' based on the division of labour, which would replace the 'mechanical solidarity' of small-scale community based on kinship (Durkheim, 1933), and, even more radically of an 'egoistic society' (Durkheim, 1952) in which values were located in the minds of separate individuals. Finally Weber saw in Calvinist religion and the Protestant ethic the end-point of an increasingly rationalistic trend in religion and, together with that, the development of political leadership based on rational legal authority (Weber, 1930).

Moral and legal systems of an abstract character thus were seen by all these authors as governing the social evolution of the modern state and of a formally rational capitalist economy. This is how what Parsons calls the Hobbesian problem of order (i.e. of how to avoid a war of all against all) was solved. This too is the significance of Furnivall's observation that the common will which charac-terised European capitalism was absent in Indonesia. It is under colonialism that we find what Marx called 'the callous cash nexus'. Economic and political institutions in Europe were embodied in what one might term 'the civic culture'.

The development of this 'civic culture' (e.g. the abstract public morality, law and religion) by no means implied the disappearance of folk morality, folk culture and folk religion. These now came to fulfil new functions. On the one hand they bound men together in separate communities into which individuals were socialised and within which they achieved their social identities. On the other they provided for what Parsons called 'pattern maintenance and tension management'. Living in a larger world with abstract moral principles was, so Parsons believed, only psychologically possible if individuals had the possibility of a retreat where they could enjoy more intimate relations and 'let their hair down'.

The ideal of the multicultural society which I have outlined above really presupposes the evolution of the modern type of society, of which Weber and Durkheim especially wrote. In simple societies morality and kinship structures had to govern the whole range of human activity. In an abstract and impersonal society a new more abstract form of law and morality had to be developed to govern large-scale political and economic organisations, while the old folk culture and morality helped the individual to retain some sort of psychological stability through more immediate social interdependence. Thus multiculturalism in the modern world involves on the one hand the acceptance of a single culture and a single set of individual rights governing the public domain, and on the other a variety of folk cultures in the private domestic and communal domains.

With regard to Marxist sociology and political thought, I think it contains a certain duality. On the one hand, the liberation of the market from traditional restraints represents for Marx the creation of precisely that type of society without a common will to which Furnivall refers. On the other, Marx may be seen as envisaging the emergence through class struggle of a new rational socialist economic order. To the extent that he does one may see Marx too as envisaging the possibility of a new civic culture.

THE INSTITUTIONS OF THE PUBLIC DOMAIN

We must now consider more closely the institutions of the public and the private domain and the ways in which they are likely to intrude on one another. As we shall see, education intrudes into both spheres and the communal ideologies which bind people together in the private sphere may have implications for their integration or non-integration into public life.

The main institutions which constitute the public domain are those of law, politics and the economy.

Law determines the rights of any individual and the way in which he or she is incorporated into society. The very mark of the plural society is that different groups and categories of people are differentially incorporated. In our ideal multicultural society, on the other hand, we are positing that all individuals are equally incorporated and that they have equality before the law. The ideals of the multicultural society and of its civic culture are not realised insofar as any individual or category of individuals are harassed or under-protected by the police or are denied access to or the protection of the courts.

In the sphere of politics again, in the plural society different groups have differing degrees of political power. In the ideal multicultural society each individual and group is deemed to have the same right to exercise political power through the vote or by other means. This does not exclude the notion of conflict but no individual or group should find the rules governing such conflict stacked against him. Participation in such a political system is part of the multicultural ideal.

The economy refers in the first place to the institution of the market. This involves the processes of bargaining and competition, and the sole sanction which an individual may use against the other is the threat to go to another supplier. The market should exclude the use of force and fraud. But while it is a rule-governed institution it excludes by definition the concept of 'charity'. This concept belongs to the world of community and folk morality. What is involved in market behaviour is the more abstract morality of sticking to the rules of peaceful market bargaining. The maintenance of such a system is another and quite central part of the civic culture and the multicultural ideal.

This is not to say that a market economy cannot be replaced by another type of allocation system or what is sometimes called the command economy, where certain abstract goals are made explicit and organisations are set up to advance them. But the best that such a system can achieve is formal justice. Here, as in the market economy, there is no principle of charity, which is again assigned to the folk community.

To say that these are the macro-institutions which are required in the civic culture of a multicultural society is not to say that such a society will always by totally harmonious and peaceful. The pursuit of directly political goals involves conflict, and markets, too, break down and give way to collective bargaining and political conflict. All that I wish to claim is that it is to be assumed in a multicultural society that no individual has more or less rights than another or a greater or lesser capacity to operate in this world of conflict because of his or her ethnic category.

Any suggestion that individuals or groups should receive differential treatment in the public domain is a move away from the multicultural ideal towards the plural society of colonialism. It would mean that groups were differentially incorporated *de facto* if not *de jure*. And this is true even in an atmosphere of paternalism. This would be the case, for example, if, while other groups had their needs provided by separate functional departments, all the needs of the minority were provided by a single Department of Minority Affairs.

It may perhaps be suggested here that the efflorescence of race relations programmes at local level reflects not a genuine multiculturalism but this trend towards different and separate provision. It is moreover a process which is very difficult to stop once in train, because a considerable number of individuals from minority groups may be rewarded for staffing it.

THE BOUNDARIES OF THE PUBLIC DOMAIN

So far I have discussed the institutions of law, politics and the economy as institutions of the public domain, and I have suggested that matters relating to the family, to morality and religion belong in the private sphere. However, the public domain is often extended through bureaucratic state activity in matters of the family and morality, particularly in the welfare state.

Two kinds of barriers are breached in the modern state. On the one hand it intervenes in the economic sphere through ownership, through control, and through subsidies to ensure efficient productions. But on the other hand it intervenes in what are essentially family and community matters. It directs the economy towards full employment so that all breadwinners may have jobs. It permits as well as directs trade-union activity to ensure job security. It makes provision through social insurance to ensure that individuals without employment have an income. It may build homes and let them, or subsidise the building of houses for private ownership. It may provide education for children and for adults and it may provide social work services to help in resolving personal and family problems. All of these activities involve breaches in the barrier between public and private domains. When the state provides, moreover, its provision is universally oriented. It cannot easily make its provision multicultural, or, if it does, it may provide unequally and unfairly for different groups.

Marshall (1950) has suggested that it is the mark of the modern state that in addition to legal and political rights, it provides a substantial body of social rights, and that this has led workers to feel a greater sense of loyalty to the state and nation than they do to class. In terms of my argument, however, there is an even more fundamental point. This is that much of the feeling of identification which individuals once had with the private domain and the local community is transferred to the state.

Undoubtedly functions have been lost by the family and community to the state, although there is an argument that state intervention actually supports the family and enables it to perform its primary tasks of consumption and socialisation more effectively (Fletcher, 1966). Because there is inevitably a degree of state socialist provision for family welfare in the modern world, this is an area for collaboration between public and private domains. When the state intervenes in education, however, more difficult problems arise.

EDUCATION AND THE PUBLIC AND PRIVATE DOMAINS

A modern educational system has three clear functions. *It selects individuals* on the basis of their achievement for training for various occupational roles. *It transmits important skills* necessary for survival and for work in industry. And *it also transmits moral values*. It is this third function which brings it into conflict with the private domain, for clearly one part of the socialisation process consists precisely in the transmission of moral values.

Clearly no ethnic minority will object to the selection mechanism being part of the public domain. What is important is simply that this mechanism should give equal opportunity to all. Again, if the minority is committed to living by employment in the industrial system, it will itself wish to take advantage of any skill training which is available. Moral training, however, involves other issues.

Insofar as it is concerned with the transmission of what we might call the civic morality and culture, the problems which moral training through the schools raises will be small. True, there will be doubts about the desirability of encouraging competitive and individualist values, because, taken out of context, these conflict with the principles of charity and mutual aid underlying local communities and the private domain. But this is an inherent tension in industrial society and one with which industrial man has learned to live. Moreover there are parts of the civic morality which are of value and importance to minorities. Especially this is true of the notion of equality of opportunity. Much more important than any objection to this aspect of the school's moral role is the objection to its interference in matters which are thought of as private or as involving individual choice. This is true of all matters relating to sex, marriage, the family and religion.

It is arguable that schools ought not to intervene in these matters at all or to do so only on the most general and basic level. Such an argument turns upon showing that a variety of practices in these spheres in no way prevents the proper functioning of the state and may positively assist it. The counter-argument is that it is of concern to the state how family matters are arranged, both because the state is concerned with the law of inheritance and because it has to uphold individual rights even against the family.

On family matters, however, there are considerable tensions between minority communities and the school in contemporary Britain. Amongst Asians, for example, there is a great emphasis upon arranged marriage and the relative exclusion and modesty of females. Neither the official curriculum of British schools nor the peer-group culture in which minority children inevitably participate foster the relevant values. Sometimes schools may be unnecessarily provocative, as when some of these require participation of girls in mixed swimming classes, but more generally the whole ethos of the school, based as it is on the encouragement of individual choice and free competition, strikes at the root of any tight-knit marriage and family system.

There is often a fundamental clash of values on these matters in any modern society. The notion of equality of opportunity appears to point to the rights not merely of families but to those of individuals, male and female, against the constraints imposed by families. Feminism has made the issues here especially sharp. It is unacceptable in terms of feminist values that a woman should be forced into a marriage or that girls should be denied the maximum degree of education because of some preconceived notion of the female role.

Such emphases in the argument are, however, quite misleading from the point of view of Asian parents and they fail to take notice of the fact that an arranged marriage reflects the care which the family shows towards its daughters, guaranteeing them a dowry far more substantial than anything which an English girl might get from her parents. Indeed it can be said that the whole system gives the bride more rights than does the notion of marriage based upon random selection and romantic love. Much more than this, however, the assertion of freedom in the sexual sphere is bound up with a whole set of values about the marketability of sex which is reflected in the media and in sex shops. The feminist demand for greater freedom is therefore seen as part of this larger package which offends against all Asian concepts of modesty and love.

There is no point in my seeking to resolve this clash of values here. It is simply important to note that it exists and that in a society which seeks to achieve equality of opportunity *and* the toleration of cultural diversity, institutional arrangements will evolve to deal with this tension. Parents will often identify with what the schools have to offer by way of equality of opportunity, but may seek to limit its role by the withdrawal of children from certain kinds of activity and by providing supplementary moral education outside the school.

Another potential source of discord is religion. Here, however, the way has been prepared in a Christian society for dealing with potential conflicts. Because the various Christian sects and denominations have engaged in conflicts, even in international and civil wars which have threatened the unity of the state, most nominally Christian societies have already downgraded religion to a matter of minor importance towards which there was no danger in exercising toleration. Once Roman Catholics were given the right to teach their own religion in schools there was no barrier principle to allowing Islam or Sikhism or Hinduism to be taught in a similar way. Difficulties only seemed to arise with quasi-religious movements like Rastafarianism because of their strong political content.

Wider than the religious question was that of instruction in minority cultures thought by many to be the key issue in any programme of multicultural education. But such innovations are often far from popular with minority communities, who see them as diverting energies from subjects more important to examination success, and in any case as caricatures of their culture. The strong preference of minority people is that unless such teaching can be carried out by minority teachers in schools, it is be done outside school-hours. While minority children learn about majority culture, perhaps provision should also be made for majority children to learn about minority culture, since this will foster equality by encouraging equal respect for other cultures.

The question of language creates greater dilemmas. Teaching in mother-tongue and teaching of mother-tongues have both been seen to be important in minority communities. Teaching in mother-tongue is vital at the outset for those who do not speak the main school language. If they are simply confronted by this other language on entering school, children's education is likely to be seriously retarded. What is required therefore is initial teaching in the mother-tongue with the main language gradually introduced until it replaces mother-tongue as a medium of instruction. Paradoxically, using mother-tongue as an initial medium of instruction can facilitate assimilation. Much more important, however, is the fact that it promotes equality of opportunity.

Systematic provision for the teaching of mother-tongue is beyond the means of most minority communities, and if it were literally left to mother, the mother-tongue would simply become a restricted ghetto language. What minority people want is financial support for language that could be used to enlarge the cultural experiences of the group. In the kind of society we are discussing it can never attain equality with the main language in some sort of bilingual state. But there is no reason why minority people should not be able to express themselves and communicate with each other about their experiences in their own language.

Once we recognise the inherent tensions to be found in the educational system, because it is at once part of the public and private domain it is possible to envisage a balance of control. The school should be concerned as the agent of the public domain with selection, with the transmission of skills and with what we have called here the civic morality. The community should control education in all matters having to do with their own language, with religion and with family affairs. In a multicultural society, the state should provide financial support for this.

The other alternative is to take education out of the public domain and make it an intra-communal matter. This is what has been done in England in the case of Catholic schools and, in principle, no new ground is opened up if, say, Muslim or Hindu schools receive similar recognition. Obviously there would be a danger in such schools that the task fulfilled by the mainstream schools would be subordinated to the inculcation of communal values, but it is also possible that a balance could be struck in which the controllers of minority schools themselves recognised the instrumental value of education in a modern society along with education in its own culture. In fact if this were recognised it might be more possible to achieve the right balance in a school controlled by the minority than in normal majority schools which find themselves in tension with minority cultures.

THE PROBLEM OF ETHNIC SOCIAL WORK

Clearly education is a sphere in which the distinction between that which is necessary from the point of view of maintaining the culture of minorities and that which is necessary from the point of view of a large-scale society is difficult to draw. Another even more difficult area is that which arises in connection with social welfare and social work. Social workers have sometimes claimed that what is necessary in dealing with minorities is a special kind of multicultural social work. If, however, the problems of minority people are so different would it not be possible for the community to be subsidised so that it could take care of its own? Alternatively is the problem not that of *combining* professional standards with sensitivity to community values? In that case would not the answer be to train social workers from the minority communities so that they could add professionalism to their existing sensitivity? Trying to train majority social workers in sensitivity is much more difficult than that of training already sensitive minority people in professional standards.

THE STRUCTURES OF THE PRIVATE DOMAIN

The nature of the sociological problem with which we have to deal is as follows. For a member of the majority the world of the family and the primary community is an integrated structural part of the whole network of social relations which constitute his or her society. It is also a functional sub-system of the whole and its culture continuous with that of the main society. Amongst ethnic minorities the situation is wholly different. For such minorities the family and community are part of another social system and another culture. In that system the extended kinship group probably carried much more weight than it does in industrial society and in some cases provided the whole of the social structure.

The most important function of the immigrant minority kinship group is, of course, primary socialisation. In the case of the majority this function is performed by the family and the family exists in relative isolation from any larger community network. In the case of the minority communities on the other hand the family is part of a wider network of communal and associational ties, the socialising community is large and more people are involved in the child's socialisation.

The extended family is not, however, solely a socialising agency. It also provides a unit for economic mobilisation and this function may even be performed when members are separated from one another by migration. The family and kin-group has an estate to which members may be expected to contribute either in terms of property or in terms of skills and qualifications. An event like marriage is not, and cannot be, solely a matter of individual choice. It involves the transfer of capital from one group to another and, as a result, the linking of two groups. At the same time the new family constituted by marriage starts with a carefully husbanded inheritance of material and social capital.

Because extended kinship is seriously damaged by the fact of migration, the networks within which family life occurs come to depend more on artificial structures which are thought of as associations, but which are actually structures through which the wider community life is expressed. In my study of Sparkbrook (Rex and Moore, 1967) I suggested that these associations had four functions. They helped individuals to overcome social isolation;

they did pastoral work amongst their members and helped them to deal with moral and social problems; they served as a kind of trade union defending the interests of the group; and it was through them that values and beliefs were affirmed and religious and political ideologies perpetuated.

Of particular importance is the role of the association in the affirmation of values and beliefs. Included in this is the offering to the individual of beliefs about himself, that is to say identity options or ideas about who he or she is. Naturally it is not the case that individuals automatically accept these options, but the associations are flexible instruments through which new identities appropriate to the new situation are suggested as possible.

Values and beliefs, however, cohere around the more systematic teachings of minority religions. Such religions have belief systems which go far beyond explaining man's relation to nature and to his fellow-man. As such they can never be simply functional in a modern society. Nevertheless, whatever their particular content, these religions provide a metaphysical underpinning for beliefs of all kinds and therefore help to provide the psychological security which the whole community structure gives.

To a very large extent the kinship structures, the associations and the religions of the minorities may be seen as acting together to perform a function for the larger society. It is the function Parsons (1952) calls 'pattern maintenance and tension management'. Sociological jargon apart, however, we may say that they provide the individual with a concept of who he is as he embarks on action in the outside world and also give him or her moral and material support in coping with that world. To the extent that they perform these functions, communal structures and belief systems become a functioning part of the larger society, whatever the particular form of the social structure and whatever the content of its culture.

Minority communities and minority cultures do not threaten the unity of society. Nor do they imply inequality between groups. They can have their place within a society which is committed in its main structures to equality of opportunity. What I have tried to suggest is that a multicultural society must find a place for both diversity and equality of opportunity. Emphasis upon the first without allowing for the second could lead to segregationism, inequality and differential incorporation. Emphasis upon the second at the expense of the first could lead to an authoritarian form of assimilationism. Both of these are at odds with the ideal of the multicultural society.

CONFLICT AND COMPROMISE IN THE MULTICULTURAL SOCIETY

As a last word let me qualify what I have said about the functionality of minority structures. I believe that we would do an injustice to the religious, cultural and political ideas of minority groups if we saw them as fitting easily and snugly into the social status quo. Sometimes their ideas and their institutions may be revolutionary or secessionist. Sometimes they are not addressed to the problems of the society settlement at all, but to those of the original homeland. Should this mean that they are dangerous and should be repressed?

I think not. After all, British culture is by no means unitary. It can be and I think should be interpreted in terms of class struggle. The working classes nationally and regionally have developed solidary forms of organisation and revolutionary notions of social solidarity which challenge the social order and the culture of the ruling classes. The result of all this, however, is that what I have called the civic culture includes the notion of conflict. The social order which we have is the result of social conflict. I see no reason why there should not be a similar process as between majority and minority groups. Ours is a society which has produced institutions to deal with the injustices of capitalism. Surely it is not impossible to envisage a similar outcome to the struggle initiated by Rastafarianism which seeks to set right the injustices of the past 400 years. The only belief system which must be outlawed in the multicultural society is that which seeks to impose inequality of opportunity on individuals or groups. That is why the multicultural society must be an anti-racist society.

SUMMARY: THE ESSENTIALS OF A MULTICULTURAL SOCIETY

(1) The multicultural ideal is to be distinguished from the notion of a plural society.

(2) In a multicultural society we should distinguish between the public domain in which there is a single culture based upon the notion of equality between individuals, and the private domain, which permits diversity between groups.

(3) The public domain includes the world of law, politics and economics. It also includes education insofar as this is concerned with selection, the transmission of skills and the perpetuation of the civic culture.

(4) Moral education, primary socialisation and the inculcation of religious belief belong to the private domain.

(5) The structure of the private domain amongst immigrant minority communities includes extended kinship extending back into a homeland, a network of associations and a system of religious organisation and belief. This structure provides a valuable means in an impersonal society of providing a home and source of identity for individuals.

(6) None the less minority communities at any one time may conflict with and challenge the existing order as have communities based upon social class in the past. The new social order of the multicultural society is an emergent one which will result from the dialogue and the conflict between cultures.

Is a society of this kind likely to come into being in Britain? I think not. The concept of a multicultural society which is now in vogue is too confused for that. It might lead much more readily to 'differential incorporation'. Moreover there are still many to whom the very idea of multiculturalism is anathema and they would oppose the emphasis on diversity which I have advocated. But it never was the task of a sociologist to provide happy endings. All he can do is to clarify his value standpoint and indicate what institutional arrangements are necessary for its realisation.

2 The Political Sociology of a Multicultural Society[*]

Although a few right-wing Conservative spokesmen have recently challenged the notion that Britain should be a multicultural society and have received some support from intellectuals of the New Right (Honeyford, 1988), the idea that we now do have a multicultural society, and that this is not only inevitable but desirable, is widely accepted. Unfortunately it is not at all clear what exactly the term means. Although it purports to being a sociological description, sociologists have done little to clarify the kinds of structure to which it refers. This chapter will, therefore seek to set out the basis for a political sociology of the multicultural society both as an ideal and as a reality, and, while dealing primarily with Britain, indicate what the principal variables are, so laying the basis for a more generally applicable theory.

MULTICULTURAL AND PLURAL SOCIETIES

In the first place the notion of a multicultural society has to be distinguished from that of the plural society, on which there is considerable literature. Furnivall, who first used this concept, used it to refer to a society, such as that which was to be found in colonial Indonesia, in which a number of ethnic groups encountered each other only in the market place, and in which, while each of the separate groups was tightly bound together internally by its own morality and culture, this encounter in the market place was marked by an absence of a 'common will' such as had underpinned

[*]Originally published in *European Journal for Intercultural Studies*, vol. 2, no. 1 (Rex, 1991a).

market relations in Europe (Furnivall, 1939). M. G. Smith, using Malinowski's notion of a society as a system of interrelated institutions, argued that in the British West Indies the various ethnic groups which constituted many of these societies each has its own separate and nearly complete institutional set, their incompleteness lying in the fact that they were bound together by a single political system based upon the domination of a ruling group (Smith, 1965). Later Smith was to refer to the *de jure* and *de facto* differential incorporation of the ethnic groups (Smith, 1974). Other writers have sought to apply the theory to African societies in a modified form (Smith and Kuper, 1969) and there has also been a Marxist critique of Smith's and Furnivall's theory which lays emphasis upon the mode and the social relations of production as the element which binds the groups together (Rex, 1986a).

What all these theories of the plural society have in common is that they emphasise the inequalities of economic and political power between the society's constituent groups. Thus the South African system popularly referred to as 'Apartheid' is seen to be a clear instance of the plural society. Obviously, therefore, when the notion of a multicultural society is discussed as an ideal in the British context, what is being suggested is something sociologically quite different from this, although it may well be the case that the widespread acceptance of the idea of the multicultural society has something to do with the fact that some of its supporters envisage a system, in which minority cultures are treated as inferior and in which members of minority groups have unequal rights.

Another type of society from which the multicultural society in Britain has to be distinguished is that in which several ethnic groups or nations live together through a system of power-sharing. This does not imply inequality, but the major groups are thought of as maintaining their separate corporate existence while sharing in the exercise of political power. This is the case in Canada where the British and French 'founding nations' have shared control of the state, and in Belgium where the Flemish and Walloon populations coexist in terms of a balance of power. It can also be argued that there is power-sharing in some colonial societies, such as Malaysia. where one group, the Malay, controls the political system, and another, the Chinese, controls the world of business. Neither of these types of social and political system can be envisaged in Britain and the concept of a multicultural society clearly does not imply them.

CULTURAL DIVERSITY AND EQUALITY OF OPPORTUNITY: THE JENKINS FORMULA

The first official British response to the presence of large numbers of immigrants distinguished by their skin-colour, their language, their religion and their culture was simply to declare that they must be assimilated to a unitary British culture. Thus the Commonwealth Immigrants Advisory Council, referring to educational provision, argued in 1964 that 'a national system cannot be expected to perpetuate the different values of immigrant groups' (Commonwealth Immigrants Advisory Council, 1964). This policy was very quickly abandoned, however, and in 1968 the Home Secretary, Roy Jenkins, said that what he envisaged was 'not a flattening process of uniformity, but cultural diversity, coupled with equal opportunity, in an atmosphere of mutual tolerance' (Patterson, 1968). Since these policy aims have never been formally abandoned, it may be assumed that, in some degree at least, they still influence government policy. In trying to decide what is meant in sociological terms by the concept of a multicultural society in the British case, therefore, the Jenkins formula provides us with a starting point.

Equality of Opportunity and the Shared Political Culture of the Public Domain

The most important point to notice about Jenkins's statement is that the notion of cultural diversity is clearly coupled to the distinct notion of equality of opportunity. If, then, it is taken as indicating the British ideal of the multicultural society, it is clear that this ideal is not satisfied in any system in which members of the society distinguished by their culture have unequal rights. Presumably, too, the notion of cultural *diversity* does not refer to a situation in which different cultures are thought of as having unequal worth, as is suggested by Honeyford (1988) when he attacks the notion of 'cultural relativism'.

It is also to be noted, however, that Jenkins speaks only of equality of opportunity and not of equality of outcome or of social rights. Given this minimal commitment, it is not surprising that the formula should have proved acceptable to his Conservative successors. More radical, though it is undoubtedly vague, is the ideal informing French policy, the long-established one of 'Liberty, Equality and Fraternity'; and even more radical is the conception of social rights which has enjoyed considerable currency in Britain since the publication of T. H. Marshall's *Citizenship and Social Class* (1950).

Marshall argued that the British working class, having previously won the legal rights of equality before the courts and the political rights which were secured through universal adult suffrage, had, in the welfare state, now also won a bundle of social rights. For Marshall, the range of these new social rights was still quite limited, but when a Conservative government succeeded Labour in 1951 and did not reverse its social policies, it was widely thought that there was now a new consensus around certain policies, including planning for full employment, welfare benefits for the sick and unemployed, free collective bargaining over wages, and the provision of basic social benefits in the form of a free National Health Service, cheap housing for rent and primary and secondary education for all. The radical commitment which such a set of policies involved was, of course, largely abandoned in the 1980s, but it is clear that at times the notion of equal social rights for all citizens in Britain has gone well beyond the limited notion of equality of opportunity enshrined in the Jenkins formula.

The other important point in Marshall's thesis was that, with the achievement of social rights, the primary loyalty of the individual, and his or her primary form of belonging, would in the future be not to a class but to the nation. Citizenship rather than class membership was to be the leading concept of Britain's future political sociology. This suggested that whatever the culture and forms of belonging experienced by individuals as a result of their membership of communal, regional, class, religious and ethnic groups, there was now a shared political culture of the public domain embodied in the idea of citizenship. Such a culture was necessarily unitary and could not be challenged by any concept of multiculturalism. This is a notion which is implicit in the Jenkins formula when it couples cultural diversity with equality of opportunity.

Cultural Diversity in the Private and Communal Domain

The fact that the Jenkins formula coupled the notion of cultural diversity with equality of opportunity should not, however, be taken to imply that it was not primarily about cultural diversity, but the coupling of these two ideals does involve an inherent difficulty. To insist upon a shared culture of the public domain which emphasises equality does appear *prima facie* to be at odds with defending the rights of immigrants and ethnic minorities to be different, and it is interesting to notice that in France the emphasis, even in anti-racist organisations such as SOS Racisme, and France Plus, has been placed on ensuring that members of the ethnic minorities attain the rights of citizenship. Very often this has meant a fear of, or even positive hostility to, immigrant cultures, as when a Black headmaster refused to admit a group of Muslim girls to his school because they were wearing their traditional Muslim scarves.

In Britain what has happened is that recognition has been given to the continuance of minority cultures in the 'private' domain of the family and community. Minority groups are thought of as having the right to speak their own languages, to practise their own religions, to have their own domestic and communal cultures, and to have their own family arrangements. It has been thought that these forms of diversity can be tolerated and even encouraged since they do not impinge on the public sphere, and also have positive value in that they provide social and psychological support for the individual in what otherwise appears as a harsh, individualist and competitive society. Some would also add that the flourishing of diverse cultures on this level actually 'enriches' British culture outside the political and economic sphere.

The doctrine of the two cultural domains was one which was widely shared in discussions of the multicultural society, including that by the present author (Rex, 1986b). The notion of equality and citizenship appeared to be saved by declaring it part of the public political domain, while that of cultural diversity was preserved as part of the private communal domain. Those who took this view therefore seemed able to get the best of both worlds. Embarrassingly for them it was also taken up by some of those who did not accept the claims of minority cultures to equal esteem (Honeyford, 1988). For them, however, what the two-domains thesis means is that, though the diverse cultures of the minorities may be inferior and even noxious, they may be tolerated so long as the public domain is insulated from them. Moreover, for them, the culture of the public domain is usually represented not simply as the shared political culture which has been described above, but an all-inclusive British national culture.

DIFFICULTIES IN THE TWO-DOMAINS THESIS

Having stated the two-domains thesis as a starting point for this discussion, it is now necessary to say that it is all too naive and simplistic. It involves intellectual difficulties, because *prima facie* it appears to be at odds with accepted assumptions in sociological theory, and it involves practical difficulties, especially when applied to education, but also in a number of substantive political ways. We should now deal with each of these difficulties in turn.

The Problem of the Two-Domains Thesis in Sociological Theory

The mainstream tradition in sociological theory has always been in some sense functionalist. That is to say, it has argued that the various institutions which constitute a sociocultural system are all necessarily interrelated so that each helps to sustain the others. Moreover, even the critics of functionalism, who have raised the possibility of inter-institutional or systemic contradictions, have envisaged these very contradictions as leading to systemic change (Lockwood, 1964), while those who have based their sociology on the notion of class conflict have still analysed the internal culture and social organisation of the separate classes in functionalist terms (Rex, 1961). There seems to be no place within such sociologies for the idea of two separate sociocultural domains which have no impact or effect on one another. The moral values inculcated by the family, for example, are looked at in terms of their functionality or dysfunctionality for performances in the political and economic spheres.

There is, however, also another tradition in sociological and historical thinking. This is that of the secularisation thesis. According to this thesis, in the process of modernisation, such forms of social organisation and culture as the market, bureaucracy and modern technology and science have been gradually but systematically liberated from the controls previously exercised over them by religion, morality and the family. Now, if anything, the liberated institutions come to dominate others, but at least they are able to insulate themselves from their effect. Herein lies the basis of tolerance. What the secularisation thesis does not allow for, however, is the extent to which the modernising values of the market place penetrate communal values, or how, on the other hand, the world of the market place depends upon individuals being socialised within the family and community, and upon their providing a retreat from its rigours (Parsons calls this the Pattern Maintenance and Tension Management System: Parsons, 1952).

Practical Difficulties in the Education System

Schools in modern societies cannot be simply located in the two domains. On the one hand, they are part of the selective system of an industrial or post-industrial society, submitting their students to competitive testing, and having necessarily to inculcate the values of such a competitive system and of the wider society; on the other, they are concerned with moral education, transmitting the values which are necessary for the individual to become socialised at all, as well as for sustaining communal cultures.

Two kinds of debate go on within the education system. One is about equality of opportunity, with almost all groups demanding that their children should be able to acquire the skills and the qualifications necessary for them to obtain the best occupational positions in their adult lives. Such demands have been made in the past by the working class, despite their former solidary culture induced by the process of class struggle, and they are made equally by immigrant groups, the rationale of whose immigration has been to ensure their children's advancement and increase their earning power. The other is about the preservation of communal values, which are threatened both by the individualism inherent in the selective process and the economic system, and by the possibility of the host society's communal values being imposed.

Immigrant groups in Britain are almost always committed to the idea of equality of opportunity. Afro-Caribbean parents complain about racism and racist bias in the selective system which prevents their children from obtaining the best results, while Asian parents, even though their children, in most groups, are doing reasonably well, still usually have a highly instrumental attitude to education, and to the possibility that it raises of their children entering the professions or succeeding in business. At the same time, racism expresses itself not simply in unfair selection processes but also in the denigration of minority values. Afro-Caribbean leaders sometimes attribute the apparently poor performance of their children to this denigration of their culture, while Asians fear that the values which are essential for maintaining the solidarity of their communities will be corrupted by the school.

Investigation of these matters in England was carried out by the Rampton and Swann Committees (Department of Education and Science, 1981, 1985), but inevitably these committees were given a confused brief. They were required to deal both with the special problem of disadvantage amongst West Indian children and with the problem of potential culture conflict which affected Asian children in particular. Their surprising and somewhat convoluted conclusions were: that the poor performance of some ethnic minority children was due in the first place to disadvantage which they shared with poor White working-class children, but that they suffered a double disadvantage in that, in addition to sharing these working-class disadvantages, they also suffered from racism, both in the wider society and in the schools themselves; that the educational system could amend this situation in part at least by its own practice; and that the way to do this was, on the one hand, to eliminate all elements of racism from the curriculum and from selective processes, and using the disciplinary system to eliminate racist behaviour by teachers and students, and, on the other, to increase respect for minority cultures by introducing all children, including indigenous English children, to them.

Interestingly much of the criticism which has been directed against the Swann Report (see Troyna, 1987; Modgil *et al.*, 1987; Verma, 1989; Chivers, 1987) has suggested that it failed to move beyond a multicultural to an anti-racist approach. In fact what this shows is that there was a powerful movement amongst educational theorists and sociologists in favour of greater equality of opportunity, and this movement was certainly right in claiming that the actual proposals for overcoming racism in the report were overwhelmed by the main proposal to teach all children about minority cultures. But what is usually less noticed is that the report had little to say about the value of education in minority cultures for minority children. This concern was displaced by the radical proposal that all children should be educated in minority as well as majority cultures and thereby equipped to live in an ill-defined multicultural society.

In fact the story of the Rampton and Swann Committees is less important than it might have been for the future shape of British society, because its recommendations were not fully acceptable to government, and were at best very partially implemented. Actual policies in schools depended far more on the statements of policy and attempts to implement these statements made by local education authorities. These statements themselves differ enormously in their proposals and reflect many of the confusions of the Rampton and Swann Committees.

The concern of this chapter, however, is not to assess the findings of Rampton and Swann, but to examine the role of the schools in contributing to the creation of a multicultural society. On this all that can be said is that the schools were the principal site of the conflicts inherent in the concept of the multicultural society itself, and experience shows that it is here above all that the contradictions and difficulties of the two-domains thesis become obvious. While it could be argued that the schools could contribute to the sustaining of minority cultures by being places of socialisation and retreat, and also offer all children equality of opportunity regardless of race, cultural background, religion or ethnicity, this is not what has happened, and parents and children themselves have been left to work out the best balance between the two goals. Perhaps some Asian families have produced the most viable solution in combining through their own efforts the maintenance of a strong family organisation and culture with a very instrumental attitude towards school education and educational success.

The Swann Committee, of course, has in effect proposed the most radical form of social engineering by suggesting that, as distinct from learning to participate in present majority and minority cultures, all children should acquire a new culture which is an enriched amalgam of all of them. What seems to be the case where this has been tried is that it has simply produced a backlash on the part of majority parents. While it is true that British culture in its non-political aspects is subject to continuous change, it seems unlikely that a new multiculturally based British culture will be produced by social engineering in the schools.

A final word in this section should be added about Muslim children in schools. More than other groups, the more devout sections of the Muslim community have found difficulty in adapting to the school regime. The absence of provision for religious worship and instruction, the failure of the school meals service to provide halal food, the required exposure of girls' bodies in physical education and swimming lessons, and the inaccessibility of single-sex education, have all stood in the way of such adaptation. Where these demands have been met, Muslim parents have been prepared to regard education instrumentally as a means of material advancement, but some, in any case, have demanded more than this, and have sought, through the development of separate schools, to prepare their children for living primarily as Muslims, albeit within a secular world.

Further Substantive Difficulties in the Way of Creating a Multicultural Society

Host Culture, National Culture and Class and Status Cultures

The ideal of a multicultural society spelled out in terms of the two-domains thesis sees British society as involving simply a confrontation between private familial and communal cultures, on the one hand, and the shared political culture of the public domain, on the other, and, in our discussion so far, what we have had in mind in the private sphere have been principally ethnic minority cultures. In much public debate, however, the confrontation is seen as being between 'British culture' in the public domain and immigrant culture in the private, and this 'British culture' is not thought of in political terms at all. Rather it is thought of as itself a whole way of life which distinguishes the British from other nations.

National culture in this sense is often bound up with war and international relations as well as with international sport. It is supposed to be a focus of loyalty and patriotism. Those who feel this loyalty most strongly regard immigrant and ethnic minority culture as a threat. This was nicely expressed by the Conservative MP Norman Tebbit when, in the course of expressing his doubts about the possibility of a multicultural society, he proposed what he called a 'cricket test' asking for whom immigrant groups cheered during cricket matches.

Although the national culture is thought of as involving a host of familiar cultural practices which distinguish the British from, say, the Germans and the French, such familiar practices, and such a way of life, are often thought of also in more restricted class terms. British culture tends to be dominated by ways of life developed amongst its upper-status groups and fostered in elite schools and universities. These status groups employ what Parkin (1979), following Weber, calls strategies of 'closure', which exclude lower-status groups from participation in their way of life. Here the contrast is not with other nations but with other status groups.

Status groups are concerned, as Weber saw, with the differential apportionment of honour (Weber, 1968), but they also come to exercise power. In the British case they exercise considerable control over the Civil Service and over Members of Parliament, and also form alliances with the business classes through which they exercise economic power. While the business classes seek legitimation of their own position through marital alliances and through sending their children to elite schools, the upper classes become members of Boards of Directors.

As against these strategies of closure and class alliance, other status groups develop their own distinct cultures. T. S. Eliot in his *Notes Towards a Definition of Culture* (1948), which was primarily a defence of upper-class culture, noted that the working classes developed cultures of their own, often of a regional sort; Raymond Williams in his *Culture and Society* (1963) spoke of a 'common culture' distinct from the restricted culture of ruling groups; and Richard Hoggart in his *Uses of Literacy* (1957) gave an evocative account of the cultural and moral values of working-class culture in Hunslet in Leeds.

Just as the culture of upper-status groups becomes intertwined with the class culture of the business classes, so this popular culture becomes intertwined with the culture of the working classes, understood in a more political sense. A working-class culture emerges in the course of defensive and offensive class struggles based upon strong themes of solidarity, and this is projected on to a national stage through the Labour Party. Such a culture disputes the claim of the upper-status groups and classes to being a national culture.

Finally, one should note the importance of the culture of the middle classes. Members of these classes often reject the solidarity of working-class culture and emphasise individualism and self-help, without themselves becoming incorporated into the closed culture of upper-status groups and classes.

In Britain, therefore, there is not a unitary British culture but rather a hierarchy of cultures, which to some extent constitute cultural strata but which are also based upon the political fact of class struggle. This is the culture which immigrant and ethnic minority cultures confront.

The Disputed Political Culture of the Public Domain

Earlier we spoke of a shared culture of the public domain. We can now see that there is a considerable degree of dispute within this culture. The upper-status groups use strategies of closure; the business classes seek entry into the world of their status superiors; the working classes emphasise the virtues of solidarity and equality; and the middle classes emphasise equality of opportunity.

The shared political culture of the public domain arises out of the compromises which are made between these various tendencies. It is based upon the notion of hard-won rights centring on the notions of equality of opportunity and equality of outcome. Political parties are bound to make some reference to these ideals. However much upper-class conservatives may wish to defend their closed class culture and their class rule, the Conservative Party is bound to subscribe to the ideal of equality of opportunity, or even, recently, to the idea of a classless society. Labour, on the other hand, emphasises equality of outcome. Sometimes one ideal gains the ascendancy, sometimes the other, but over the longer term what emerges is a new compromise based upon the idea of a minimum which is equally available to all, coupled with superior rewards for some, conceived of as a reward for effort.

The relationship of immigrant and ethnic minority cultures to this system is necessarily complex. On the one hand, they find their own cultures placed within a hierarchy of cultures, and their individual members having to face not only the strategies of closure of the upper classes, but also those based upon what Parkin (1979) calls the strategies of usurpatory culture of the working classes. On the other, their members must make what claims they can within whatever is the going system of rights available in the public domain. They may seek to preserve their own solidary cultures while seeking in an instrumental way to benefit from equal opportunity policies, or they may come to share some of the values of the working classes, the middle classes or the business classes.

Race relations legislation in Britain complicates these problems. It is primarily designed to secure equality of opportunity for members of ethnic minority groups, but it also sometimes seems to be aiming at equality of outcome imposed by what Honeyford (1988) calls a regulatory bureaucracy. Inevitably, therefore, it produces resentment, both among the middle classes whose ideal is simply equality of opportunity, and among the working classes whose rights have been won not through the interventions of a benevolent government, but, much more, through hard political struggle. Thus, however much ethnic minority groups might seek participation in the shared political culture of the public domain, they find themselves faced with additional suspicions and hostility.

Religion in the Public Domain

Another questionable assumption in the ideal model of a multicultural society, which we have outlined, is that Britain is a secular state, and that religion is a private matter. There is some truth in this in that it is in no sense a theocracy, and that a variety of forms of religious belief and practice are tolerated, but the notions of secular state and secular state education are not nearly as clearly defined as they are, for instance, in France.

In fact the Anglican Church in Britain has a privileged position and even some symbolic power. The Archbishop of Canterbury actually crowns the Monarch, and the Church endorses state institutions on many public occasions, especially those connected with war. Not surprisingly the Archbishop was criticised by the Prime Minister for having failed to strike a sufficient note of triumph in his sermon at a memorial service after the successful completion of the Falklands War.

The various churches also provide supernatural recognition of individual life events, such as birth, marriage, and death, and their religious functionaries provide a counselling service for many people at times of individual and family crisis; the schools provide occasions for Christian religious worship and instruction; and Church spokesmen are expected to make statements on social and political matters such as the plight of the homeless or of inner-city people generally, even though these are expected to avoid any kind of party political commitment (see, for example, *Faith in the City*, the report of the Archbishop's Committee on Urban Priority Areas: ACUPA, 1985).

None of this, of course, adds up to more than the exercise of symbolic power by the churches, and in return for this symbolic power they are kept firmly in their place. Although the Monarch is crowned by the Archbishop, she is also known as the Supreme Governor of his Church; the Church is expected to support the interests of the nation in wartime; and where it does make apparently political interventions, these are expected to be of a general moral kind rather than being precise political directives to legislators in Parliament.

None the less the special role of the Christian churches, and the Anglican church in particular, does have some significance for any attempt to create a multicultural society. They appear to endorse a national and nationalist culture rather than a society based upon a plurality of cultures; they have a privileged position in the schools, and they even have the protection of a law against blasphemy, which is at odds with the general commitment of the political culture of the public domain to freedom of speech.

From the point of view of immigrant and ethnic minorities this privileged position of Christianity does make their integration into British society more difficult. Though they have formally established their right to opt out of religious worship in schools and to have worship of their own, they have in fact to struggle and argue to enforce this right, and on the major question of protecting their religions against blasphemy, they have been sharply reminded, since the publication of Rushdie's *The Satanic Verses* (1988), that their religions do not enjoy the protection accorded to Christianity. As some of their more devout members see it, they are cultural and religious aliens in a Christian society, while from the point of view of cultural equality they face a national culture with a religious endorsement which is not available to minority cultures.

Human Rights and Minority Cultures

In Britain, in common with other advanced industrial societies, discourse within the public domain does not usually stop at the discussion of equality of opportunity or of equal social rights in the Marshallian sense. It also extends to the question of individual human rights, and it is here that it brings the very foundations of ethnic minority social organisation and culture into question. This is particularly true of the discourse of feminism. To many feminists the position of women in the minority cultures appears unacceptable, and they see themselves as having a concern for the liberation of wives and daughters from the domination of their menfolk. Though ethnic minority spokesmen may claim that they are concerned to protect their womenfolk from the corruption of a secular capitalist society, and that their forms of arranged marriage and extended kinship are essential strengths in their community organisation, they are likely to find their cultures continually under attack from these quarters. There is a certain irony in this in that feminists often see their campaigns on questions of gender equality as paralleling campaigns for the equality of ethnic minorities.

Demands by Ethnic Minorities in the Public Domain

The model of the multicultural society based upon the two-domains does not, however, encounter only those difficulties which arise from the British side. For some minority groups and minority religions, and particularly Islam, the division between public and private domains appears unacceptable. For most Muslims, Islam is not merely a private matter but a whole way of life. Some Muslims, though by no means all, Muslims believe in the idea of an Islamic state; there is a widespread expectation that the state should protect religion; Islam has its own economic ethics, which are in some ways at odds with capitalism; it has its own ideas about education; and, not least, as we have seen in the previous section, it has its own views on the position of women and the family.

In fact Islam has a long history and Muslims have in the past found ways of living in non-Muslim and secular societies. They do not necessarily all share the belief, to be found in the teachings like those of Maududi, the founder of Jamaat-i-Islami, in the ideal of an Islamic state; they have found ways of pursuing their banking and business in capitalist societies; they have found ways of adjusting to predominantly secular education; and even on the question of the rights of women their discourse is by no means as reactionary and patriarchal as many Western feminists assume. It is misleading therefore to suggest that anyone who practises Islam is a so-called 'fundamentalist' whose irrationality makes it impossible for him to live in a multicultural society.

To say this, however, certainly does not mean that there are no difficulties in the way of finding a place for Islam in British society. In the immediate future it may well be that some extreme Muslims may make demands which appear unacceptable to most British people, as is evident from the recent publication of *The Muslim Manifesto* (Muslim Institute, 1990(a)) by a relatively small and unrepresentative body called The Muslim Institute, which calls for the establishment of a Muslim Assembly, and a speech by the Institute's leader, Kalim Siddiqui (Siddiqui, 1990(b)) calling for a special relationship between British Muslims and the state of Iran. On the other hand the tendency to dismiss all Islam as 'fundamentalist' may make it impossible even for the more moderate to be accepted as legitimate citizens. In the immediate future, then, considerable religious and ethnic conflict seems likely, even though, in the longer run, dialogue and negotiation might lead to the discovery that Muslim and Christian/British notions of the public domain are not incompatible.

Other ethnic and religious minorities have found it easier to come to terms with living in Britain than have Muslims. However, even though they might adapt very readily to living in Britain and taking the economic opportunities which living there offers, many of them may remain oriented in their thinking to homeland politics. Sikhs may use their British base to campaign for a separate state of Khalistan, Mirpuris may campaign for what they see as the liberation of Kashmir, and many West Indians, finding themselves rejected in what appears to them to be a racist Britain, may hunger for an African Zion. A multicultural Britain might have to recognise that the continuance of such commitments is part of the culture of the private domain and can be tolerated, even though they prevent some ethnic minority members from becoming completely and finally British.

POSSIBLE OUTCOMES

The aim of this chapter has not been one of simple advocacy. What it does, having outlined an ideal model, is to consider some of the difficulties which stand in the way of its realisation. It is an exercise in political sociology, and the task of sociologists is not simply to provide happy endings. All they can do is to suggest possible outcomes, leaving it to activists to pursue this or that political ideal, including that of the multicultural society. It is to the task of considering realistically what these outcomes may be that we must now, finally, turn.

One important possibility which should not be neglected is that over several generations present problems and difficulties may grow less acute. Many of the descendants of immigrants may become less concerned with the perpetuation of their own cultures and more concerned with economic success in Britain. They may also find themselves affiliating to the class cultures and organisations of their indigenous peers. It would be 'optimistic' to believe that this process will occur as easily and smoothly as it has over two or three generations amongst European immigrants in America, because, at least so far as British Asian immigrants are concerned, they have great cultural and organisational strengths, based on cultures and religions in their homelands, more different from those indigenous to Britain than were the cultures of America's European immigrants from those of the United States. None the less this does not mean that there will be no process of adaptation and acculturation.

The second more immediate and likely possibility is the continuance of conflict on all the levels we have discussed. Conflict will go on about the place of multiculturalism in education; British nationalism and racism are likely to continue in ways which deny ethnic minority cultures recognition and individual members of these minorities equality of opportunity; efforts to ensure equality of opportunity and equality of outcome for ethnic minority members will continue to provoke a backlash in the indigenous community; many members of the indigenous working-class will continue to pursue strategies of usurpationary closure against the minorities, particularly if economic circumstances are such that their own livelihood seems threatened; ethnic minority cultures may continue to be attacked by human rights activists; and, finally, minority cultures may be slow to adapt to living in a secular multicultural society, the more so if their adherents feel that they are not fully members of that society.

If, however, societies attempting to be multicultural are likely to be societies in conflict for the foreseeable future, it should not be thought that this necessarily means everlasting riots and street demonstrations, even though there may be substantial and violent disturbances.

Just as, in earlier times, class conflicts which started in circumstances of riot and disorder gave way to processes of negotiation and compromise, so the relationship of ethnic minorities to British society will be renegotiated. This will include not merely a redefinition of the extent to which differences in the private and communal sphere are tolerated or encouraged, but also a renegotiation of the political culture of the public domain. So far as this latter is concerned, what may occur is that the political ideals of the minority, as well as their ideas about human rights, will not be so different from those of the majority. Muslims, for example, may be very supportive, for their own religious reasons, of the idea of the welfare state. On the other hand, British class-based cultures may be seen as matters of private preference rather than as demanding some sort of overall hegemony, while the privileged role of Christian religion might also come to be questioned in a secular state.

To recognise this third possibility does not, however, point to an inevitable happy ending. But it records the fact that in a society which has to deal with cultural diversity, while there may be continuing conflicts there may also be dialogue, and, arising out of such dialogue, negotiations and compromise. The actuality as opposed to the ideal of the multicultural society will, in fact, be found in a continuing process of both conflict and compromise.

3 Conceptual and Practical Problems of Multiculturalism in Europe*

THE RANGE OF MULTICULTURAL POLITICAL SITUATIONS

Much confusion is introduced into the debate about multiculturalism in Europe by the failure to distinguish between a number of different political situations in the modern world loosely referred to as multicultural. It seems necessary at the outset of this chapter, therefore, to distinguish between seven different types of situation of this sort. These are:

(1) Colonial societies in which a ruling nation establishes political control over one or more indigenous and immigrant groups who play different economic roles and are differentially incorporated, e.g. almost all the former British, French, Dutch, Spanish and Portuguese colonies.

(2) Post-Colonial societies in which, after the withdrawal of the imperial nation from its political position, control passes to one of the other groups or to all these groups collectively. In this case there may be some degree of commitment to the notion of a democracy of all individuals, yet, frequently, at the same time

---

*A paper delivered to a symposium on Multi-Cultural Society organised by the Swedish Ministry of Culture, Vasteras, Sweden, June 1994.

the maintenance of inequality and differential incorporation of different ethnic groups, e.g. South Africa, Malaysia, Senegal, Indonesia, Mexico or Brazil.

(3) Situations in which after the ending of empires, settlers from the former imperial metropolis remain conscious of their common nationhood with the metropolitan community, leading to irredentist movements in the metropolis and a specific type of ethnic conflict in the former colonial dependency, e.g the position of Russians in the former territories of the Soviet Union, of Serbs in Bosnia, or of Hungarians in Romania or Slovakia

(4) Situations in which autochthonous minorities located within a larger political territory claim varying degrees of political or cultural autonomy for their regional territories, and at one extreme may seek secession, sometimes using violence in pursuit of this goal, e.g the Basques in Spain and France, the Scots and the Irish in Britain, the Albanians in Kossovo or Yugoslav Macedonia, or the Tartars in Russia.

(5) The situation of immigrants in societies in which being an immigrant is normal or even prestigious, but in which one or more of the early immigrant groups has established its language and culture as that of the new nation, e.g. the United States, Canada, Australia or Israel.

(6) The situation of immigrants and their descendants in societies in which there is a long-established national language and culture and in which, although immigration is recognised as economically necessary, immigrant status is in no sense prestigious, and is commonly the basis of discrimination and stigma, e.g. the situation of immigrants in West European societies.

(7) The situation of refugees in any of the above mentioned types of society. In the case of societies such as those included in (6) above, they are accepted with varying degrees of benevolence or reluctance and, in any case, they and host governments are uncertain about their long-term future.

In what follows, I shall be concerned primarily with situations (6) and (7) and will emphasise the distinctiveness of their problems, yet at the same time I will draw attention to aspects of these situations which reflect elements of Situations (1) to (5).

THE RANGE OF RESPONSES OF EUROPEAN SOCIETIES TO THE ARRIVAL OF IMMIGRANTS AND REFUGEES

There have been three broad responses to the arrival of immigrants in West European societies. The first is exemplified in the German-speaking countries by the notion of the 'gastarbeider'. In these countries, even though large numbers of foreign workers are necessary for the maintenance of industry, the very notion that these are immigrants is rejected. In principle they are thought of as temporary residents, 'auslanders', who will return to their own countries and, who, in the meantime, while they may have a claim to minimal social rights, are denied full citizenship. It is true, of course, in this case that the reality is often at odds with the theory, since many foreign workers do settle with their families and some, with difficulty, become naturalised, but the theory does have considerable effect in that these societies have very large minorities who are, on the legal and political level, 'differentially incorporated'. Paradoxically, however, in such societies there is some tolerance of cultural diversity, since residents who are foreigners may even be encouraged to maintain their original cultures so that their eventual return might be facilitated. At least there will be no pressure on them to adopt the culture of the country of their settlement.

The second alternative is represented by French thinking about immigration. In the extreme republican or Jacobin view, all should have equal citizenship regardless of national or ethnic origin, but this very emphasis upon equal citizenship means that the cultural diversity of ethnic groups is not encouraged. In the public sphere even religious diversity amongst Christians is not recognised and the ideal in education is that of 'l'école laique'. The well-known 'foulard' incident nicely symbolised French thinking, when a head teacher from Guadeloupe, thinking of himself as French, excluded Muslim girls from his school because they were wearing their traditional scarves. As in the German case, of course, though perhaps even more so, French policy makes pragmatic adjustments, and ethnic groups and ethnic minority cultures have to be recognised in the development of social policy particularly at local level. On the other hand, too, it is by no means the case that all French people are willing to extend the Jacobin principle of equal rights to all immigrant groups. There is a strong movement for repatriation and France, after all, is the home of one of the strongest anti-immigrant movements, that of the Le Pen's Front National.

The third alternative emphasis in policy, and that which most concerns us here, is that which goes under the name of multi-culturalism. This is an idea which receives widespread support among both liberals and conservatives, the former accepting cultural diversity along with the equality of all individuals, the latter recognising such diversity without insisting upon equality or even, indeed, making cultural diversity a marker for unequal treatment. What is evident in the Netherlands, Britain and Sweden, however, is the existence of strong pressure among liberal policy-makers and among immigrants themselves for the recognition of both cultural diversity and the right to equality of all individuals. The structural and political implications of this ideal as well as the practical difficulties of implementing it will be discussed in subsequent sections.

Refugee policies and immigration policies are, of course, subject to different considerations. Immigrants have been accepted, albeit often reluctantly, because they have been seen as necessary for the functioning of the economy. There is no economic compulsion to accept refugees. In principle their applications are applications for asylum, and the West European countries are bound to consider these applications because of their obligations under the Geneva Convention. This obligation is a legal and moral one.

Such a legal and moral obligation is fulfilled with varying degrees of generosity. The former Federal Republic of West Germany developed a generous policy, primarily because of its concern for Germans on the other side of the former Iron Curtain, and its willingness to accommodate refugees from Communism. Such a policy was enshrined in the constitution and was extended to people other than ethnic Germans and refugees from Communism. Of the other countries, Sweden in the 1980s was generally regarded as having the most generous policies toward asylum-seekers for more idealistic reasons. Other countries like Britain were less generous in their handling of asylum applications, but insisted that they were still fulfilling their obligations under the Geneva Convention.

In all the West European countries, however, it was difficult to distinguish true refugees from others, and it was the way in which this distinction was made, as much as anything, which led to the scale of generosity. A 'true refugee' under the Geneva Convention was one who, if he or she returned to his or her country would be in personal danger. But many of those who sought asylum did not fit easily into this category. Very often they were simply fleeing from overall situations of violence and civil war or ecological disaster, and some, like immigrants, were just seeking a better life and job opportunities than their country of origin could provide. Notably, after the collapse of Communism, many who during the Communist period would have been able to make legitimate claims to asylum, now had no such claim and were regarded as immigrants.

The scale of generosity came to turn on the question of how narrowly the category of Convention refugees was defined in practice and, no less, on what was to be done with those whose applications failed. The more restrictive countries were those who defined true refugee status very narrowly, required visas from asylum-seekers, imposed penalties on those who carried asylum seekers without them, and were more willing to expel failed applicants to their countries of origin or to third countries. Faced with the possibility of a flood of asylum claimants after 1989, all countries, including Germany and Sweden, came to adopt more restrictive policies along these lines.

One reason for generosity, however, was a less than idealistic one. After the immigration stop of the 1970s, countries which still needed immigrants but could not admit to doing so because of 'racist' and xenophobic responses in the political mainstream, found it convenient to use refugees as replacement workers. Refugees, indeed, became the new immigrants, and despite the uncertainties arising from a myth of possible return, shared by governments and the refugees themselves, their problems and those of recognised immigrants and guest-workers tended to become merged. Thus the problematic of immigrant policy and, within it, of multiculturalism, becomes the central one for considering the relation of refugees as well as true immigrants to their societies of settlement.

THE STRUCTURAL DEFINITION OF THE DEMOCRATIC MULTICULTURAL IDEAL

As I have suggested above, the Netherlands, Sweden and Britain were the countries in which an ideal of multiculturalism most strongly influenced policy. While it is necessary to emphasise again here that there was in all countries some difference between the ideal and the reality, none the less the ideals enunciated in these countries were not simply rhetorical verbiage and they do provide something of a yardstick against which actual policies can be measured, if their structural implications are clearly spelt out.

The Dutch alternative arises in the first place from the radical attempt made originally to deal with the problem of religious pluralism. This was stated in terms of a policy of 'pillarisation'. Under this policy the different Christian faiths were each recognised as having the right to develop their own educational institutions and their media with full state support. The same confessional distinction developed within the trades unions and the political parties. The question which then arose was how far separate institutional pillars could be recognised in relation to the new immigrant communities and their cultures. It is probably not true to say that such new separate pillars were developed, but none the less the pillarisation policy led to a predisposition, first, to recognise foreign-born residents as immigrants rather than guest-workers, and, second, to recognise their right to maintain their own cultures. Considerable emphasis was placed upon equality of opportunity for all, and there was much concern about the danger of the development of an 'underclass' among new immigrants, particularly among Moroccan youth (Roeland and Schuster, 1990), but this was coupled with two government reports in 1980 and 1991 which dealt with and recognised multiculturalism (Netherlands, 1979, 1990).

Swedish policy developed within a benevolent social democratic tradition, and the outsider is struck by the fact that government policy discussions there tend to start, not with treating immigrants as problems, but with a concern for developing appropriate social services through which immigrants might obtain social rights. The guiding principles of this policy were said to be those of ensuring 'freedom of choice, equality and co-operation' (Hammar, 1983).

These ideals were often thought of as being the equivalent of the French Revolutionary slogan of 'Liberty, Equality and Fraternity', but freedom of choice does appear to refer to something not included in the French ideal, namely the acceptance under the heading of 'freedom of choice' of the right to follow a particular culture, though this is coupled with a notion of equality, held even more strongly in Social Democratic Sweden than in France.

The themes of Dutch and Swedish policy recur in the British context. Although there was never the same strong policy of 'pillarisation' as there was in the Netherlands, there was a recognition within the education system of state subsidy of separate religious schools, and the legal situation was, as in the Netherlands, that Muslim schools could apply for this support. (In fact no such Muslim schools have achieved recognition in Britain, but Muslims claim that this is an unacceptable form of discrimination and a denial of their legal rights.)

The problem of multiculturalism has, however, been posed in more general terms than this. After the Labour government of 1965 had endorsed selective and racially biased forms of immigration control, one of its members stated that while unfortunately 'integration without immigration control is impossible, control without integration (i.e. of those already admitted) (my parenthesis) is morally indefensible'.

Following this through, the next problem was that of what was meant by 'integration'. Probably to most of the Labour Party it simply meant equality and nothing more, and in 1964 a government advisory body, the Commonwealth Immigrants Advisory Council, had in fact argued that immigrants to Britain should not expect that their cultures should be perpetuated in the educational system.

In the troubled situation of 1968 when the Conservative politician Enoch Powell had made a series of speeches denying that an Indian could ever become an Englishman the then Labour Home Secretary, Roy Jenkins, sought to define the notion of 'integration' in terms which have provided a kind of charter for democratic multiculturalism and which provide a convenient text for the more general European debate (Rex and Tomlinson, 1979; Layton-Henry, 1984, 1992).

Jenkins defined integration 'not as a flattening process of uniformity, but of cultural diversity, coupled with equality of opportunity in an atmosphere of mutual tolerance'. Clearly, here, as in the Swedish and Dutch version, the democratic notion of multiculturalism combines the notion of cultural diversity with that of individual equality for all and, *per contra*, suggests that the emphasis upon equality does not preclude the recognition and encouragement of diverse cultural forms.

Some ten years ago I sought to spell out what this statement of an ideal meant in structural and sociological terms (Rex, 1986b, 1991a). I argued that it seemed to imply that in a democratic multicultural society there were two separate cultural domains. On the one hand there was a shared political culture in the public domain, centring on the idea of equality, which was binding on every member of the society; on the other there were private or communal cultures which involved separate languages, religions, and family and other cultural practices. As I will argue below, I now see that the contract between immigrant groups and a national society involves more than this and that what I said was something of an oversimplification. None the less the notions of equality and the recognition of cultural diversity do have some significance, and it is worth developing them further.

It should be noted that Jenkins calls for no more than equality of opportunity. But this is a somewhat conservative position, and one which in the present day United States would be regarded almost as reactionary by many of those campaigning on behalf of Black Americans. It is also one which would be quite acceptable to British Conservatives after the undermining of the welfare state in the 1980s. Clearly, however there are many who would argue, with T. H Marshall (1950), that the working class, having earlier won legal and political rights, had in the post-war world begun to enjoy the basic rights of *social* citizenship, and that this social citizenship was, in the post-war world, the principle bond between men (and women) and their society.

While there is an argument about this, and in the present market-structured world little more than equality of opportunity is agreed to, it is of considerable interest to note that in the United States, committed though it is to the market and individualism, so far as the development of civil rights and race equality policies are concerned there has been a considerable amount of bureaucratic intervention designed to ensure not merely equality of opportunity but equality of outcome through Affirmative Action programmes. In Britain, moreover, American models were applied in setting up institutions to combat racial discrimination and inequality, and these were sometimes based on the notion of equality of outcome as the test of public policy. Compared with other European countries, Britain has perhaps gone furthest in setting up institutions of this kind. Other countries are more inclined simply to rely on the courts to protect the individual against discrimination, and the Swedish response was to appoint an Ombudsman. However, there is, in every case, some notion of a public political culture based on the notion of equality regardless of race or ethnic background.

Given such a shared public culture to which all indigenous as well as immigrant groups are required to adhere, what should be the scope of separate cultures and why are they necessary at all?

I have suggested that the binding elements of these separate communal cultures are to be found in language, religion and family and other cultural practices and that there are three reasons for maintaining them. First, I think that such cultures should be encouraged because they may be of value in themselves. Their distinctive cultural achievements should be preserved because they may be of value to the whole society. Secondly, I have made what I call the Durkheimian point, that in a complex impersonal market-oriented society human beings need the security of having an intervening form of belonging between that provided by the family and the state. Durkheim believed somewhat romantically that this form of belonging would be provided by occupational groups like guilds, yet it is clear that the one type of group which has played the role which he envisaged is the ethnic community or the ethnic colony. Thirdly, one should note that if immigrant groups are to be able to mobilise to fight for rights they need the sort of solidarity which ethnic community offers as a resource. Marx imagined that classes could arise *ab intitio* on the basis of nothing other than the perception of common interest. In fact he was wrong even about classes, who often draw upon regional and local solidarity to bind their members together. Even more, ethnic groups engaged in struggle call upon their ethnic solidarity.

SOME SOCIAL SCIENTISTS' CRITICISMS OF THE CONCEPT OF DEMOCRATIC MULTICULTURALISM

It seemed to me when I first put forward this theory of a democratic multicultural society and the notion of two cultural domains that it had much to contribute to the theory of contemporary political democracy. In fact I still think it does. I am surprised therefore to find that it has been greeted with suspicion by many of my social science colleagues in Europe and I should like, therefore, before continuing with my main argument, to deal with some of these as they were put forward at a recent conference on Ethnic Mobilisation in Europe (Rex and Drury, 1994). They included the following:

Michel Wieviorka argues that the very concept of ethnicity has to be viewed with suspicion. As he saw it, ethnicity was something which we in Europe attributed to inferior newcomers. They are thought of as having ethnicity. We are not. Thus seeing people as ethnics is a way of treating them as inferior. A similar argument is put forward by the Dutch sociologist, Jan Rath, who argues that what multicultural policy has done is to 'minorise' groups of people and thereby mark them for unequal treatment (Rath, 1991). Frank-Olaf Radtke, having looked at the development of an elaborate multicultural policy in Frankfurt, argues that what this policy does is to foster minority cultures because they are exotic, without noticing that they are often regressive and reactionary in terms of modern democratic values. Finally, Schierup and Alund in Sweden have seen multiculturalism as a manipulative policy through which the state seeks to control minorities through selected elders, reifying and rendering static the notion of minority cultures. As they see it, individuals, particularly younger individuals, from the minorities are actually continually developing their culture and forming links with individuals from other minority, as well as indigenous, groups. Multicultural policy therefore is not adapted to meeting the needs of these individuals (Schierup and Alund, 1987, 1990).

I take all these criticisms seriously, but I do not believe that they undermine the democratic multicultural idea, which I have put forward. I should like therefore to answer them seriatim.

I think that the concept of ethnicity which Wieviorka discusses is one derived from popular political discourse rather than from social science. As I use the term, we all have ethnicity. In this sense it does not imply inferiority. The real problem is to discover the ways in which different ethnicities interact and to ensure that they do not involve inequality.

In Rath's case, I think that he overlooks a fundamental feature of the theory of ethnicity. This is, that while it is true that ethnicity is often ascribed to individuals by others, and usually in a hostile or derogatory way, it is also, separately and very differently, something self-chosen. By concentrating on ethnicity ascribed by the state, therefore, and then rejecting it, he actually ignores the claims which are being made by the minorities themselves. His theory of the state seems to me to assume an institution with fixed purposes which allocates roles and resources accordingly. As I see it a democratic state is a site of struggle in which different groups seek to make their demands heard. Ethnic mobilisation is a means to this end, rather than something invented by the state.

So far as Radtke's view is concerned, I think there is something to be said for it, but not everything. It is true that there are reactionary and regressive elements in some minority cultures, as indeed there are in the indigenous majority culture. What I am seeking to do is to argue for the maintenance of those elements in minority culture and social organisation which give psychological support to their members and which, in enabling them to fight effectively for equality, actually contribute to the life of democracy.

Schierup and Alund I take most seriously of all. What they say is essentially true, and I would wish to modify my conception of multiculturalism to include the recognition of the changing syncretic cultures developing among the young. I imagine that most governments also find it simpler and politically convenient to reify the cultural and social organisational forms of the community elders and to deal only with them. I would, however, go on to add that I think that it is both misleading and derogatory to dismiss all traditional elements in minority cultures as though they were simply the prejudices of a few reactionary old men. I believe that often there is great value in the traditional elements of minority cultures, and that these deserve equal recognition with the fashionable elements to be found in the new syncretic cultures of the young. I have to recognise this as a sociologist. It may seem less important in the new discipline of Cultural Studies which often seeks to displace sociology.

SUBSTANTIAL PROBLEMS IN THE CONTRACT BETWEEN IMMIGRANT MINORITIES AND THE NATION STATE

Of course, policy, even in the countries whose governments formally profess multiculturalism, is also subject to other influences. Some of these are simply based upon hostility to and contempt for the minorities, attitudes commonly referred to as xenophobic and racist, and there are also some who, while' not guilty of such attitudes, none the less have a different view of their society from that of the multiculturalists. They argue that there is a national culture, language and religion which should be preserved and which is threatened by the appearance of minority cultures and may even see these cultures as subversive and unpatriotic. They are particularly concerned that it is this national culture which should be perpetuated in the schools. Those who hold these ideas may have a considerable influence both on the formation of policy and the way in which it is actually implemented.

In this chapter, I would simply argue that views of this kind are not acceptable. The multicultural ideal is one which has to be fought for against them. Since what we have been discussing is a pure ideal only, we must now pass to a more realistic view of the constraints made on this ideal, not by racists and xenophobes or cultural nationalists, but by the needs of the modern nation state. We now look at the kind of implicit contract which comes to be established between immigrant communities and the nation state within whose territory they settle. In a later section I shall deal with the question of the position of minorities in a supranational entity like the European Union, but for the moment I will accept that, at present, any realistic multicultural policy has to operate within the bounds of nation states. In the sub-sections which follow, I deal with some of the most important of these constraints.

The Further Requirements of the Public Domain in the Nation State

The Problem of a National Language

In the formulation of the basic multicultural ideal, I suggested that language was a matter for the separate private communal domain and the separate cultures. It is clear, however, that the public domain also has to have its own language or languages. Thus the Netherlands conducts its public business in Dutch, Sweden employs Swedish, and Britain, English. In the United States, too, English is the language of the state. Some other countries such as Belgium and Canada are formally bilingual, of course, but here there is also a distinction between the languages of public business and those spoken privately in the separate immigrant communities. Thus immigrants have to accept that, in order fully to participate in their society of settlement and in order to enjoy its benefits, they must interact with the majority via the medium of the national language or languages.

Such a constraint by no means implies that minority languages must be extinguished. They will still remain the languages of their communities, and, as part of the policy of sustaining cultural diversity, it can and should be part of public policy to provide the means for their maintenance. It may also be the case that where there are regional concentrations of minorities, the public language employed in these regions should be supplemented by the use of the language of the relevant minority. This is necessary from the point of view of the minorities and from the point of view of the national state. Moreover, anyone accused of a criminal offence should normally be given the benefit of interpretation in hearing the charges against them, and more positively should be able to understand the various welfare rights available to them. From the state's point of view, public business is best conducted if its purposes can be fully communicated to its subjects. All of these adjustments are possible without challenging the special role of the national language or languages. A multicultural society does not have to be a Babel.

The Problem of a National Culture and Religion

Somewhat similar arguments, if weaker ones, apply in regard to the established national culture and religion. A strong multicultural view would see this allegedly national culture or religion simply as one amongst many. In England, for example, traditional English culture and religion would be practised by those who chose to practise it, but it would not be required of immigrants from the Indian sub-continent or from the Caribbean or Africa that they should adhere to it, practise it, or even understand it. For myself I do not think that this a realistic or tenable position. One feature of an immigrant's situation is that he or she has to accept, and indeed most do accept, that apart from the private cultures of the separate communities there should be a shared culture of the public domain, and although this shared culture will no doubt change and be renegotiated over the longer term, the simplest alternative is for minorities to learn to understand, and operate in terms of, the established national culture. Similar problems, in fact, face regional and class-based minorities. They retain their own regional and class customs but are also aware that in the larger public world they must accept the idea of a common national culture, though here, of course, in its political aspects, this culture has emerged from a process of political negotiation.

So far as religion is concerned, the strong multiculturalist view would be that no religion should have pre-eminence. One way of achieving this would be to insist that the state itself should be purely secular, as is the case in France and the United States. From this point of view, the notion of an established church enjoying privileges, and sometimes an income, from the state would be unacceptable. So would a special position for the established church in education.

There is much to be said for this view, but it can still be asked whether the role of the church in Britain or in Sweden is entirely incompatible with multiculturalism. It can play a role in the administration of welfare and in giving symbolic support to national institutions, without denying the right of minorities to practise their own religions. Also one cannot realistically hope that the position of these established national religions will in some way be abolished. What is perhaps desirable, if freedom of religion is to be positively affirmed, is that there should be inter-faith dialogue, leading to a religion more widely based than is that of the established church taken by itself.

There does appear to be a considerable area of argument about the place of religion in a multicultural society, and it will go on. What should not be at issue, however, is religious tolerance, and it does not surprise me that Muslims in Britain protested, with at least symbolic violence, when it emerged that Islam did not enjoy equal protection against blasphemy with the Christian churches.

The Structure of a Modern Economy and Polity

Further problems arise from the fact that West European nation states exist in 'modern' societies. That is to say that the basic institutions of the economy and the polity are of a secular impersonal kind. Two elements are involved. One is the growing importance of markets as the basic means of economic provision. The other is that of the development of formal bureaucratic structures in both government and private enterprise. These two forms of modernisation are of course at odds with each other, and that is what most of the argument between left and right in the politics of the modern state is about. Whether the market or the bureaucratic element is emphasised in the institutions of the economy and the polity, both are at odds with any system in which rights and services are dispensed in terms of particularistic positions, or as personal favours. In the modern economy the distribution of rights and favours in this way is seen as corruption. The modern world, to use Talcott Parsons' terms, is based on a universalist achievement pattern rather than on a particularistic and ascriptive one (Parsons, 1952).

To say this, of course, involves little more than what we have already emphasised, namely, that in a modern democratic multicultural society the notion of cultural diversity has to be coupled with the idea of equality of opportunity (in the right-wing version) or at least a minimum of equality of outcome (in various left-wing versions). This means that when ethnic minority people with strong solidary cultures come to live in modern societies, they must be, as it were, morally bilingual, learning two different moralities, and yet knowing which is relevant in particular circumstances.

Law in the Public Domain

The maintenance of these modern institutions as well as the notion of the individual human rights of citizens means that the structure of society as a whole is governed by a body of civil and criminal law, and, clearly, living in such a society implies that all of its members, including those joining it as immigrants, must accept this. This is not to say, of course, that such a system of law is unchangeable. It can be altered both by legislation and by the recognition of new precedents in the courts. Thus, when particular laws are regarded as unjust by immigrants or anybody else, it is to be expected that they will lead to political and legal action.

One question which does arise in this sphere is that of whether it is possible for the courts to recognise different laws applying within different communities, particularly in matters of domestic and family law. On this basis some Muslims would argue that their marriage arrangements should be governed by the Sharia law. This, however, is difficult to concede because this law is seen as incompatible with human rights recognised in mainstream jurisprudence, and because it raises in a sharp form the question of who belongs and does not belong to a particular community. What has begun to occur in Britain to deal with these questions is the emergence of shadow Sharia courts which, although they have no legal standing, may give a religious endorsement to decisions relating to such matters as divorce reached in the normal courts.

The Ethical Limits to Cultural Diversity

Beyond the bounds of formal law it is sometimes suggested that there are certain practices tolerated within minority cultures, which cannot and should not be accepted in a humane and democratic society. Such, for instance, might be the practice of female circumcision. This does suggest that my original formulation, which suggested that family and other customary practices should be purely a matter of the private or communal domain, is questionable. Certainly in any modern society there will be a human rights movement and, particularly, a feminist movement, which seek to intervene in the regulation of these customs. All we should note, however, is that such movements do exist and that they will give rise to conflict. We should not assume that they are necessarily right. One important area of argument, for example, concerns the acceptability of arranged marriage. This is something to which many modern human rights activists are strongly opposed, but many minority leaders, while being capable of being persuaded that forced marriage is unacceptable, will none the less argue for the social benefits of arrangement. What we should say, therefore, is that while there are some practices which a modern humane and democratic society cannot and should not tolerate, there are others which are likely to be a matter of conflict or at least of dialogue between mainstream society and minority communities.

Schools and Multicultural Education

Many of the problems discussed in the previous sections are particularly evident in relation to schools and the educational system. On the one hand, schools prepare children for their participation in the public world of the market place and the economy, but, on the other, they are concerned in the early years at least with moral education, which is also the special concern of minority ethnic cultures. The difficult question to answer, therefore, is whether, if the schools do concern themselves with moral education, they should recognise cultural diversity. The French model of 'l'école laique' suggests that they should not. But some in Britain suggest that they should, and that religion itself should be taught in the schools on a multi-faith basis. It is also suggested by these proponents of a multicultural society that multicultural education is essential for the achievement of the third and least discussed of the elements in the Jenkins formula discussed above, namely that of 'mutual tolerance'. The argument here is that the study of the culture of other communities can produce this tolerance. (For a discussion of this whole question of multicultural education in Britain, see Lord Swann's report entitled *Education for All*, Department of Education and Science, 1985. An equivalent discussion of the problem in the Netherlands is to found in part of the report of The Netherlands Scientific Council for Government Policy, entitled *Immigrant Policy* (1990).)

None of these are closed arguments by any means, and apart from those in the majority community in Britain who oppose multiculturalism in the schools, there are those in the minority communities who have argued against it on the ground that it might conflict with the education which really matters, namely that which prepares children for successful competition in the world of work (Stone, 1981). But this is an argument about whether cultural diversity should be reflected in the school syllabus. What would not be at issue for more moderate proponents of multiculturalism is the notion that the perpetuation of minority cultures should be tolerated and publicly supported in some place, even if outside the school.

The Role of Literary, Aesthetic or High Culture

In all that has been said above we have referred to the anthropological concept of culture, meaning in effect the customary practices, norms, and patterns of social relations in everyday life. These are clearly of first importance in the sociology of democratic multicultural societies, and should not be regarded as secondary by those who are interested in another debate, and one which often seems most important to literary intellectuals, namely the relation between the 'high' cultures of various groups. Here, 'culture' does not simply refer to traditional practice, but to the intellectual pursuits of writers, artists and others in various communities, which, almost by definition, transcend tradition.

Clearly each of the separate communities in a multicultural society will have its own cultural achievements in this other sense. But writers, artists and others who transcend tradition within their own culture will also see the new situation of culture contact as a challenge and something to be explored. Of course there will be those in the indigenous as well as in immigrant communities who seek to preserve established cultural forms (i.e. not merely traditions, but cultural products, in the second sense) at all costs. But in doing so they produce only cultural fossils. The intellectuals of all cultures in a modern society reflect on and respond to new experiences, and not least among these are the experiences which arise in the contact between group and group. As a result, an important part of the shared culture of the public domain is likely to involve a shared aesthetic culture. There will. of course, still be those who act as the guardians or priests of tradition and who confine themselves to the maintenance of tradition, but one cannot ignore the question of the interaction of creative intellectuals drawn from different groups.

The Problem of Political Loyalty

Overriding all the questions discussed in the sections above is the question of political loyalty. Any individual entering the society of a nation state, however much he or she remains committed to his or her own culture has to accept a certain political duty towards that society. Such a duty or allegiance has to take precedence over any other national allegiance, and the individual is required not to commit treasonable acts. This duty or allegiance may even include a duty to serve in the armed forces of the nation state in the country of settlement. It may seem that in saying this I am failing to recognise the ideal of liberal internationalism and, on one level, I would not wish to do this. Indeed, I have always been impressed by the Stoic notion that, with the collapse of the polis, we should all identify with the international community of the wise. But the question which we are dealing with here is a sociological one. The nation state has not yet collapsed and what we are discussing is the sort of contract which must be entered into by the immigrant to the territory of such a state.

This contractual duty, however, is a moral and legal one. It does not imply a strong patriotic commitment of an emotional kind such as is generated in war or in international sport (which no doubt the sociologist Georg Simmel would have seen as the play-form of international relations: Simmel, 1959). An absurd claim of this kind was recently made by a Conservative leader in Britain who suggested that immigrants should be subject to a 'cricket test' to see whether they supported England rather than their own country of origin in international cricket matches. I do not believe that this kind of loyalty should form part of the immigrant's contract with his country of settlement.

Limits to the Private and Communal Domain

The section above discuss the various ways in which the culture of the public domain extends beyond the simple assertion of rules of the game based upon the notion of equality, although it should be pointed out that what the ideal of the democratic multicultural society asserts is that all these aspects of the public political culture should be governed by that notion. What I now want to consider is the question of what limits have to be placed on the private and communal cultures, which I suggested involved speaking separate languages, having different religious faiths and following particular family and other customary practices. I shall therefore consider some of the issues which may lead, sometimes legitimately, to anxiety about the perpetuation of these cultures. The other side of the coin to that which recognises an extension of the public domain is that which limits the private and communal one.

Multiculturalism, Ethnic Mobilisation and Ethnic Cleansing

The case which I have argued for the recognition of cultural diversity includes the notion that political mobilisation on an ethnic basis is desirable, and can indeed contribute to the better functioning of a democratic society. But this case has come to be viewed with suspicion amongst democrats, because ethnic mobilisation is now identified with the horrific Serbian notion of 'ethnic cleansing' in the former Yugoslavia. Better, it is argued, not to encourage ethnic mobilisation at all, if there is the possibility of the creation of conflicts of this kind. Paradoxically, however, the adoption of this view leads to assimilationism, and, in a more extreme form, to ethnocide and demands for repatriation, and it is the existence of these extreme views amongst the majority, rather than the perpetuation of minority cultures, which really raises the question of ethnic cleansing. However much minority cultures may emphasise ethnic solidarity, they should also, if they are to be acceptable, include a commitment to coexistence with and participation in the society of the country of settlement.

Apartheid and Secession

In a book dealing with recent arguments about multiculturalism in the United States, Schlesinger argues that some ethnic political movements, particularly amongst Black Americans, now reject the idea of belonging to a single society and claim that their culture and society should be entirely separate. Some of them, indeed present racist arguments, stating that Black and White Americans are actually psychologically different (Schlesinger, 1992). Clearly, if this were what multiculturalists in any country were claiming it would be politically unacceptable. But this was not the claim which was formerly made by ethnic minorities in the United States, who did accept the idea of a shared public political culture, and it is certainly not widely accepted elsewhere.

What is more likely is that the politics of minority communities may remain strongly oriented to the homeland and that they may cling to a myth of return to these homelands. Insofar as they are so oriented they may well be inclined to accommodate themselves to 'gastarbeider' status. This is, however, as unacceptable in a democratic multicultural society when it is suggested by minority groups as when it is imposed by the national state. The democratic ideal of the multicultural society necessarily involves the idea of a shared political order.

The Political Loyalty of Minority Groups

Involvement with the politics of the homeland may involve political loyalties to the state or to political parties in that homeland. The possibility then arises in international relations that these political affiliations will conflict with the interests of the nation state within which a minority is settled. This may also be a problem when there is an overriding loyalty to an outside religious or linguistic group. Such a problem was clearly likely to arise in Britain during the Gulf War, when some Muslims felt that their loyalty to Islam required opposition to a war pursued by an alliance made up largely of non-Muslims against Iraq, although such disloyalty did not gain majority support, and most Muslims accepted, at least pragmatically, their political obligations to the British state. Fortunately perhaps from the point of view of maintaining the unity of that state, the question of military conscription did not arise.

The Regressiveness of Minority Cultures

Some traditional leaders of minority groups are sometimes inclined to see their own culture in reified terms, as static and unchanging, and insist on maintaining cultural practices developed in their homelands. In this situation ethnic minority communities way well be seen to be regressive. Minority cultures do, however, undergo change as they face up to the challenges of migration and relocation, and younger members of these communities while insisting that they do identify themselves with the minority cultures may none the less adhere to these cultures in flexible and developing forms. The notion of democratic multiculturalism recognises this and cannot be based upon the notion of reified and unchanging cultures led by traditional leaders.

THE IMPLICATIONS OF THESE POLITICAL CONSTRAINTS FOR MULTICULTURALISM IN THE NATION STATES OF WESTERN EUROPE

It may seem that, given all these constraints, not much of the ideal of multiculturalism as enunciated in the first part of this chapter remains. I do believe, however, that there is a distinctive multicultural, as opposed to an assimilationist, approach to the problem of the integration of minorities. This approach will be governed by the Jenkins formula and involve the three elements of cultural diversity, equality and mutual tolerance. One thing which it rules out is the inherent superiority of majority indigenous culture, something which Schlesinger seems to suggest when he argues at the end of his book that American society must be based upon the superior cultural achievements of an essentially European culture, and which the British writer Honeyford argues for when he rejects what he calls 'cultural relativism' (Honeyford, 1988). Both assimilationism and the notion of a hierarchy of cultures, dominated by one which is held to be morally superior to others, is likely to give rise to much more severe conflicts than a culture which rests upon mutual tolerance and co-existence.

More positively it is necessary to repeat here the reasons which I gave earlier for maintaining cultural diversity. We should not suppress potentially significant cultural achievements in any group; we should recognise the value of maintaining structures intermediate between the individual family and the state which provide psychological security for those involved in them; and we should recognise that ethnic solidarity is a valuable resource as immigrant groups struggle to achieve equality for their members.

A final question which we should consider is that of the permanence of multiculturalism. In my own view, I think it is wrong to suggest that European societies will move from being monocultural to being permanently multicultural. Indeed I do not think it desirable that they should be. What is likely to happen over three or four generations is that some members of minorities will voluntarily enter the mainstream and that, as they do, they may well modify the shared culture of the society. What will remain will be the symbolic ethnicity which is common amongst those descended from European immigrant groups in the United States. This will involve the continuation of festivals of various kinds which help to define the identities of individuals, and which are almost universally thought of as enriching rather than politically threatening to the national culture.

MULTICULTURALISM IN A SUPRANATIONAL EUROPE

When the question of multiculturalism is discussed at a supranational level in Europe, two problems are often confused. One is that of the relation between the cultures of the constituent nation states; the other is that of the relation between immigrant minority cultures sometimes organised on a transnational basis and the political culture of a multinational Europe.

The first of these problems is similar to that of Canada and Belgium and, in a lesser way, to that of what is called the United Kingdom. In Canada, the national state of the present day is based upon two 'founding nations'. In Belgium two distinct ethnic nations, the Walloons and the Flemings, control the national state. Both of these states are officially bilingual. In the case of the United Kingdom, while the constituent states are formally united politically and the question of linguistic diversity is a relatively minor one, in fact the notion of the Kingdom being united is contested in varying degrees, and nationalist movements press for varying degrees of autonomy or secession.

The constituent nation states of Europe are its 'founding nations'. They start with regional autonomy and seek to create a supranational political entity. In these circumstances, it is to be expected that, just as movements for secession or autonomy develop within incompletely unitary nation states, so here there will be national resistance to the development of the new supranational identity. Attempts will be made, however, to fashion a shared European identity and culture, and from this point of view the question of how far national cultures can be preserved will arise. Realistically, it seems to be recognised that this Europe will be multicultural because it will remain multinational. Moreover, so far as language is concerned, the problem is much greater than it is within Canada or Belgium. There are not one or two official languages, but, presently, at least ten. As a result the model of the new Europe risks being not that of Canada or Belgium but the Tower of Babel. There is, of course, a complex process of development of political, legal and bureaucratic institutions, and there are some unifying symbolic elements like a flag and an anthem, but it remains to be seen whether these unifying developments will be strong enough to deal with the present resistance of the nation states with future secessionist movements.

Meanwhile this complex supranational entity has had to develop a policy with regard to the integration of ethnic minorities, incompletely integrated in their countries of settlement, and sometimes transnationally organised, so that some feared that they might become a kind of thirteenth state in the Europe of the early 1990s. The European Parliament has responded to this situation by declaring itself against racism and xenophobia, a position which might be supportive either of assimilationism or of tolerance of cultural diversity. Meanwhile, however, the Council of Ministers and meetings of civil servants of the constituent have sought to harmonise immigration and refugee policy on a very restrictive basis, and the bureaucracy of the European Commission has been left to devise practical policies for the integration of minorities on the European level.

The policies of the Commission have had to be planned to deal with two problems. One is that of the rights of non-EU citizens, such as the 'gastarbeiders' of the German-speaking countries; the other is that of disadvantaged and sometimes culturally distinct minorities, who often have the rights of citizens in their countries of settlement. These two quite distinct groups have been merged in the creation of what is called the Migrants' Forum. So far, this body has addressed itself to the problems of immigration and of disadvantage at the social level of both citizens and non-citizens amongst ethnic minorities, without dealing with either the special problems of the non-citizen 'gastarbeiders', or that of cultural diversity. It is difficult in these circumstances to envisage the emergence of a democratic and multicultural Europe, in the sense in which I have discussed that notion in this chapter. This problem has been largely left to the separate nation states and the most optimistic scenario for Europe would appear to be one which unites a number of separate democratic multicultural societies. The least optimistic scenario would be that in which all minorities are thought of as non-citizens or guest-workers.

NORTH AMERICAN APPROACHES TO MULTICULTURALISM

Since most attempts to develop a political sociology of multiculturalism draw upon the observations of North American social scientists, it is desirable, finally, to say something of the differences between the way in which the problem of multiculturalism has been posed in Canada and the United States as compared with its discussion in Europe.

Both these countries fall into the category of those in which the core political culture derives not from a long-established nation but from a set of institutions established by the earliest immigrants, but in which nonetheless being an immigrant, especially from the European countries, is a relatively desirable, even prestigious status.

Canada's definition of its problem of multiculturalism begins with the fact that it has to hold together the two founding nations. Thus the recognition of a problem of multiculturalism actually followed the production of a report on bilingualism and biculturalism designed to deal with the problem of Quebec. When this was seen to involve the recognition of the problems of ethnically distinct societies, it appeared to government, as it did to other immigrant minorities, that these other minorities should also have rights and, importantly, government funding. Thus a policy of multiculturalism was developed and a variety of immigrant minority cultures received funding. On the whole this policy has not had to deal with issues of a divisive political kind, but rather with the fostering of languages and of symbolic ethnicity. It is now widely recognised, however, that this policy does not deal with what are sometimes called the problems of the visible minorities or the problem of race relations, nor with the problems of the native peoples. Such problems of course take a sharper political form, in that they involve resisting racism and dealing with the heritage of colonialism, and they tend to intrude into any discussion of a relatively benign multiculturalism or into that of the settlement of the problems of Quebec. It is of some interest that the so-called Meech Lake Accord, which was supposed to deal with the problem of Quebec as a distinct society, was not ratified largely because of a filibuster by a representative of the native people in the Manitoba legislature.

Problems in the United States are of a different kind. Basically they arise because the settlement of colonial America involved two kinds of immigrants: on the one hand, the largely European immigrants coming to a society established by English settlers, and, on the other, the forced immigrants who came as slaves. In addition to these groups, however, there are three other groups, namely the native people, the Chicanos and other Hispanic-speaking people, and immigrants from various parts of Asia.

The earlier discussion of issues of immigration, equality and multiculturalism dealt with two problems. One was that of the European immigrants, who mobilised under political bosses and fought their way into a democratic political system, providing in fact a model of ethnic mobilisation in a democratic society; the other was that of Black America and the discrimination, exploitation and marginalisation which Black Americans suffered. A commonly held view was that over several generations the European minorities disappeared into a 'melting pot', save for a purely symbolic ethnicity, and became Americans, while the Blacks remained oppressed and marginalised. The civil rights movement was thought of as bringing Blacks into the mainstream and giving them access to the melting pot. It was, of course, a Swede, Gunnar Myrdal, who, called upon to give an objective outsiders view, saw that there was an 'American Dilemma', in which, while universalistic ideal aims were expressed in the constitution, the rights to which they led had not been extended to Black Americans (Myrdal, 1944).

The major aims of the civil rights movement were thus concerned with equality rather than with multiculturalism, but two processes then occurred. One was the relative failure of the move towards Affirmative Action on behalf of the Blacks. The other was the coming of immigrants from the poorer countries and particularly from the Hispanic countries of Central and Latin America.

For the Black American sociologist, William Julius Wilson, the problem was that while Affirmative Action had benefited a minority of Blacks the vast majority were left in poverty in the ghetto. His first major book was called *The Declining Significance of Race* and pointed to what was in effect a class problem amongst the Blacks (Wilson, 1978). The White American, Andrew Hacker, on the other hand, wrote a book entitled *Two Nations*, which despite the implicit reference to Disraeli in the title, did not envisage the emergence of One Nation, but rather recounted, with chilling objectivity, the way in which the political cultures of Black and White America pointed in opposite and conflicting directions (Hacker, 1992). In a more radical account, Steinberg's book, *The Ethnic Myth*, denied that the different trajectories of the various ethnic minorities were due to cultural differences, attributing them rather to the material position at which these different groups had entered the economy (Steinberg, 1981). He also went on, in an important article to argue that Black Americans had suffered unique disadvantages which distinguished them even from other sections of the underclass (Steinberg, 1990).

None of these texts really discuss the problem of multiculturalism except to dismiss it. This is why the book by Schlesinger mentioned above is of some importance, even though he comes down firmly against multiculturalism. Two things had happened in the United States in the few years before Schlesinger wrote. One was the posing of the problem of multiculturalism by the coming of the Hispanics. The other was the claim by some Black intellectuals that part of the failure of their people to achieve equality was the result of a monocultural educational curriculum which gave inadequate recognition to Black or Afro-American culture. Drawing his own inspiration from de Tocqueville, Schlesinger shows both that much of what is being written by these Black intellectuals is actually false, but, more important, that both they and Hispanic Americans, calling for bilingualism in public affairs, are breaking up the unity of the United States. Multiculturalism is seen as a divisive movement and one which has to be countered by emphasising the valuable European nature of American political culture. It is to be noted that Schlesinger ignores the alternative, which Myrdal recognised, of pointing to a political culture born out of struggle, which had produced a distinctively American political culture.

Clearly Schlesinger is right to point out that much current and highly politicised discussion of multiculturalism is divisive and incompatible with the unity of a nation state. But he is not right to propose the continued dominance of European immigrant culture. In fact neither he nor the Black intellectuals he criticises stand for the kind of multiculturalism which has been discussed in this chapter.

CONCLUSION

It has not been my purpose in this chapter to offer a general theory of multiculturalism applicable to all times, places and nations. I have introduced the above discussion of North American thinking primarily in order to point out that Western Europe's situation is a distinct one. Its problem is that of the integration of immigrant minorities and their descendants into long-established national societies. I have sought to spell out an ideal of multiculturalism in sociological terms which is relevant to that situation, while at the same time giving a realistic account of the problems involved in making it a reality in the context of the European nation states, and in a supranational Europe. My hope is that having made some of the elements in this specific historical context clear, I will have contributed to an understanding of the way in which these elements, regrouped, might serve to lay the basis for a general theory.

4 Ethnic Minorities and the Nation State: The Political Sociology of Multicultural Societies[*]

The question of ethnic and national identity is one which is addressed in two separate theoretical discourses. One is that of contemporary general sociological theory where it seems to be central to debates about Late Modernism, Post-Modernism and Globalisation. The other is in a much more empirically oriented branch of political sociology which is concerned with forms of solidarity and division in the nation state. This chapter will be primarily located within the second type of discourse, but its aim is to suggest that its formulation of concepts is highly relevant to the clarification of issues in general sociological theory.

IDENTITY, NATION, AND ETHNICITY IN CONTEMPORARY SOCIOLOGICAL THEORY

The following propositions seem to have fairly wide acceptance amongst contemporary sociological theorists:

(1) The sociology of our contemporary world has to recognise fundamental changes in the very nature of the individual's relationship with society. These are indicated by the use of such terms as Pre-Modern, Modern, Late Modern and Post-Modern, as well as by the cross-cutting notion of Globalisation.

*A paper delivered to the Theory Committee of the International Sociological Association, XIII World Conference of Sociology in Bielefeld, Germany, 1994. Published in 1995 in *Social Identities*, vol. 1, no. 1, Carfax, Oxford.

(2) Parallel to these changes it has to be recognised that the notion of the identity of the subject, which has to be central in sociology, has had to undergo radical revision. The enlightenment assumed the existence of the pure individual who was the principal subject of history; in the twentieth century the concept of identity which this implied was superseded by a more sociological conception in which the individual was assumed to be the creation of society, and identity was assumed to be socially created; but in the present Late Modern or Post Modern period this kind of clear and monolithically conceived identity has been replaced by the notion of multiple identities and a de-centred subject defining his/her selfhood only through a belief in a pesonal narrative (Hall, 1992).

(3) Separate from this process of changing forms of identity, is that in which the bounding of social life by such political units as nation-states has been superseded by a state of affairs, in which the social relations and networks in which individuals are involved, as well as the cultural influences to which they are subject, tend to have a global, rather than a purely national, character. This process is, however, incomplete, and forms of identity appropriate to an earlier stage linger on in conflict with the overall trend, and, moreover, are sometimes reasserted as a form of resistance. The revival of ethnicity and religious and ethnic 'fundamentalism' has to be undertood in these terms.

(4) The kinds of political processes which had a master role in determining the course of politics in the nation state and in the earlier modern period are also superseded. Most important, classes and class struggle, central to Marxist and quasi-Marxist political sociology, have been replaced by a variety of social movements, including ecological movements, women's movements, gay and lesbian movements, youth movements, the peace movement, and ethnic movements. Unlike classes which were based on conflicts of interest (albeit of a resolvable kind), these movements are about identity and are not resolvable in any simple way (see Touraine, 1971, 1977; Melucci, 1989; Scott, 1992).

Those, like the present author, who actually do empirical research on questions of ethnicity and nationalism find many of the concepts which are used here very unclear, even though irritatingly close to those which they themselves must use, and also that the highly general conclusions to which they lead are at odds with empirical reality.

At the centre of these difficulties is the use made of the concept of identity. This concept is a difficult one, and for many sociologists has a reference to problems of both social psychology and sociology. It is also a normative concept, since having identity tends to be contrasted with not having succeeded in achieving it. It is usually not clear where contemporary sociological theory stands on the important questions involved here, because they are being subordinated to another really quite different question in philosophy and history, namely that of how the subjects or agents of social change are to be conceived. While this is an important issue in the formulation of concepts of social action, interaction and social relations, it actually throws little light on such empirical questions as those of ethnic and national identity; and, *per contra*, research on these questions cannot resolve the theoretical and philosophical question as to how the agents of human action are best conceived. In what follows, because the problems surrounding the use of the concept of ethnicity are, in fact, complex ones, we will not make them the starting point of our analysis, but will introduce them as part of the discussion of the nature of ethnicity and nationalism.

A further set of questions relates to the replacement of some of the traditional structural concepts of sociology like class and status and class and status conflict with those derived from the theory of social movements. Certainly it can be conceded that the form of the social relations of production has changed, that control of knowledge now occupies the role formerly occupied by control of the means of production, and that the size of the employed 'working class' has now diminished to a point at which it is no longer possible to imagine the parties which represent this class taking power by themselves. But this, of itself, does not mean that there are no longer groups in society with differing and distinct interests. Further, while it was always the case that the mobilisation of the working class did not result purely from rational agreement about common interests and was deeply dependent upon the cultural ties and organisational forms to be found amongst class members, this does not imply that cultural bonding and perception of common interest were separable processes. It is absurd therefore to suggest that whereas in the past men and women united because of their perception that they had common interests, in the present they do so purely on the basis of culture. Yet something like this is precisely what the theory of social movements suggests.

There is, of course, considerable disagreement amongst social movement theorists about the relationship between social movements and social classes. Nonetheless two points are commonly made. One is that the social classes of the past were, in fact, social movements, important more because of the cultural bonding of their members than for their pursuit of common interests. The other is that the new social movements are more concerned with creating space in civil society for the expression of their members' beliefs, than with forming parties in order to control and use state power. Another way of expressing this is to say that they are concerned with 'identity', a term whose lack of clarity has been indicated in the previous paragraph.

Now, of course, there is a need in political sociology to give some account of movements like those concerned with ecological issues, the position of women and homosexuals and the peace movement. The British sociologist, Parkin, for instance, dealing with the Campaign for Nuclear Disarmament many years ago, recognised the existence of a middle-class radicalism which cross-cut the better understood class conflicts in British politics (Parkin, 1969), and clearly the sociology of the contemporary world calls for an analysis of the way in which such movements are effective or ineffective in a political system, structured traditionally in terms of class conflict. This, however, should be a matter of empirical study, and it is by no means to be assumed that such movements are solely concerned with opening up an identity space for their members. What is true of the peace movement is true also for the ecological, women's, youth and homosexual movements. Each of these has to be investigated empirically and cannot be adequately covered by a single generalisation. Each has its own way of influencing the political system.

Even if it is conceded that the movements mentioned above are about opening up an identity space, it can seriously be questioned whether the same is true of ethnic mobilisation and ethnic movements. One would have thought that a global perspective, and the recognition of an international division of labour, might have led to asking whether immigrant workers and entrepeneurs did not have, in this perspective, a class-like position, even if it were true that they relied upon the cultural resource of their ethnicity to provide them with solidarity in their struggles; and also whether, in the knowledge-based society, there was not also a dual labour market in which those, like immigrants, who inhabited the less privileged positions, still faced class-like problems because of their relation to the means of production. In the sections which follow we will seek precisely to consider the nature of the ethnicity of immigrant minorities from this point of view.

Perhaps the most fundamental difficulty which one has with contemporary sociology, however, is that of the terms in which it seeks to describe the social world. On this, the perspective taken in this chapter is essentially that of Max Weber. It assumes that what we have to do in sociology is to describe structures of social relations, that is to say the kinds of social relations which exist between individuals within different groups and within different institutions, and between groups and institutions within larger, usually politically defined, systems. Such a view, of course, does not rule out an interest in the cultural goals of groups or in the kind of cultural bonding which exists between individuals, but it does see this as tied into the business of creating structures of social relations. In these terms, Weber, and others in the Weberian tradition, sought to describe social classes and status groups. The important question which the theory of social movements has to face is that of the structures of social relations in these movements and between them and the larger political society. Related to this is the question of what we mean by ethnicity and ethnic groups. The argument here is that such groups should not be thought of simply as involving reactive responses to modernism, concerned with the preservation of identity. Rather they should be seen as forms of mobilisation in pursuit of political and economic interests. What follows below is an account of the nature of ethnicity and the development of ethnic groups, ethnies, nations, ethnic nations, and migrant groups in these terms. Within this context it will also be possible to discuss the psychological question of how and why individuals come to attach themselves to groups, that is to say, to discuss the question of identity.

The Nature of Ethnicity and Ethnies

A commonly held view in sociology, as well as in popular political discourse, is that, apart from other types of groups, such as those of class and status, there are some which are purely 'ethnic'. What is actually meant by ethnic in this sense is often not clear and sometimes it is claimed to have a mysterious quality of 'primordiality'. It is essential if we are to develop adequate concepts in this field that we should demystify this notion.

The primordial account of ethnicity is clearly stated by the American anthropologist Geertz in his earlier work. He contrasts social relations which arise from kinship, neighbourhood, commonality of language, religious belief, and customs, with those which are based upon 'personal attraction, tactical necessity, common interest or incurred moral obligation' (Geertz, 1963).

The first of these kinds of social relation, Geertz describes as simply 'given' as 'ipso facto', as 'unaccountable' and as having an overpowering force 'in and of themselves'. If, however, we are to understand and describe such social relations for sociological purposes, it is precisely necessary that we should demystify them and make them accountable.

The first point to notice is that these types of social relation are 'given' in one very special sense. They constitute the network into which human individuals are born. Thus, apart from so-called 'feral' children brought up by animals, every human infant or young child finds itself a member of a kinship group and of a neighbourhood, as well as sharing with some others a language, religious beliefs and customary practices. Each of these forms of membership, in fact, has a different potential span, and of themselves they do not coincide. Particularly, linguistic and religious communities extend far beyond the range of the groups based on kinship or common residence. Before one can speak of a group, therefore, it must be shown how they are made to coincide.

Three things, perhaps, are important in this business of group creation. One is that those who are its members gain some emotional satisfaction or a feeling of emotional warmth from belonging to the group. A second is that they share a belief in a myth of origin or the history of the group and that this myth makes clear the boundaries of the group. A third is that they regard the social relations within which they live as 'sacred' and as including not merely the living but the dead. It is because of these features of the situation, not mentioned by Geertz, that these groups have their special and overpowering quality. Moreover, while linguistic and religious ties may extend far beyond the group and suggest much wider memberships, speaking a common language and sharing religious beliefs are appropriated for its own purposes by the small group as criteria of membership.

Such small groups into which we all enter at birth are sometimes called 'ethnic' and, in this sense, we all have 'ethnicity'. But it does not matter whether we use the term 'ethnic'; we could, for example, speak simply of primordial or infantile communities. What matters is that all human beings as infants must have had an experience of this type of satisfying and sacred group membership.

It is, however, a further feature of the human condition that individuals do not merely enter this infantile ethnic trap; they also grow up, and growing up can involve two separate processes. One is that the individual who emerges from the infantile community develops his or her individual personality and interacts with other individuals from other groups on a different basis. The other is that he or she might find that there are those who suggest that the satisfying features of infantile ethnicity can be reproduced in much larger groups.

So far as the first of these processes are concerned what happens is the social psychological process of socialisation through which the significant others of the infantile community 'enter the heads' of the individual. What happens here, to express it in less graphic terms, is the sort of process of personality formation described by Durkheim, Freud, Mead, and others. There thus emerges the second social type of 'identity' referred to in the sociological theories discussed above. It refers back to the group in which the individual is socialised, but it also becomes the subject or agent of action in the wider world.

The social relations of this wider world may be of a different kind from that of the infantile group. They may, indeed, be of the non-primordial kind to which Geertz refers, being based upon 'personal attraction, tactical necessity, common interest or incurred moral obligation'. But there will be some individuals who take the opportunity of joining a more extended community which has some of the qualities of the small infantile one, and even those who have moved into a more individualised world may also seek the satisfaction some of the time of experiencing such membership. Durkheim opened up the discussion of these problems with his concepts of mechanical and organic solidarity (Durkheim, 1933). What we are suggesting here is that although some adults may move completely into a world of organic solidarity there are others who find more extended forms of mechanical solidarity, or who find a way of living in terms of both organic and continuing mechanical solidarity.

A group which extends the solidarity of the infantile group to a larger population is sometimes called an ethnie. The definition of an ethnie, therefore, is that it is a group, membership of which has some of the qualities of the simplest type of infantile group, and which is thought of as having the same kind of emotional warmth and sacredness. Its members share a common language, religion, and culture but are distinguished from some others who also share these characteristics by the fact that they believe in a myth or history of origin and of past collective action. Immediate kin and neighbourhood are not essential to defining the bounds of this group but they adopt symbols which stand for these simpler types of belonging.

A further feature of the ethnie is that membership also implies the possibility of non-membership and the notion that non-members are also organised in ethnies. Relations with members of these other ethnies lack the feelings of emotional warmth and sacredness which were experienced in the original one, and may be regarded as neutral, but commonly involve actual enmity. We should also note here that the self-chosen ethnicity of any group is contrasted with the ethnicity attributed to it by outsiders.

Groups of this kind belong in what Tonnies called the world of *Gemeinschaft* rather than *Gesellschaft* (Tonnies, 1955). They are, that is to say, not purposive in character, but exist for their own sake. Yet a different theory of ethnicity from that of Geertz suggests that their actual boundaries depend upon the situation in which they are operating. This is the approach of Barth (1959, 1969) who suggested that whether any particular individual belonged or did not belong to an ethnie, like the Pathans whom he studied, depended on the purpose in hand. According to this view, while it is still not claimed that ethnies are purposive associations, they are shaped by projects of one kind or another. We may call this the situationist theory of ethnic boundaries. Perhaps unconsciously, the groups formed in this way serve particular purposes.

A rather more cynical view emphasises the role of leaders who do not simply use symbols to evoke a feeling of ethnic belonging for its own sake, but, having conscious purposes, deliberately draw selectively on an ethnic heritage in order to unite the members of a collectivity in the service of some purpose. This is the theory of ethnogenesis which suggests that ethnicity was not 'given', but was more or less deliberately created in order to create a solidary group to pursue a project. Such a view is taken in a recent book, called *Creating Ethnicity*, by Eugene Roosens (1989).

Whether or not this rather more cynical view is correct, it does seem that the ethnie often comes into being in connection with some political project. Clearly this will be the case when an ethnie is at war with its neighbouring ethnies, war serving to intensify latent forms of ethnic bonding. But even short of this, there seem to be two ethnic projects which are of great importance. One is the claim to sovereignty over a territory; the other is migration. We shall have to return to the question of migration in due course, but first we must consider the question of territorial claims.

Of course, as we saw, territory is an element even of infantile ethnicity and, apart from the commonalities which we have mentioned in drawing the boundaries of an ethnie, this process usually, though not always, involves attachment to a territory. A further step is taken, however, when sovereignty is claimed over that territory. At this point the 'ethnie' becomes an ethnic nation.

Nations and Nationalism

Despite what has just been said, what are often called nations do not emerge in this way. In the history of European nationalism, the nation is seen as part of a modernising project. It is based not on an appeal to ethnicity or to emotional feelings of belonging, but, in the first place, on rationalistic notions like citizenship or participation in a market. Nations of this kind belong primarily in the world of Tonnies' *Gesellschaft*. Particularistic ethnic ties have no place in a nation of this kind, and commonly it sets out to erode ethnicity where it exists. The clearest case of a conception of the nation in these terms is to be found in French Republican and Jacobin thought, but it is a notion that is repeated in the making of other European nations.

A nation conceived in these terms, however, does still face two problems. One is the cutting off of any trans-national or extra-national ties which members may have through the market, through shared language or shared religion, and ensuring that the economic activity, the language and religion which occur have a functional relation to the purposes of the nation state. This kind of nation is thought of ideally as a bounded functional system contained within its own territory. The other problem is that, while it denies particularistic ethnic loyalties or subordinates them, it has itself to create its own sense of belonging, and it often does this by using the same kind of symbols as ethnies do, referring for instance to the mother country or the fatherland.

It may be thought that if a nation state has to do these things in order to create the new nation, it is not, sociologically speaking, so different from the sort of ethnic nation which we discussed earlier. But there does seem to be a crucial difference of emphasis and priorities. The ethnic nation is primarily a community which may then develop associative features when it embarks on the project of establishing sovereignty over a territory. The modernising nation is in the first place an association which then has to create a community and a new type of belonging.

This kind of basically rational modernising nation is in fact rare. In many cases the state comes into being after one ethnie has conquered another. The ruling ethnie maintains its own consciousness and structure, and may either destroy other ethnies, making their members second-class citizens, or simply dominate and subordinate them as groups. When this occurs, one of the features of the nation state might well be the mobilisation of the subordinate ethnies as ethnic nations, seeking varying degrees of autonomy, secession or independence.

Such ethnic mobilisation might also occur in the case of a new non-ethnic modernising state. While in this case the state is not simply imposing the rule of one ethnic group upon another, it does none the less offer an alternative focus of loyalty to the various ethnies, and this may well lead to an intensification of ethnicity in the subordinate groups as they struggle to survive. On the other hand, the members of the various ethnies might adjust to the situation by developing dual loyalties. They may still have a sense of belonging to their own group, but also enter into the new modern world of the market place and the polity. When they do this they will become accustomed to having multiple identities. Such multiple identities are not therefore to be thought of simply as a feature of post-modern society. They are inevitably involved in the integration of ethnic groups in the nation state.

We can see, then, that the emergence of the nation state is a complex process, and that whether it emerges as a result of modernising and rational trends, or through domination by one ethnie of others which it subordinates, there are many different types of group membership and many different and conflicting identities produced, which are too easily confused in discourses about nationalism. This situation is made even more complex with the emergence of multinational states and empires, and with what happens when they break up.

Nations, Empires and Post-Imperial Nationalism

Nations conquer other nations, and, when they do, the victorious nation establishes its rule over the defeated ones through imperial bureaucracies and armies. It may also open up the markets of the defeated nation to its own entrepeneurs and allow its own members to settle in the conquered territories. The establishment of these forms of domination is then likely to be met with resistance from the nationalisms of the subordinated nations.

When such imperial and multinational systems break up, two major consequences occur. One is that the subordinated nations reassert their sovereignty over their own territory and, *inter alia*, must establish control over their own subordinate ethnies; the other is that the settlers from the former dominant nation seek protection from the former imperial centre, and, in that centre, movements may occur, seeking to protect its settler members. Thus the history of imperialism and post-imperialism is marked by the emergence of both secessionist movements and irredentist movements and both of these are commonly referrred to as forms of nationalism, even though they are very different.

The Project of Ethnic Migration

Ethnicity, however, is not always related to the assertion of sovereignty over a territory. A quite different project from that of the nationalist one is that of migration. In this case, some members of an ethnic or national group, whether for economic reasons or because of political persecution, leave their own territory and seek to establish themselves in other territories over which they do not seek to establish political control. More than this, they may migrate to a number of territories within which they have varying economic opportunities. A good example of such migration is that of migrants from the Punjab who have settled across the world from Fiji to California.

One way of describing the total world of such migrating groups is to say that they live in the diaspora. This is a term which can be used in a narrower or a broader sense. In the narrow sense, in which the term is used of the Jews and Afro-Americans, it implies that the dispersal was due to some politically traumatic event and that those involved seek to return to the homeland. This, however, is not the case with many migrating communities, like the Punjabis, and it is perhaps misleading to use the term to describe them. Certainly if one speaks of the Punjabi diaspora one is using the term in a wider and looser sense.

Migrant communities of this kind have a number of distinct points of reference. They are seeking to maximise their economic opportunities in a range of territories across the world, often moving from one country of settlement to another if better opportunities are available in the latter. (Thus Punjabi settlers in Britain, for instance, may move on to the United States when they have accumulated enough money.) Secondly, however, they are oriented to securing their position and winning rights in their country of present settlement. Thirdly, they may seek to retain their own culture, if in a modified form, as a resource in any of their struggles. Finally they may have some kind of 'myth of return' to their homeland, may seek to acquire property there, and may retain an interest in its politics, using their position in the country of settlement as a base to support some political interest, which governments prevent in the homeland itself.

The most immediate form of membership in such an internationally dispersed community is usually the extended family and the most immediate form of economic interest is the protection and enlargement of the family estate. A family group and estate might be based right across the territories of migration. (A Punjabi settler in Britain might have familial obligations to relatives in the Punjab itself or to others in Canada or the United States or to both.) Familial connections also exist within a larger bounding framework of a migrant ethnic community defined in terms of language, religion, custom and historical myth. Such a community is today at least as important as membership of a nation. In the sections below we shall deal with one aspect of the total situation of international migrant communities, namely that of their relationship to national states in which their members settle.

The Response of National Societies to Migrant Communities

What we now frequently find in the new globalised world is a confrontation between two types of society and community. One is the community of the national state; the other is the migrant community. The major political problem is then that of how the national state responds to the existence of what it sees as ethnic minority communities and the ways in which they are integrated or not integrated.

There are, of course, some societies which consist primarily or solely of immigrants. When, however, a new nation is formed from such groups, one of them provides the framework within which all later arrivals have to work. Thus the United States includes all kinds of immigrants, but it has at least a national language which the later arrivals have to accept as the national language.

It also has to be noted that national societies are not necessarily culturally and economically united prior to arrival of immigrants. They are often divided in terms of classes and status groups, and any national culture will often rest upon some kind of compromise negotiated between these groups.

A number of responses to incoming immigrants are possible from members of the so-called 'host society'. They may seek to keep them out, to expel them or to attack and kill them; they may see their presence as temporary, regarding them as 'Gastarbeiders' and second-class citizens; they may demand that the incomers should abandon their own culture and identity and become assimilated; or they may pursue a policy of multiculturalism. It is this fourth alternative which is the primary concern of this chapter, so far as migrating ethnic groups are concerned.

The Concept of a Multicultural Society

There are actually two possibilities in societies which see themselves as multicultural. One is that although the immigrant communities and their cultures are seen as having a right to exist they are not necessarily accorded equal rights, and may be regarded as culturally inferior; the other, however, is that some ideal of equal citizenship, previously negotiated between the classes and status groups in the host society, is extended to the immigrant groups, even though their right to retain their own culture is recognised.

As a matter of empirical fact this ideal of an egalitarian multicultural society has probably never been fully recognised. None the less it is an important political ideal and can provide an ideological framework within which minority groups can operate in adjusting to settlement in another nation state.

Such an ideal was enunciated in Britain by the Home Secretary of 1968, Roy Jenkins, when he defined 'integration', 'not as flattening process of uniformity, but as cultural diversity, coupled with equality of opportunity, in an atmosphere of mutual tolerance' (Rex and Tomlinson, 1979). This ideal, I have argued elsewhere (Rex, 1986b), suggests that there are two cultural domains, and two forms of belonging, in the multicultural society. One is a public political culture and a political society based on the idea of equality of opportunity, but often also on a conception of at least a minimum of social rights for all, i.e. equality of outcome (Marshall, 1950). This, of course, is the ideal of the Welfare State, achieved in varying degrees by most West European states, and surviving to some extent even after the move towards more free-market-based societies in the 1980s. Such an ideal, where it is held, cannot be brought into question because of the coming of immigrants. The indigenous community and the immigrant ethnic minority communities are equally called upon to accept it.

Given this shared political ideal, however, the question which remains open is whether the culture and social organisation of diverse groups is to be allowed to continue, or whether they should be forced to assimilate to a single and homogeneous national culture. What the multicultural alternative suggests is that it is possible, without threat to the overall political unity of the national society, to recognise that minorities have the right to their own language in family and community contexts, the right to practise their own religion, the right to organise domestic and family relations in their own way, and the right to maintain communal customs.

There are three basic reasons, it is argued, why such cultural diversity should be accepted. The first is the simple one that the separate cultures may have values which are important in their own right, and actually enrich the overall society; the second is that the social organisation and cultural forms of the minorities provide them with the protection and emotional support of a community standing between the individual family and the state, something which was recognised by Durkheim in *The Division of Labour in Society* (1933), where he was concerned with the ways in which a society based on 'organic solidarity' differed from a state of anomie or anarchic individualism; the third is that ethnicity can provide the kind of solidarity in a group which enables it to fight more effectively to defend the rights of its members. Taking these three points together the suggestion is made that, far from threatening democratic societies, the recognition of cultural diversity actually enriches and strengthens democracy.

Of course, in an increasingly globalised world, immigrant communities also have other points of reference. They may, as we suggested, use their location in a country of settlement as a base to pursue political interests in their homelands or to assist those who have gone on to other countries of settlement. Because of this, they may be regarded as troublesome or dangerous, and nation states in their countries of settlement tend to be suspicious of any transnational organisations to which they affiliate. Thus, it often becomes a condition of their acceptance that they should be loyal to the state and refrain from treasonable acts. This was an important question during the Gulf War when Muslim immigrants in Europe were thought likely to support Iraq as a Muslim state against an alliance led by non-Muslims.

In this case and in others, however, minorities, when forced to choose, have accepted their obligation of political loyalty to their country of settlement.

Multiculturalism and Democratic Political Theory

A recent symposium on *Ethnic Mobilisation in a Multicultural Europe* held in the University of Warwick showed that the idea of multiculturalism raised important problems and anxieties amongst European social scientists (Rex and Drury, 1994). In fact such an idea does not fit easily within the framework of the largely shared political theory of a social democratic welfare state. The problems raised in the symposium were of two kinds. One suggested that the ways of handling of the ethnic problem which were likely to emerge were at odds with the kinds of procedure for handling conflicts of interest which social democratic welfare states had evolved. The other was that the actual kinds of institution which were likely to be set up would, far from enhancing democracy, actually provide governments with new means of manipulation and control.

In the most thoroughly argued of these criticisms, Radtke (1994) suggests that, whereas the social democratic welfare state is based upon a pluralist society in which different interest groups negotiate about their interests and rights, what is proposed in the idea of multiculturalism is a system in which any member of an ethnic minority group must represent himself or herself as culturally different, and this is likely actually to prevent the resolution of conflicts. The kind of ethnicity which will then be defended is likely to be reactionary and regressive and to present irresolvable problems. Wieviorka (1994), again, argues that the very concept of ethnicity is an alien concept in a modern society, and one which is only introduced in dealing with inferior groups. Similarly, on this point, Jan Rath, in a separate thesis, offers a critique of multicultural policy in the Netherlands (Rath, 1991) arguing that what this policy does is to 'minorise' individuals, marking them for unequal treatment. All of these criticisms suggest that what multiculturalism does is to place minorities outside the normal political process in social democratic welfare states.

In Sweden, Schierup and Alund, making a rather different point (Schierup and Alund, 1987 and 1990; Schierup, 1994) have drawn attention to the diversity to be found in the situation of different individuals, and particularly young individuals, drawn from the same group. While national policy deals with the traditional elders of immigrant communities and reifies immigrant culture, many young people from these groups are forming syncretic links with members of both other immigrant communities and the indigeneous society. Like Rath, Schierup and Alund see official multicultural policy as essentially manipulative and in no way conducive to democracy which is seen as resting either on class conflict and compromise or on new social movements.

There is undoubtedly truth in all of these criticisms so far as the actual forms of multiculturalism which have been developed by governments are concerned. But against them two things may be said. The first is that most of them in effect argue for the maintenance of existing political forms and for the absorption of immigrant groups into normal and established political processes (though Schierup and Alund modify this traditional social democratic position, through the recognition of modern social movements). The second is that they assume that the definition of ethnicity rests simply with the state and take no account of the actual forms of ethnic mobilisation and the minorities' own goals.

Such criticism and responses are very much less valid if the nature of ethnicity amongst migrants outlined here is fully understood. What we have sought to show, in fact, is that this ethnicity is complex, many-sided and changing and should not be reified. It includes as part of ethnic self-definition the notion of fighting in a democratic way for equal rights, and it accepts that there can be a diversity of response by different members of a minority community. It also accepts that some members of minority communities will move away from their traditional culture and that they may follow a strategy of working with or in indigenous organisations in addition to or instead of relying solely on ethnic organisations. We should not, however, over-simplify in the opposite direction and imagine that ethnicity and ethnic mobilisation do not exist. The real problem of the political sociology of multiculturalism is to do justice both to ethnic mobilisation and 'normal' political processes and to show how these are interrelated.

Inevitably in such a situation individuals belong to different social groups and different cultural systems simultaneously and are used to the fact of multiple identities. This does not mean 'living between two cultures' and breaking down under the strain. It is a normal part of social and political life. Nor, we should note again, is this simply a feature of the post-modern condition.

CONCLUSION: A MORE EMPIRICAL APPROACH TO THE PROBLEMS OF ETHNICITY AND IDENTITY

Clearly, from all that has been said above, the resurgence of ethnicity which has followed the break-up of empires, the global nature of migration processes and the formation of worldwide migrant communities, and the complexity of the process of the political integration of minorities, all point to the need to revise the dominant theories of political sociology which have arisen in West European welfare states. What this revision has to do is to base itself on a careful analysis of the actual empirical and historical processes which have occurred with regard to nationalism and migration. The crucial difference between this discourse and that of recent highly sophisticated forms of sociological theory is that it does not depend upon some notion of a new and remarkable transformation of the nature of society, in which what are seen as the old problems of class and conflict give way to a new and mysterious situation in which ethnic politics, together with other kinds of politics, come for the first time to be based purely and solely on 'identity'. What we really need is a careful historical and empirical analysis of the forms of ethnicity and ethnic belonging which occur in the course of national conflicts and the processes of migration. It does not seem particularly useful to refer to these processes as late modern or post-modern. They do not take an easy place in such a meta-narrative. They are simply concerned with some of the most important political processes of the present day and sometimes, indeed, involve very old and recurrent types of group formation and conflict, albeit on a more global scale. The task of sociological theory should be to systematise what is involved in these empirically studied processes, not to mystify them through the use of a confusingly defined concept of identity.

5 Transnational Migrant Communities and Ethnic Minorities in Modern Multicultural Societies[*]

THE FEAR OF ETHNICITY

Ethnicity today is in ill repute. With the collapse of the bipolar world system after 1989 the various groups, nations and communities which had been held together by the quasi-imperial systems of the superpowers were left to fight for themselves and amongst themselves. In the name of ethnicity, nationalism or ethnic nationalism they fought brutally for territory, and the Serbian notion of 'ethnic cleansing' came to provoke something of the horror felt towards the Nazi holocaust fifty years earlier. Meanwhile, even though they were not engaged in nationalist projects, migrant ethnic minorities became the focus of suspicion and hostility in their countries of settlement.

In these circumstances it has not been easy to argue for the political ideal of multiculturalism in Western European societies. It is an ideal which is regarded with grave suspicion in the media, amongst politicians and social scientists and in public opinion generally, as well as amongst educated members of the migrant

---

[*]Published in 1994 in a special issue of *Innovation*, vol. 7, no. 3, Carfax Publications, Oxford.

communities themselves who fear that their labelling as 'ethnic' necessarily involves their assignment to inferiority.

Although the unitary nature of Western European nations and their cultures can be exaggerated, since historically they themselves have been ethnically diverse, and divided in terms of class and status, it is nonetheless true that, allowing for this diversity, the range of permissible cultural and political variation has been limited and the culture of new immigrant groups, coming often from long distances and having distinct languages, religions and customs, is seen as 'alien'.

Those members of migrant communities who have been successful in adapting to the demands of their host societies understandably fear that if they represent themselves as culturally different they will be treated as inferior and denied equal rights, and they are often supported by democrats who see the setting-up of separate multicultural arrangements as something which will undermine established and familiar democratic political procedures.

There are a number of ways in which this democratic and universalistic response of democrats affects the thinking of social scientists. From a simple Marxist point of view, ethnic conscious-ness is seen as false consciousness and a diversion from the class struggle and class politics which are taken to be normal. Liberals and republicans also see any deviation from the notion of universal and equal citizenship as politically dangerous, while social demo-crats, with their notion of the reconciliation of conflicting class interests in the welfare state compromise, find it difficult to accept the setting-up of special and separate institutions for dealing with minorities. More widely, those who see existing societies as based upon a delicate balance between the cultures of status groups, rather than simply on a class compromise, are inclined to see the coming of more distant and alien cultures as upsetting this balance (Rex and Drury, 1995).

These fears are understandable and it is to be expected that European social scientists and politicians will wish to defend institutions which have been slowly and painfully established in political struggles of the past two centuries. Nonetheless such attitudes are literally prejudiced in that they prejudge the nature of ethnic minority cultures and the goals which ethnic minority communities set themselves. What is necessary for a serious sociology of multicultural societies is an empirical as well as a theoretical study of the nature of migrant ethnic minority groups, based not on the way in which these groups are categorised and classified by the state but on the way in which they see themselves. This is the object of this chapter. What we shall do is, first, look at the nature of ethnicity in general; second, look at the way in which the two major projects of ethnicity and nationalism branch from this general ethnic stem; and third, look in more detail at the actual structure of migrant ethnic minority communities and their relationship to modern nation states.

The Simplest Forms of Ethnicity

In the literature on ethnicity and nationalism the first major division is that between 'primordial' and 'situational' or 'instrumental' theory. According to the former, ethnic bonds are quite unlike all others; they are recurrent, largely inexplicable, and have an overpowering emotional and non-rational quality (Geertz, 1963). According to the latter, they are, if not wholly invented by political leaders and intellectuals for purposes of social manipulation, at least related to specific social and political projects (Roosens, 1989; Barth, 1959, 1969).

It is important that we should understand why the primordialist view can be maintained at all, even if ultimately we reject it as an adequate account of ethnicity and nationalism. What we need to do is to consider the difference between two types of group affiliation, namely one which involves a strong sense of emotional belonging, and even of sacredness, and another in which such affiliation is related in some way to ulterior and rationally formulable purposes. To do this we must consider, first, the very simplest form of ethnicity into which children are born, and, second, the formation of more extensive groups, now commonly referred to as 'ethnies'.

Our human condition is necessarily a social one. Apart from the so-called feral children, brought up by animals, any human infant finds himself or herself caught up at birth in what I have called 'the infantile ethnic trap' (Rex, 1995). Such an infant finds himself or herself as caught up in a kin network in which named and categorised individuals play specific roles, and in relation to whom the infant has clearly defined rights and duties. He or she will also belong to a neighbourhood group which may coincide with the kingroup, but often simply intersects with it. Such groups as these will also share a language as well as religious beliefs and customs.

On a social psychological level these simple groups will be seen as generating positive warm emotions and as possessing some supernatural qualities. The dead as well as the living are thought of as belonging to the group, and its origins and history are explained in terms of some kind of myth or narrative which is taught to the young as truth.

It should be noted here that language and religion present special problems in that they are often shared with a wider range of people who are not members of the group. None the less, within these larger linguistic and religious communities, smaller groups are differentiated in terms of kin, neighbourhood, customs and history. Language may be modified by dialect and religious beliefs may be reinterpreted and appropriated to reflect the more specific beliefs of the smaller group.

From this initial base members go on to enter a wider world in two ways. Firstly, through the socialisation process (as described in different ways by Freud, Mead, Durkheim and others) the external role players 'enter the head' of the individual whose very personal identity is then a social creation so that he or she acts not simply as a Hobbesian individual but as an ethnic individual. Such an individual may then go on to enter into relations with other individuals of different ethnicity just as his or her ethnic group enters into relations with other groups. Secondly, however, it is possible that the individual will find that there are larger groups than his original one which can give him or her some of the same feeling of belonging and sacredness. It is these larger groups that we refer to as 'ethnies'.

The ethnie is differentiated from the simpler type of kin and neighbourhood based group by the fact that there is no precise definition of the roles of one member *vis-à-vis* another. Rather the group is constituted, as Smith has suggested (A. Smith, 1986), by the fact that it has a name, shared symbols and a myth of origin. These elements, however, do mean that the ethnie claims something of the strong sense of emotional belonging and sacredness which is to be found in the smaller group.

This is not to say that the ethnie does not have its own structure of social relations. Usually there is some sort of status and economic differentiation and complementarity between its members, and there will be some type of role differentiation of those who exercise authority of a political and religious sort. What differentiates the ethnie from a modern political nation, however, is that these economic and political structures are subordinated to the community structure. Characteristically a priesthood exercises more authority than it would in the nation state.

Smith also tells us that the ethnie normally has some sort of attachment to a territory, even though it does not set up the administrative structures to be found in the modern state which claim authority throughout that territory. Ethnies will, of course, vary in their size and complexity and the term should probably be extended to cover a range of possibilities, including, at one extreme, a group which has little more than a name, a myth of origin and a shared culture, and, at the other, one which has some of the features of the nation state.

The ethnie's own self-definition may not be the same as that used in referring to it by other ethnies. Generally its self-definition involves the notion of moral worthiness, while other groups might describe it in quite derogatory terms. On the other hand it should not be thought that ethnies are of their very nature forced into conflict with one another. They may be, if conflict over control of a territory or other resources is disputed, but it is perfectly possible for different ethnies to live at peace with each other.

The primordialist view of the ethnie would be that it exists largely for it own sake. The alternative 'situationist' view deriving from the work of Barth, however, would suggest that the boundaries of such an ethnie depend on the situation or on the project in which the group is engaged. There is truth in both these positions, particularly when control of a territory is involved. In this case we should say that the boundaries of the group are at least partly determined by a political project, even though it may call on the solidarity of the pre-existing ethnie as a resource. We will next deal with the case in which the project is the creation of a nation. In the latter part of the chapter we will deal with groups whose project is almost the opposite of laying claim to a territory in the business of migration.

The Nation State, Nationalism and Ethnic Nationalism

The sort of discourse with which we have been concerned above derives largely from social anthropology, social psychology and history. A quite different discourse, however, has dominated thinking about nationalism and the nation state. In this discourse the nation state is thought of as coming into being almost *ab initio* as part of a modernising project.

Gellner's account (Gellner, 1983) of this modernising project, of nationalism and the nation state, is probably too narrow. According to him, the nation depends upon a political and intellectual elite imposing a shared culture on the whole population in a territory, particularly through a national education system which ensures that all members of the nation have a minimum of competence and a degree of flexibility so that they can fulfil a variety of roles. Such a culture and such an education system is, in Gellner's view, essential to the operation of an industrial society.

There is, however, more to be said about modernisation than this. Most important is the fact that the polity and the economy are released from their subordination to the communal institutions and the culture of the ethnie. Instead they come to dominate it or to erode the very basis of its existence.

In fact, however, in this conception of the nation, it is the polity which is dominant. It rules and administers the whole of a given territory and, in so doing, faces a problem in that the economy, language and religion have to be brought under its control. The natural tendency of the modern nation state so far as the economy is concerned is towards economic autarchy. On the linguistic front, it has to ensure that, however much minority languages are tolerated for communal purposes, there is a shared official national language. Finally, so far as religion is concerned the priesthood must in some way come to terms with the state and cannot be allowed to encourage loyalty to some wider community of co-religionists.

Such a nation state is also bound to encounter resistance from ethnies within its borders. It may deal with this either by destroying the ethnies and their culture or granting them a degree of subordinate autonomy. If it fails to do either of these the ethnies themselves may develop in the direction of ethnic nationalism, seeking to establish their own states, whether of a modernising or traditional sort. Thus the nation state is likely to foster other nationalisms apart from its own.

The modern nation also rarely rests content with the bonding of its own members simply as individual citizens. It needs to create a national sentiment and a sense of belonging to the nation. To some extent it can do this by converting its population to the ideology of nationalism, but this will probably only be possible amongst an elite. It also therefore has to create its own symbols, mythology and sense of sacredness and belonging. In doing this it will be using many of techniques used by pre-modern ethnies. This is what is happening when the national leaders speak of the mother country or the fatherland.

What the theory of nationalism has to do therefore is to describe a complex process of interaction between modernising nation states, ethnies and ethnic nationalism. Thus the business of creating the modern nation state is always incomplete, and what is loosely called nationalism covers a variety of interacting types.

Finally, we have to consider under the heading of nationalism the fact of imperialism and the creation of multinational states. Nations conquer nations and when they do new imperial structures extending beyond the boundaries of the conquering nation come into being. An imperial bureaucracy is created, metropolitan entrepreneurs gain access to the productive system and the markets of subordinate nations, and settlers from the conquering metropolis go to live and work in the subordinated territories.

Just as the creation of the individual nation provokes resistance from ethnies and ethnic nationalism, however, so imperial conquest provokes resistance from subordinate nations. If then the metropolitan power becomes weaker for any reason, or if its rule is overthrown, old nationalisms will be released and will flourish in the formerly subordinate territories. In fact they will be stronger than ever in national sentiment as they add to their myths the story of their resistance and their successful national revolutions. At the same time they may still have their own internal problems of dealing with the resistance of their own ethnies and ethnic nationalisms. All of these problems are evident in the wake of the break-up of the Soviet Empire and the USSR.

The Second Project of Ethnicity: Migration

Although much of the theoretical writing about ethnicity has been concerned with the attachment of an ethnic group to a territory, in fact ethnic communities are often concerned precisely with their *detachment* from a territory, that is to say with the business of international migration.

In attempting to relate such groups to the theory of nationalism, a commonly used notion is that of diaspora. A diaspora is said to exist when an ethnie or nation suffers some kind of traumatic event which leads to the dispersal of its members, who nonetheless continue to aspire to return to the homeland. Diasporic nationalism is thus seen as one kind of nationalism. It is exemplified by Jews seeking a return to Zion, Black Americans seeking to return to Africa and Armenians seeking a return to Armenia.

The term 'diaspora' has also been loosely used, however, to refer to any national or ethnic group dispersed across several countries and this may be misleading, since many such groups have not suffered a clear traumatic experience, and are not primarily concerned with a return to some kind of Zion. They are not in fact nationalist at all, even though they have some kind of transnational community as a point of reference. There are three cases to be distinguished.

Firstly there are groups of migrants from economically backward to economically successful countries. Individuals from the former migrate to the latter in order to seek work. Some may have no strong desire to return to their country of origin and simply seek assimilation in the country of settlement. Quite commonly, however, they may send remittances home and plan to return there, and even those who are destined *de facto* to remain in the country of settlement and bring up their children there, may retain some kind of myth of return.

Secondly, there are those who are part of more extensive migration movements, who migrate to a number of countries and who intend to go on living abroad and exploiting whatever opportunities are available within the several countries. For them there is an international community distinct both from the community of the homeland and that of the nations in whose territories they are temporarily or permanently settled. Often such communities consist of secondary colonialists for whom opportunities open up within another country's former empire. Such is the position of Indians from the Punjab settled in countries ranging from South East Asia, though Europe, to North America.

Thirdly, there are communities of refugees whose situations vary enormously. They may constitute diasporas of a kind and, seeing their immediate situation as temporary, envisage a return to the homeland when political circumstances change, but given that they are often fleeing from their fellow nationals they are not necessarily nationalistic in outlook. There will, moreover, be many who cannot envisage such a change in political circumstances at home and are committed to finding a new life in the countries of refuge.

Separately from these cases is one which is more closely related to nationalism and occurs after the break-up of empires. In this case there are often settlers in the colonised territories who now look for protection to the former metropolis, and in that metropolis there will be those who feel the need to protect or gather-in the former settlers. This is best described as irredentist nationalism. It occurs amongst White settlers from the former European Empires in Africa and Asia and is happening in the case of Russians living in the former territories of the USSR. It is misleading in these cases to speak of diasporas.

In understanding the second project of nationalism the most important case is the second of those mentioned above. In order to grasp its structure, it may be helpful to consider the case of Punjabi migration and particularly Punjabi Sikh migration by way of illustration.

Looking first at the country of origin, we have to note that the territory of the Punjab, within which the principle language is Punjabi, is divided between India and Pakistan. Huge population transfers occurred there at the time of the partition of the sub-continent and it is possible to distinguish Pakistani and Indian Punjabi migrants, primarily in terms of their religion. Even if we concentrate on the Indian Punjab, the population is divided in religious terms between Sikhs and Hindus and there are separate migrant networks deriving from the two communities. Punjabi Sikhs also support a nationalist movement, the most extreme version of which seeks to establish a separate state of Khalistan.

This movement has led to violence and terrorism both in India itself and abroad.

There are further divisions amongst the Punjabi Sikhs based upon caste and class. The most important of the caste divisions, at least amongst migrants, is that between the Jats, who hold, or seek to hold, land, and the Ramgarias who were originally carpenters. So far as class is concerned, there is division between those for whom the nationalist movement is most important and those who support either one of the Indian Communist parties or the Indian Congress Party.

Even if we confine our attention to Punjabi Sikhs, it is clear that Punjabi Sikhism is not a unitary phenomenon. Nonetheless there is a shared religiously based culture which is a point of reference for all Punjabi Sikhs, even including the Marxists.

The political position of the Punjabi Sikhs was profoundly affected by the fact that they did not support the Mutiny within British India in 1857. They therefore enjoyed a somewhat privileged position within India and also had the necessary skills to enable them to play a role within the wider British Empire, particularly in the development of East Africa, but later in Britain itself. From these bases they were able to seek still further opportunities in other parts of the Empire and in other countries in North America and Europe. It is against this background that the ethnic community of Punjabi Sikhs can be understood.

The basic unit within the international Punjabi Sikh community is probably the extended family. Such an extended family may be thought of as trying to increase its family estate. This may involve remittances and saving with a view to obtaining land or starting a business in the Punjab itself, but this relationship with the homeland is only one possibility. A Punjabi family in Britain might well envisage further migration to North America and it might have relatives there as well as in the Punjab.

Beyond the family there are, however, other social and cultural links. Even those who are not particularly religious may participate in the life of the temples or gurdwara, at least so far as dealing with the life crises of birth, marriage and death are concerned, and many men will still display the five symbols of Sikhism as well as wear turbans. Thus Sikhism remains an important point of reference within the transnational community. Such wider cultural links help to produce a degree of solidarity even amongst families who would otherwise be simply competitors, and in planning their affairs the separate extended families will be able to rely on the networks which these cultural links provide. Of course there is conflict within the community but there is also a basis for solidarity *vis-à-vis* the indigenous communities in the land of settlement.

Given such solidarity, the Sikh community has still to develop relationships with the various modernising nation states within which its members settle. It has the experience and skills to do this. The development of class-based industrial and political organisations is not something new to the Sikhs and they are quite capable of exploiting the opportunities available to them within the politics of the nation state of settlement. Part of the total political culture of the community is concerned precisely with ensuring that its members have maximum rights in their country of settlement. We are not dealing with a simple traditional ethnie facing a modernising nation. Rather what we have is a community with a changing and developing political culture with a strong modernising element within it.

It can be argued that Punjabi Sikhs are a special case. But so are most transnational migrant communities. What can be seen in this case, moreover, are certain generalisable elements. First, despite the immense internal complexity of the community, even before migration, it still has reference points, particularly those based on religion, which give it an overall unity. Second, this community is now located across the world and intends to go on living across the world and exploiting whatever economic opportunities the world provides. Third, the existence of this community does not mean that there is not scope for individual family enterprise. Fourth, it has to be part of the political culture of this community that it produces its own modernising ways of dealing with a modern nation state. Finally, it is a part of this overall world-based outlook that some kind of interest is retained in the homeland, taking the economic form of remittances and investment in the homeland and the political form of support for the various nationalist and class-based factions and parties in the homeland. (This last point does suggest some applicablity of the concept of a nationalist diaspora, but the point which is being made here is that this is balanced by the seeking of whatever economic opportunities are available in the transnational community.)

Of course the business of dealing with various nation states and their social and political institutions involves some cost to the community. Success in the land of settlement may well mean that some of those who succeed within this system may leave the community altogether, and there is strong evidence in the case of Punjabi Sikhs in Britain that some of their successful young members are doing just this. Having achieved educational, business or professional success they find that they can hold their own in British society and become, to all intents and purposes, British. But even though this may be the case, this very success depends at the outset on the maintenance of communal solidarity and that same communal solidarity projected across the world also provides wider opportunities. There may still be advantages, even for an acculturated British Sikh, in using his or her networks to participate in a wider transnational system. Thus, for example, many professionals and business men in Britain may still use their ethnic networks to improve their position still further in North America. It is quite possible in fact to take advantage of membership in two societies and communities, one being that of the nation in the country of settlement, the other that of the transnational ethnic community.

Looking more widely at the other minorities in Britain and Western Europe, one can, of course, see that there are a number of possible variations from the type suggested for the Punjabi Sikhs, although most of the Asian minorities in Britain reproduce the structural and cultural features mentioned (e.g. Punjabi Hindus, Gujaratis, Kashmiris, Pakistanis and Bangladeshis). In the case of migrants to the Caribbean there is a diasporic element or at least a diasporic myth of return to Africa, although for many the possibilities presented by migration to Britain, Canada or the United States are more important than any such return, and the homeland to which they refer is more likely to be a West Indian island than Africa. In the case of the Turks in Germany mobility to other countries as well as citizenship in Germany is restricted by guestworker status and the main points of reference are simply Turkey and Germany. Algerians find themselves in a dependent post-colonial relationship with France. The Moroccan situation is more like that of the Punjabis though the migrants are more likely to be in poorer occupations. Finally, there are the Southern Europeans, who on the one hand can fairly readily assimilate culturally to their countries of settlement, yet are close enough to their sending societies to maintain social and cultural links with them. In all cases much will depend upon the range of occupations which are open to migrants and the skills they have to exploit them.

Despite all this variation it is clear that in all cases we are dealing with transnational communities which are not primarily nationalist in their orientation (except in relation to surviving homeland issues) and in which an element of diasporic yearning for return is not the overwhelming uniting political factor.

The Response of Nation States to Immigrant Ethnic Minorities

The other party to the relationship in which these immigrant communities are involved is, of course, the nation state, and it is to its reaction to immigrant settlement that we must now turn. It is here that we have to deal with the problems of nationalism, particularly nationalism of the modernising sort.

There are two aspects to the nationalism of European states. On the one hand, they define their own national identity in relation to each other and to their empires and colonial territories, such notions of identity having been reinforced by wars, economic competition and resistance to colonial liberation. On the other, they have created a national cultural and political consensus out of conflicting class and status cultures. In Britain, Marshall (1950) suggested that with the acquisition of social rights in addition to legal and political rights, British workers now had reason to identify more strongly with their national citizenship than with social class as Marx had predicted. Williams also suggested in his book, *The Long Revolution* (1961), that these workers were now also beginning to win their cultural rights.

The notions of legal and social citizenship are central to the modern nation state. In the French Republican tradition it is the legal equality of citizenship which is crucial. Two hundred years after the French Revolution, however, social rights have become more central and most European societies see themselves as having achieved some kind of political compromise between contending classes through the establishment of the Welfare State. In any case the central theme of the political culture of these societies involves the recognition of equality of opportunity and, up to a minimum level, equality of outcome. There are, of course, those in most countries who would prefer to define the national culture and identity in terms of upper class culture, but it is the notion of equality which is the central ideological element in the modernising nation state.

Given an ideological consensus of this kind these societies also tend to recognise the possibility of separate cultures, thought of as private matters in which the state does not interfere. Religious tolerance is therefore the norm. This is achieved in France through the secularisation of politics and education, while in the Netherlands the policy of 'pillarisation' recognised the right of the separate faiths to control considerable institutional areas. It is less completely achieved in Britain and in North European countries where there is an established church with special duties and privileges.

But the social structure of the nation state is not determined simply by the creation of social equality. There has to be a national language for the conduct of official business; there is a national economy over which the government seeks to retain control even in the face of international markets and multinational business corporations; there is a civil and a criminal legal system to which all are required to conform, even if, through the political process and through the courts themselves, laws which are thought to be unjust can be changed; there is a national educational system concerned with developing the skills of the population as well as imparting shared national values; finally, there is also a developing national literary and aesthetic culture.

The question with which we are concerned is that of how a nation which defines itself in these terms reacts to the presence of immigrant communities and their cultures and how these communities themselves fit into the national system.

Two reactions which are to be expected in the receiving society are those of xenophobia and racism on the one hand and assimilationism on the other. The terms 'xenophobia' and 'racism' are probably too loosely used, but as they are used here they refer to reactions to immigrant communities which involve demands for their expulsion, physical attacks, racial and cultural abuse and racial and ethnic discrimination which gives the immigrants less rights than those of full citizens. All these elements have been involved in the political reactions of European societies to post-war immigrants. Sometimes they occur simply in the propaganda and activities of anti-democratic parties but they have also influenced the policies of governments. Of particular importance here is that, in the German speaking countries, while measures may be taken to ensure the legal and social rights of immigrants, they are not accorded political rights.

The assimilationist alternative has been more prominent in France. There is a widespread belief that minority cultures and minority identities threaten French national culture and identity and that while minority members should have equal rights as citizens they should be discouraged from maintaining their own cultures. Politically they should be expected to work through the mainstream parties and there should be no intrusion of minority culture and values into the secular national schools.

The third alternative to the policies of racial and ethnic exclusion on the one hand and assimilationism on the other is multi-culturalism. Such a policy, which is professed in Britain, the Netherlands and in Sweden even if it is imperfectly practised, involves both the attempt to ensure the full rights of citizens to minorities and the recognition of their right to maintain their separate cultures.

Our next question is that of how migrant ethnic minorities are likely to react to these various regimes. Obviously, so far as the first is concerned, they will organise to fight against 'racism' in all its forms, but in doing this they are likely to have the support of many indigenous democrats. So far as the second is concerned there will be some who are prepared to accept the hard bargain which is offered if it brings sufficient rewards to individual minority members, but generally the attempt simply to destroy minority culture is likely to provoke resistance, both because of the psychological cost in terms of the threat to the identity of minority members, and because of the destruction of helpful community networks which it involves.

Clearly it is the third alternative, multiculturalism, which provides most scope for the immigrant minority to attain its own goals. The question is whether it can do this without threatening the society as a whole.

Usually multiculturalism recognises that there is a private and communal sphere in which there is no need for government to interfere. This is thought to include the speaking of minority languages within the community, the practising of minority religions and the maintenance of minority customs in matters relating to the family and marriage. There are, however, problems even about this restrictive definition of the private and communal sphere. Whatever minority customs there may be in relation to family matters there are no cases in which such customs are backed by the law, despite an occasionally expressed demand by Muslims that their family affairs should be in accordance with the sharia law. Often, too, these customs are criticised by human rights activists and feminists who believe that they should be a matter of public concern. There is also often an unwillingness to admit that the propagation of minority cultures should have any place within the educational systems or even be subsidised by the state outside of it. Minority religions might also be denied facilities through such means as planning regulations.

Usually, however, ethnic minority cultures and social organisation can be preserved in these circumstances, though minority organisations will usually have to work to maximise their area of independence. They will do this in order to maintain their community structure nationally and internationally, but if they enjoy a reasonable measure of tolerance, it is likely that their main concern will be to fight against racism and racial discrimination and for social equality.

But ethnic minorities will also have to accept more than this as part of the implied contract into which they enter with the host nation. They will have to accept that there is an official language and that they will have to use it in their dealings with the public authorities; they will have to recognise the criminal and civil law; they will have to recognise that existing national values will be taught within the educational system; and they may have to accept that there is an established religion which has special privileges.

Most ethnic minority members do accept some contract of this kind. They see it as part of the cost of living in a particular society of settlement, which has to be set against the real gains which migration brings. What is likely, however, is that there will be some members of their communities who are more committed to their cultures than this. These cannot be called nationalists. What they are concerned with is achieving what they think of as adequate recognition and respect for their cultures. They may organise public demonstrations against any perceived insult to their culture and religion, as in the case of the Rushdie affair, and they may ask either for separate schools or for adequate recognition of their religion and customs in the state schools. They may also seek to present their own literary and aesthetic culture in the public sphere. Thus what one may expect is the emergence of minority cultural movements pursued with varying degrees of aggression and militancy.

The existence of movements such as these hardly threatens the national society. They can easily be tolerated. They only become problematic if they lead to overt political disloyalty. Such disloyalty or the suggestion of a prior loyalty to some other state has been advocated by a few extreme Muslim organisations in Britain. There are also groups which advocate violence and terrorism in their homeland and are prepared to use the migrant community as a base for organisations. It is bound to be the case that national governments will do whatever they can to repress such activities.

What we are examining in this chapter is the nature of ethnicity in the project of migration. We have seen that such ethnicity is not primarily concerned with the project of nationalism, but with the maintenance of a transnational community in which economic advantages can be pursued. It also has to come to terms with modernising national societies and is usually easily able to do so. In any particular country of settlement there is likely to be the emergence of cultural movements trying to strengthen adherence to the culture and enlarge its area of operation. The existence of such movements can easily be tolerated and negotiated with as part and parcel of the working of a democratic society. The most important problems arise in connection with those movements which deliberately foster political disloyalty or which engage in violent and terrorist politics on an international scale. It is to be expected that any such movements and activities will be suppressed in a nation state. On the other hand it would be wrong to assume that they are typical of ethnic minority communities and their political culture.

We should remember here, however, that immigrant ethnic minority groups do not normally only have to face the problem of fitting into a society committed to multiculturalism. Even in the societies in which such a policy is professed there will be many individuals and often political movements who are hostile to or suspicious of ethnic minority communities and their cultures. Where this is the case ethnic minority movements will not simply be concerned with the preservation of their culture and networks, but will pursue active policies against racism and racial discrimination. Not surprisingly in Britain there is a dispute in the ethnic minority communities between those who fight primarily for multiculturalism and those in more radical movements who see their main task as fighting racism.

It has been assumed in this chapter that ethnic minority communities may have a more or less permanent existence on an international basis. This may well be true in some cases. But in other cases, ethnic minority organisations and movements may be of a more transitional kind. They may exist for a few generations while there is still a need to fight for equality and for cultural respect. But after that, what may remain, given religious tolerance, is a purely symbolic ethnicity involving such things as festivals and special occasions as well as some attempt at preservation of the minority language. Such purely symbolic ethnicity is something which troubles nobody and is usually regarded by an indigenous population merely as an exotic enrichment of their own culture.

Going beyond such purely symbolic ethnicity, however, neither the maintenance of the transnational migrant community nor the development of defensive community organisations are really incompatible with the maintenance of the institutions of a modernising national state. It is very important therefore that what has been called here the second project of ethnicity should not be confused with the nationalist projects discussed earlier. What has been happening in the former Yugoslavia holds no lessons relevant to the way in which Blacks and Asians in Britain or Turks and Maghrebians in various parts of Europe have to be treated by their host societies. The real focus of the problematic of nationalism in these cases has to be in the majority nationalism of the host societies.

6 Multiculturalism in Europe and North America

THE WIDER CONTEXT OF THE PROBLEM OF MULTICULTURALISM

The problem of multiculturalism in Europe and North America has to be understood within a wider world context involving the changes which have gone on since 1945 and since 1989 in the relations between the so-called first, second and third worlds. After 1945 the process of uneven economic development led to large-scale migration within and to the countries of the first world, including Western Europe, The United States and the economically advanced settler-dominated territories of the former European empires, such as Canada and Australia. This migration process was halted in Europe after the early 1970s except for family completion as far as workers were concerned; Japan came to join the first world countries as a centre of economic growth; and, as capital went in search of labour rather than bringing labour to it, new intermediate areas of economic growth came into existence, most obviously in oil-rich countries of the Middle East, and in the Pacific rim. The so-called second world consisting of the Communist countries remained outside this migration system except for small numbers of political refugees, until after 1989, when the breakdown of Communism produced economic and political collapse, forcing

---

*Keynote address to a conference on Comparative Perspectives on Ethnic Relations and Social Incorporation in Europe and North America organised by The Robert F. Harney Program in Ethnic, Immigration and Pluralism Studies, University of Toronto, September 29th to October 1st, 1994.

many of the citizens of these countries to flee from political disorder or to grasp the better economic opportunities which opened up to them in Western Europe and North America.

This chapter is concerned with a part of this total problem, namely that of the place of various immigrant, refugee and quasi-refugee communities who settled in the economically advanced countries of Europe and North America. These countries grew rich and concentrated on their own prosperity, leaving large parts of Asia, Africa and Latin America to constitute the new Third World marked by increasing relative poverty. It is this gap which constitutes the major political problem of the world today. Migration, however, had left the advanced and economically successful countries with their own internal problem of the place which immigrants and their children were to occupy within their political, economic, social and cultural systems.

Nation States and Migrant Communities

The nation states within whose territories immigrants had settled were based upon capitalist economies, even though these were modified by the creation in varying degrees of welfare states, and, on the political level, upon some sort of multi-party democracy. So far as their ethnic and cultural composition was concerned they also saw themselves as having national cultures, even though these cultures may have emerged from earlier migrations. The European nations had long historic traditions, while in the more recently constituted societies of North America the earliest immigrants had succeeded in imposing their languages and cultures. This did not of course exclude the possibility of two or more ethnic or national groups sharing in this domination, as in the case of Belgium, Switzerland and Canada, or of some regionally located groups being accorded a degree of autonomy or even of struggling for independence, as in the cases of the United Kingdom and Spain.

The various migrant groups had their own social, cultural and religious points of reference external to the countries in which they settled. They could not, however, be understood as nationalist groups, or even as diasporic communities, necessarily intending a return to some homeland Zion. Unlike the ethnic nationalist groups which re-emerged in the post-Communist world, they were not seeking secession from their countries of settlement in order to form their own nation states. Rather they were committed to the project of living in other people's countries and the last thing they wished to do was to secede from them.

So far as the concept of 'diaspora' is concerned, these groups probably all had some concept of possible return to a homeland, and they would, *inter alia*, maintain their contacts with that homeland. But at the same time they were likely to be seeking to maximise their opportunities through their kin and cultural networks in their present and possible future countries of settlement, and for some such transnational communities, this, rather than a diasporic return, was a dominant motive.

A good example of such a transnational migrant community is provided by migrants from the Punjab. They constitute a worldwide community whose members use their international networks to improve their economic position, even while maintaining some sense of connection with the homeland. There are, however, other possibilities. Some migrants may have relatively strong diasporic yearnings for return to a reconstituted homeland and many at least have some kind of 'myth of return', albeit often an unrealistic one; others operate on a less worldwide scale, migrating only to one or to a few countries and retaining realistic homeland links; and, finally, there are a number of diverse situations amongst refugees, who may be aware that they have no prospect of return and must perforce make the best of the opportunities available to them, but who may, on the other hand, look forward to returning when the injustices imposed on them by some of their fellow countrymen have been brought to an end (see Rex, 1994b).

If migrant communities have these transnational points of reference, they must also necessarily come to terms with their present societies of settlement. To this end they have to mobilise and negotiate collectively even though they may lose some of their more successful younger members who become acculturated to, and assimilated into, the society of settlement.

The problem of a multicultural society may therefore be presented as follows. The host nation will have to decide how far immigrant minorities should be allowed to enjoy the full rights of citizens, and whether they should be required to give up their own culture; or whether, if they preserve their own cultures, their cultural distinctiveness should act as a marker for separate kinds of treatment and control. Looking at matters from the point of view of the migrant communities, the struggle for equality might involve forsaking their own culture and networks and losing their more successful younger members. This is the problem we now discuss in relation to West European and North American societies.

In the above paragraphs I have attempted to make a general theoretical statement about the kinds of multicultural contact that we are facing in Europe and North America today. Any such attempt inevitably involves sweeping generalisations and it is relatively easy to point to the peculiarities of the problems of immigrant settlement, as between migrant groups, as between nation states in the societies of settlement, and as between larger regions. I now propose to focus on some of the differences between Europe and North America and, while still remaining on a high level of generality, to suggest, within the discussion of each of these regions, what some of the main lines of structural differentiation are.

The Pattern of Migrant Settlement in West Europe and the European Multicultural Problematic

After 1945 the economically successful countries of West Europe faced shortages of unskilled labour, and offered niches for entrepreneurs in areas of business which indigenous entrepreneurs were unwilling to occupy. They also needed professional skills which had to be provided from outside. Professional migrants were, however, not thought of as creating difficulties in their countries of settlement, representing more a problem to their sending societies, which saw themselves as suffering a brain drain. The main problem groups in the countries of settlement therefore were seen to be the largely unskilled immigrant groups and 'pariah' traders.

West European countries drew their immigrants from different countries and received different kinds of immigrants according to their historic circumstances. The United Kingdom drew upon Ireland, and then primarily on former colonial territories in the Caribbean, the Indian sub-continent, East Africa and the Mediterranean. France turned to southern European countries, particularly to Portugal, and to its former colonial territories in the Maghreb and in more distant overseas departments and former colonies, including the Caribbean, Africa and the Far East. Germany, having no former empire to turn to, recruited guest workers from Southern Europe and from Turkey. The Netherlands faced a variety of immigrant problems, including those of returning settlers and their allies from Indonesia, those of migrants with Dutch citizenship from Surinam and the Antilles, and those of Turks and Moroccans coming in as guest workers. Belgium recruited Italians and then Moroccans. Sweden, already having large numbers of Finns, also began to recruit in the same labour markets as the other North Western European countries. Additionally all these countries attracted a variety of asylum-seekers and others fleeing from conditions of political disorder.

Obviously there is great variety in these patterns of migration and this summary statement also excludes a number of smaller immigrant minority groups in each of the countries concerned. There are dangers, therefore, in any attempt to make a generalisation about all immigrant problems. What is clear, however, is that there were certain patterns in the way in which these countries defined their 'immigrant problem'. The United Kingdom was preoccupied with questions of colour, and the term 'immigrant' was a social construction referring primarily to dark-skinned people from the Caribbean, Asia and Africa, although so far as South Asians were concerned there was also cultural and religious difference. France became increasingly concerned with its Algerian immigrants and with what was often seen as the 'threat' of Islamic identities. In Germany anxieties were focused on Turkish guest workers, who were not necessarily thought of primarily as Muslims, but simply as temporary residents. In the Netherlands there was less colour-consciousness than in the United Kingdom, making it possible to assimilate the Surinamese more easily than was the case with British West Indians, but, increasingly, as can be seen from the Report of the Netherlands Scientific Council for Government Policy, entitled *Immigration Policy* (1990), the focus of attention was on the immigrant population from Morocco and Turkey.

Of course it can and should be argued that any intelligent policy towards immigrant settlement would have needed to take account one by one of the problems of, and those presented by, each separate immigrant group. Nonetheless it was clear that two related but separate problems had to be dealt with. One was the question of political, social and economic inequality. The other was the accommodation of cultural difference.

The Emergence of the Multicultural Problematic

The relatively straightforward question of inequality was dealt with in different ways in the different countries and in different policy traditions. Where there was a guest-worker policy there could, by definition, be no political equality, though it was still possible for governments and political organisations to argue about the ways in which non-citizens could have equal social rights. Where immigrants had citizenship rights, on the other hand, the primary focus of the debate about equality had to be on combating racial and ethnic discrimination.

This latter situation was most clearly evident in the United Kingdom, which, recognising the similarities between the problems of its Caribbean immigrants and those of Blacks in the United States, set up relatively elaborate institutions concerned with bringing about 'racial' equality. While such institutions were often appropriate for dealing with Black Caribbean migrants, whose situation paralleled that of Black Americans, they were extended in Britain to deal with the case of South Asians, whose migration often had a different trajectory and whose problems included those of cultural rather than racial difference. Not surprisingly there was some objection on the part of Asians to being dealt with in this way (Modood, 1994) and when it was suggested that similar institutions should be set up in continental Europe, European social scientists pointed out that the British concentration on 'racial' equality was not really relevant to their situation (Neveu, 1994). Generally they did no more than try to combat discrimination through the normal courts.

A further feature of the situation in continental Europe was an unwillingness to use the term 'race', which was thought to be disreputable after the experience of Nazism. Problems of inequality were often referred to as the inequality of ethnic rather than racial groups, though paradoxically their inequality was often explained in terms of the 'racism' of majority groups. In the United Kingdom, too, the Marxist sociologist (Miles, 1993) argued forcefully that the focus of attention should be on 'racism' rather than 'race relations' and his view was widely shared by many others who were not Marxists (Rex, 1983, 1986a, 1986b; Wieviorka, 1994).

Concern about equal treatment of the members of minority groups was shared by those influenced primarily by French republican ideas (see Wieviorka, 1994) and by socialist and social democrats committed to the ideals of the welfare state (see Radtke, 1994). These traditions were however, silent on the question of how far cultural difference should be tolerated or encouraged. Indeed, the likelihood was that any tradition which based itself on the notion of equality would be cautious about the recognition of cultural differences, which might become markers for inequality. Those who campaign for multiculturalism therefore had to show that the recognition of cultural diversity was compatible with and did not undermine those institutions which were concerned with guaranteeing equality between individuals and classes.

I have, myself, argued for an ideal concept of egalitarian multiculturalism which deals with both of these questions (Rex, 1986b). In doing this, I have found it useful to base the concept on a statement by the British Home Secretary in 1968, when he defined 'integration' as involving 'not a flattening process of uniformity', but 'cultural diversity, coupled with equal opportunity, in an atmosphere of mutual tolerance'. I have suggested that this statement involves the simultaneous recognition of two cultural domains, one a shared political culture of the public domain, centring around the idea of equality, the other that of a number of separate cultures in the private or communal domain, involving shared language, religion, customs and family practices.

What this concept of egalitarian multiculturalism seeks to avoid above all is the sort of situation imagined by left-wing critics of multicultural policies. What they argue is that multiculturalism has usually been simply a rhetoric which disguises inequality and ghettoisation, or a means of marking groups as minorities so that they can be controlled, manipulated or subject to unequal treatment (Rath, 1991). I agree with these critics that what has usually passed as multiculturalism does have these characteristics (Rex, 1991a), but this by no means brings into question the *ideal* which I have proposed. It is possible to combine the recognition of cultural diversity with a fight for individual equality, and I would argue that it is only if it does this that any concept of multiculturalism is acceptable in a democratic society.

It may still be asked why cultural diversity should be encouraged if individuals are in any case offered all the gains and benefits of equality in a modern democratic society. In answering this question I have given three reasons (Rex, 1994a, 1994b): the first is what I call the Durkheimian one, namely that some kind of intermediate group between the individual family and the state is necessary to provide the individual with moral and emotional support and to prevent a situation of anomie (Durkheim, 1933); the second is that individuals need the networks and cultural ideals which their group offers if they are to have the solidarity which is necessary in their fight for equal rights, and that it is this solidarity deriving from ethnic mobilisation, rather than the benign behaviour of governments, which can act as a guarantee of equality; the third is based on the utilitarian argument that we do not know whether new cultures may not have some objective validity, and that the possible gains of recognising them outweigh any possible dangers.

There is, of course, a danger in reifying minority cultures and I do not want to suggest that they should be recognised in unchanging traditional forms, but I know of no ethnic minority culture which has this form. What strikes me about them is that they themselves are a response to circumstances and that, while they are always in some measure concerned with maintaining cultural forms for the reasons given in the previous paragraph, they are also shaped by the experience of minority individuals in fighting to achieve equality.

A further point to be made here is that ethnic minority communities do not simply act on their own. They enter societies in which other disadvantaged groups are engaged in the struggle for equality and they must necessarily interact with and form alliances with these groups. Indeed, within an established class and party system, they cannot act without the aid of these groups. What they have to counter, however, is the process of what Parkin (1979) calls 'double closure'; that is what happens when an indigenous group fighting for equality and having made gains for itself, seeks to exclude others from benefiting from those gains. In joining in class struggles, immigrant minorities have to form parties within parties and unions within unions to ensure that their interests are defended.

One other realistic point has to be made in reviewing European experience in dealing with the question of multiculturalism. The indigenous majority culture cannot be seen simply as one amongst a number of cultures. Nor should it even be argued that this culture will inevitably be modified through absorbing into itself bits and pieces of new minority cultures. There are, of course, superficial elements of minority cultures, like those concerned with cuisine, which do affect the majority culture, but they are unlikely to transform it fundamentally, and there are many cultural and institutional features of the societies in which immigrants settle which they will, therefore, have to accept as providing the framework in which they now have to live their lives. *Inter alia*, these include the official language of the society, its economic institutions and its criminal and civil law. Accepting these and living within their constraints is the price which immigrants have to pay, and are usually willing to pay, for the advantages of immigration. On the other hand, I believe that it is to be expected that immigrant minorities will make their contribution to a developing national culture through their campaigns against injustice and through their own 'high', 'literary', or 'aesthetic' culture.

Finally, I should like to make clear what the egalitarian ideal of multiculturalism means when it uses the term 'integration'. It does not simply mean proportionate representation in educational and economic institutions, as the recent Dutch report referred to above appears to imply. Nor does it simply mean legal citizenship. For my own part, I would draw on another idea from Durkheim's *Division of Labour*. This is that he is concerned to argue that a modern society based upon organic solidarity must have a moral basis. In criticising Spencer's view of economic exchange, he writes, 'the image of the one who completes us becomes inseparable from ours . . . It thus becomes an integral and permanent part of our conscience.' Similarly, I would argue that, quite apart from the warm moral and emotional support which groups provide for their members, the nature of the relationships between minority groups and national societies on the political level has itself to be a moral one. The individuals who negotiate with one another do not simply have an external relation with each other; they become united in their consciences and their pursuit of justice. Only when this sort of relationship exists on the public level, will what I mean by integration have been achieved. Integration should therefore be seen as a moral and social psychological question.

Multiculturalism in the North American Experience

What I have said above reflects some of the issues which have arisen in the discussion of multiculturalism by politicians and social scientists in Europe (for a more detailed discussion of the arguments which have arisen amongst social scientists, see Rex and Drury, 1994; Rex, 1995). What I have found as I have discussed these issues abroad, however, is that what is being discussed is often something quite different from what is being discussed in Europe, depending as it does upon different historical circumstances. Here I will deal with the two North American cases of the United States and Canada.

The United States

In the case of the United States, the problems which emerge are those which have resulted from three different types of colonialism and several different types of immigration. The three types of colonialism are those which involved the conquest of the native peoples and the occupation of their lands, the establishment of plantations with slave labour brought involuntarily from Africa, and the settlement of wave after wave of European immigrants who were thought of as entering some kind of 'melting pot' as they gradually abandoned their own cultures in favour of a single Anglo-Saxon based one. Following this European migration, there were two other migrations, one that of Mexican and Latino workers who were more likely to retain their Spanish language as well as relatively close connections with their countries of origin, the other that of a variety of different types of Asians whose cultures were more alien from those of the first settlers than that of the Europeans had been, and many of whom came as secondary entrepreneurs.

American political ideology in the form of the American creed was largely based upon a political design of incorporating the European immigrants. This involved the notion of the 'melting pot' through which people of diverse national origins became one nation. This melting pot, however, did not deal with the problems of those descended from slaves after emancipation. As Ringer

(1983) has shown, from the very outset the notion of 'We, the people' excluded 'others', and the 'American Creed' was not thought of at its inception as applying to them. The major political issue facing the United States in 1945, at the time when Europe was coping with its diverse groups of immigrants, therefore, was that of how its Black people could achieve equality with Whites, and enter a society whose institutions had been designed to deal primarily with the situation of European immigrants. It was this movement for civil rights which came to dominate political thinking about inter-group relations, rather than that of a diversity of cultures. It was only with the coming of so-called Hispanics from Central and Latin America that the question of multiculturalism returned to the political agenda, though, as I shall argue below, in a somewhat perverse form.

The history of the United States since the 1950s has involved, first, the placing of the question of civil rights for Black Americans on the political agenda, and, secondly, disillusionment with the process, both amongst Whites who feared that positive discrimination gave an unfair advantage to Blacks, and amongst Blacks who felt that the civil rights movement had not given them real equality. At this point there was increasing hostility to Blacks amongst Whites and also a claim by Blacks that, since the civil rights movement had not given them true equality, some further initiative was needed.

For some this further initiative involved continuing to pursue ever more detailed policies of affirmative action. As against writers like Glazer who had withdrawn their support for the further continuation or elaboration of such policies (Glazer, 1983a, 1983b, 1988), or Wilson (1978, 1987) who seemed to be arguing for class-specific rather than race-specific policies, some, like Steinberg (1990), argued that the structural position of the so-called under-class amongst Blacks was different from that of other underclasses and that further structural adjustments of a race-specific kind had to be made to enable Blacks to achieve equality. The aim of these policies was to deal with the structural consequences of the historic wrong which had been done to Blacks by slavery and, subsequently, by racial discrimination.

What was remarkable about the Civil Rights Programme was that although the United States was, as compared with Europe, an individualistic and market-based society in economic matters, so far as human rights and the promotion of equality was concerned, its governments and its courts were in fact highly interventionist, and it was from the United States that Britain adopted its models, atypical in Europe, for the promotion of racial equality. Moreover, when there was disillusionment with the outcome, it was still possible to argue for continued and ever more detailed forms of interventionism.

A different response, however, began to emerge amongst some Black intellectuals in the late 1980s. This was that Blacks had not benefited from increased educational opportunities, particularly in higher education, because the curriculum in terms of which they were being educated was not sufficiently 'multicultural'. In making this point they suggested that Black American culture, rather than being simply a variant of American culture, was a distinct culture in the same sense as was that of the new Hispanic settlers.

Such views transformed the debate about equality in the United States. Previously, notwithstanding the reservations expressed by writers like Ringer to the effect that the American creed had not applied to Blacks, the predominant view was that of Myrdal, who had seen in the institutions of the Supreme Court the means whereby Blacks could claim for themselves the equality to which all Americans were entitled according to the American creed. Essentially it involved a view of the United States as one nation. This was a view very close to that which I had been arguing for in Europe. The shared political culture of the public domain was that which the Supreme Court could be called upon to guarantee, even if cultural differences amongst different immigrant and racial groups were accepted in the private and communal domain.

That these assumptions were no longer universally accepted by the late 1980s was made clear in Hacker's important book, entitled *Two Nations: Black and White: Separate, Unequal, and Hostile* (Hacker, 1992). Though the implicit reference of Hacker's title was to Disraeli, he did not indicate, as Disraeli had done, that the unity of the nation could be restored. What his account suggests is that White public opinion and Black public opinion no longer envisage a compromise. Whites have reverted to seeing Blacks as outside of their nation and Black thought has become increasingly secessionist.

There is, of course, a great deal of truth in Hacker's account of contemporary political opinion amongst intellectuals, at least amongst Whites and Blacks. But the particular point I want to make is that the argument of Black intellectuals merges the discussion of equality and inequality with that about multiculturalism. It would seem to rest upon an argument, rejected in an important book by a Black school teacher in Britain, that Black failure in the schools resulted from poor self-esteem which could be corrected by multicultural education (Stone, 1981).

The new Black radical line of argument was not simply about education. It was essentially political. Blacks were seen as constituting a distinct cultural group and, to all intents and purposes, a separate nation. It is difficult to understand what is meant by this, since it does not usually rest on the notion of a return to an African Zion. Blacks are simply seen as constituting a separate nation *within* the United States.

An important difference between the American and the European situations is that while Europeans were cautious about the use of the term 'race', all parties in the United States continue to use the term uncritically. Radical critics like Steinberg (1994) speak of 'the liberal retreat from race', and even Blacks who advocate separatism, arguing that Blacks have a separate culture, still see themselves as racially distinct. Indeed many of them adopt what Europeans would see as a 'racist' assumption, that they are culturally different because of differences of 'race'.

The response of traditional liberal opinion to Black separatist political ideologies was predictable, and it has been clearly stated by Schlesinger in his *The Disuniting of America* (1992). According to Schlesinger, American society has been created out of the merging of immigrant cultures in a new nation which is united by its acceptance of European culture and the English language. This society works because it has held together diverse groups within a single set of institutions. What he sees as happening now is a questioning of this ideal, on the one hand through the coming of the Hispanics who do not accept the dominant Anglo-Saxon culture, and, on the other, through the secessionist teachings of radical Blacks. Against this subversive tendency towards disunity, his own view is that what has held and what only can hold America together is a recognition that its political unity is to be found in adherence to a European culture (which, it was suggested during the five hundredth anniversary of Columbus's arrival in the Americas, Columbus had brought with him from Europe). The very notion of multiculturalism therefore had to be opposed.

What is questionable about Schlesinger's argument is the idea that the unity of the United States depends on its adherence to *European* culture. This is very different from the view I have suggested, that the shared political culture of the United States is to be found in the bundle of rights which have been won and could still be won through the courts. It is misleading to think of this bundle of rights as simply the product of European culture. It has been achieved through a process of struggle by classes and immigrant groups fighting for their rights and is far from being just a European import. Instead of recognising the contribution which non-European minority groups have made to the development of American political culture, Schlesinger merely dismisses them as dangerous and inferior in his final angry, and some would say 'racist', chapter.

One can none the less understand Schlesinger's argument against the disuniting of America, and stripped of its Eurocentric perspective it is one which is accepted by most Black Americans other than academics and ideologists. They do not see their hope as lying in some kind of imagined secession, but are still concerned with winning equality within a single political system.

Multiculturalism need not be, as Schlesinger imagines, a movement for disunity. Given political unity, it is an important feature of American life. The various European immigrant communities in the United States in the past have fulfilled all the functions which I suggested minority cultures and networks should do in Europe. They provided a moral and psychological home for immigrants over several generations; they provided a basis for political mobilisation in a democracy (the more important in the United States because of the relative weakness, *vis-à-vis* Europe, of class-based organisations); and they also enriched the complex new entity of American culture.

It is possible to see similarities in the possible ideal of an egalitarian and democratic form of multiculturalism which might be fought for in the United States and Europe. Indeed, it might be argued that American history has provided a better political environment for its realisation than European history has done. There is a shared political culture based on the idea of equality there, and the various immigrant cultures have been able not merely to coexist with it, but to fortify it. The disillusionment of the Blacks, and to a lesser extent of some of the new minorities, however, has brought this ideal into question and multiculturalism has, for some at least, become a disuniting ideology.

Canada

Canadian society shares some of the structural features of the United States, but does not share all of them. It also has certain distinctive problems of its own. Thus when we turn to Canada, we find the same argument about the rights of the native people, the same creation of a settler society of European immigrants, and the same fact of the later arrival of Latin Americans and Asians. It does not, however, share with the United States its history of slave plantations and of civil war between two colonial systems. Nor did its break with Britain take the form of a revolutionary war of independence.

The distinctive feature of the Canadian situation was the fact that it was not simply a British colony. Although the French were defeated militarily, there were from the outset two distinct societies or two so-called founding nations. Inevitably this meant that any discussion of multiculturalism was certain to be bound up with the question of the relationship between the two founding nations, and with the continuing resistance of Quebec to Anglophone ascendancy, and to political domination of the English. There were some parallels here to those of the multinational state in Britain, called the United Kingdom. In that case one had a nationalist movement amongst the Welsh concerned with questions of language, amongst the Scots, which was largely resolved through a degree of administrative autonomy, and in Ireland where there was overt political resistance, sometimes involving the use of violence. Potentially the relation of Quebec to the rest of Canada reflects all of these problems.

The question of multiculturalism has arisen against this specific background. In fact it arose incidentally in the course of an enquiry into the question of bilingualism and biculturalism as between French-speaking and English-speaking Canadians. Having raised this question, however, the commissioners, not being content with *ad hoc* solutions but seeking general principles, went on from dealing with the Quebec case to a more general discussion of the rights of other cultural and linguistic minorities.

There is, of course, an important difference between the position of these other minorities and that of Francophone Quebec. They are often dispersed across Canada and do not have the nationalist aspirations of the people of Quebec. Nor, one should point out, do the immigrant minorities have a political problem of a kind which presents itself to the native people. Their problem is that of later immigrants, seeking to remain in Canada, but having to define their relationship with the uneasy coalition of the two founding nations who control the political system.

The attempt to resolve these questions and to deal simultaneously with the problem of the founding nations and the native peoples, on the one hand, and that of accommodating later immigrants, on the other, was resolved in terms of a formula which suggested that Canada was a multicultural society within a framework of bilingualism.

To a very large extent this 'solution' of the problems facing of later immigrant minorities was a matter of rhetoric. While the notion of a multicultural society seemed to suggest shared control of the political system, and a modification of shared political culture of the public domain, there was never any real belief that this would be the case. What was really being suggested was simply the recognition of cultural and linguistic diversity in the private or communal domain.

Perhaps, however, there is more to it than this. The notion of two domains, one public and political, the other communal or community-based, involves a degree of oversimplification. It is largely based on the experience of European nations within which there are well-established cultural forms which cannot be regarded as belonging to one amongst many cultures. In a newer society like Canada, itself based on immigration, and in which national culture was split between French and English traditions, it was easy to accept the notion that on a non-political level the national culture could be modified by new inputs from other groups.

What was happening, then, behind a rhetoric of multiculturalism which suggested shared political control, was the benign recognition by governments of cultural diversity on a non-political level. Such diversity could easily be encouraged and funded without any threat to the political system.

The easiest things to fund in this way would be the aesthetic culture of minority groups and the purely symbolic ethnicity which takes the form of exotic festivals, which go on long after a group has settled and which threaten no-one. It is not possible, however, to deal with the associations of immigrant groups without encountering other issues of a more political sort. Immigrant communities maintain connections with homeland politics and may, through their associations, have external political goals; they will be concerned with assisting later immigrants of their own ethnicity to solve their immigration difficulties; they will be involved in social and pastoral work dealing with the family problems of their members; they may feel that they have a distinct 'identity' which they wish to preserve; and they will be concerned with fighting against ethnic discrimination. Thus what appear as innocent cultural organisations are likely to have some political dimension. On a policy level, therefore, the national and provincial governments have to decide how far they are willing to extend their funding to support activities of this more political kind. The view I have taken in relation to immigrant communities in Europe is that supporting them in this way does not threaten, and may enhance, democracy. Obviously there will always be argument between those who take this view and those who are only willing to recognise a simpler, more benign and cultural form of multicultural policy.

If there are problems of this kind in dealing with immigrant communities from Europe, they are even more likely to be evident in the case of the more visible minorities. This has proved to be true. Recognising that its Black people are liable to suffer from the racism and racial discrimination suffered by Blacks in the United States, Canada has had to supplement its multicultural institutions with others dealing specifically with the problems of visible minorities or of 'race relations'. Similarly, it has not easily been able to fit new minorities from Asia and Latin America within the framework of a purely cultural multiculturalism. Many of the political concerns which have arisen in relation to minorities who are distinguished by cultural and racial markers in Europe are likely to recur in Canada.

In international debates like this one the danger is that we can oversimplify our difficulties. Canadians sometimes suggest that they have much to teach other countries who face severe problems of ethnic conflict. Perhaps, indeed, they do, but what I am suggesting is that they will have more to teach if they do not base their case on a somewhat simplistic model of the support of ethnic minorities on a purely cultural level. On the other hand the experience of Europeans and Americans in dealing with the difficult political questions of inter-group relationships may be highly relevant to the Canadian situation.

CONCLUSION

In this chapter I have looked comparatively at the kinds of debate which have gone on about multiculturalism in three very different contexts. What emerges from this is that there can be no simple general theory of multiculturalism. This would be even more obvious if I had attempted to deal with the problems of the recently collapsed Communist world or with those of post-colonial societies. This is not to say, however, that we might not look for a much more sophisticated theory which takes account of the complex variables which are to be found in individual cases. I also conclude that there is the possibility of developing an ideal of egalitarian multi-culturalism for nation states which takes account both of the inevitability of a struggle for individual equality and of the value of cultural diversity. I would also go back to my first point, namely that these internal problems of the nation state have also to be set within a wider theoretical framework, in which, important though it still is, the nation state is not the only focus of political action.

7 The Integration of Formerly Dominant Ethnic Minorities in a Democratic Multicultural Society[*]

TYPES OF MINORITY PROBLEM

If nation states are to be established on some basis other than ethnic cleansing or the domination of one ethnic group over others, the question of the principles of a democratic multicultural society becomes one of the major questions of political theory. It may present itself as the problem of integrating immigrant ethnic minority communities whose members are committed to living in the country of their settlement; it may take the form of dealing with ethnic national minorities who seek varying degrees of regional autonomy, or, at the extreme, even political secession; or it may involve defining the position of those who were privileged immigrants during a period of external imperial rule, towards whom newly independent national governments must develop a policy. The first sort of situation is that which is to be found in the countries of the European Community; the second is that which is presented to the government of Serbia by Kossovo, to the Spanish government by the Basque question or to the British government by Irish nationalism in Northern Ireland; the third is that which faces the Baltic Republics in dealing with its Russian settlers or, less

[*]A lecture delivered to a conference sponsored by the Soros Foundation in the Institute of Philosophy and Sociology, Riga, Latvia, 1994.

obviously and severely, the government of Slovakia in dealing with its Hungarian minority.

This chapter will in the first instance look at the experience of Western Europe in dealing with the first and second types of situation, but while it is clearly true that not all of the principles developed there are applicable in the other types of situation, it is worth asking how far such principles may be modified and developed in dealing with them.

MINORITIES IN WESTERN EUROPE

North West Europe has since 1945 faced one of the major immigration movements of the past three or four centuries. While it has lost large numbers of indigenous people, and continues to do so by way of emigration, it has faced, at least in times of economic expansion and prosperity, a labour gap, which has had to be filled by immigration. As a result, there are in this region today some fifteen to twenty million people, who are either immigrants, or the descendants of immigrants who are to some extent attached to the social organisations and the culture of their immigrant parents or grandparents. The problem here is that of the terms on which these immigrant communities are to be integrated into the society of settlement, either as groups or as individuals, and the question is further complicated by the arrival of refugees from the East and from the South.

I take for granted the fact that there will be some in the indigenous population who will react to the presence of these immigrants and refugees with xenophobia and racism, and such xenophobia and racism has undoubtedly influenced the development of government policies. None the less, repatriation has rarely been a practical policy, and some at least have argued for the integration of these newcomers into the indigenous society on one basis or another. Here again, of course, one possibility is that of the unequal incorporation of these groups through an estate or caste system, but democrats have argued for their incorporation on equal terms. It is the nature of this more egalitarian concept of multiculturalism which I wish to develop here.

In fact there are three alternative responses to the problem of incoming ethnic minorities which have been developed in Western

Europe. The first is the German alternative which insists that the newcomers are not immigrants, cannot easily aspire to full citizenship, and are only temporary residents or 'gastarbeiders', who, when their labour is not needed, will return to their homelands. The second is the alternative, which is, at least partially, the basis of French policy, which calls for equal political rights for the newcomers, but which also looks forward to the relatively rapid disappearance of minority cultures. The third is that of multi-culturalism expounded as a policy ideal especially in Britain, the Netherlands and Sweden. Once again emphasising that I am talking not of the reality of the present situation which immigrants face, but with an ideal which they and their democratic allies in the indigenous community might fight for. I want now to spell out that ideal as it has been stated in Britain, and to ask what its political implications are.

THE WESTERN IDEAL OF MULTICULTURALISM

In 1968 the then British Home Secretary, Roy Jenkins, defined 'integration' as 'not a flattening process of uniformity, but cultural diversity, coupled with equal opportunity, in an atmosphere of mutual tolerance'. What does it mean, in structural and institutional terms, to combine the two notions of cultural diversity and equality of opportunity?

Some ten years ago, I suggested that the notion of multi-culturalism of a democratic sort involved the existence of two cultural domains (Rex, 1986). On the one hand there was, or ought to be, a shared public political culture which laid down the basic political 'rules of the game' and I suggested that these should centre around the idea of equality, or at least equality of opportunity, for all individuals. On the other, there should be an acceptance of a variety of communal cultures involving the right of members of separate communities to speak their own mother tongue, to follow their own religions and to have their own customs and family practices.

The idea of a shared political culture was developed in Britain particularly by the sociologist T. H. Marshall, who argued that the working class, having first gained equal legal and political rights, were now in the process of winning at least a minimum of social rights in the Welfare State (Marshall, 1950). In fact, of course, many of these rights were undermined during the 1980s with the move towards market individualism, but even those who argued for the maximum degree of individualism still found it necessary to say that they believed in equality of opportunity or the classless society. Such equality was not simply dispensed by benevolent governments but was a hard-fought right won in political or class struggle. Applying this same notion to ethnic minority communities, the ideal of equality implies preventing racial and ethnic discrimination, either through the action of governments, or through the collective pressure of the minority groups themselves.

The tolerance of cultural diversity is based upon three ideas. One is that there are cultural values which separate groups regard as worth pursuing, and which do not threaten either the culture of other groups or the shared public political culture. The second is what I call the Durkheimian point as developed in his *The Division of Labour* (Durkheim, 1933), namely that, under conditions of the modern market economy, individuals would seek the psychological and moral support of a group intermediate between the individual family and the state. It would seem that such support is found in ethnic communities rather than in the occupational guilds which Durkheim imagined would develop within modern society. The third idea is that, in order to fight for equality of their members, ethnic groups, like classes before them, rely upon ethnic solidarity as a valuable resource.

Such cultural diversity, of course, does not necessarily imply that a society will be permanently divided on a multicultural basis. The general thrust of industrial and post-industrial society is towards secularism and individualism, and, in time, the descendants of immigrants might well prefer to claim their rights as individuals. When they do, what remains is likely to be only symbolic ethnicity, involving group festivals, which do not cause any political concern, but are seen only as an exotic enrichment of the society. For the first few generations, however, the maintenance of separate cultures is a necessary and valuable means of creating a stable democracy.

The ideal I have in mind here is not to be confused with one particular pathological version of multiculturalism, where the state, claiming to recognise cultural diversity, seeks to establish a relationship with those ethnic leaders whom it chooses – usually older men – and seeks to control the separate communities through them. Clearly diversity has to be recognised within ethnic communities, as well as between the separate communities, and there must be the possibility of political expression for a variety of different types of individuals with differing types of affiliation to their own communities.

A MORE DETAILED CONSIDERATION OF MULTICULTURAL POLICY

All that I have said thus far, however, is oversimplified, and to be more realistic we must now look at what the public political culture is likely to involve. I have spoken as though it involves nothing more than a set of rules of the game involving equality. I *do* insist that such a notion of equality should underlie all that goes on in the public sphere, but one has to recognise that those entering a society as a minority will have to accept more than this.

Law and the Public Sphere

In the first place there is the requirement of acceptance of the criminal and civil law. The notion of the democratic multicultural society should not undermine the idea of the rule of law. Perhaps we should say that this rule of law has to be accepted because it is the mechanism through which human rights and equality are guaranteed. There are only two qualifications which should be made to this. One is that, since laws may be, and are often regarded as, unjust, they are therefore subject to reform. The other is that there may be areas of domestic law where courts might take account of varying customs and cultural practices.

Ethical Limits to Cultural Diversity

With regard to this last point, it is sometimes suggested that there are certain practices tolerated within ethnic cultures which cannot and should not be accepted in a humane and democratic society.

Such, for instance, might be the practice of female circumcision. But this principle of intervention on behalf of individual human rights should not be extended too far. I do not, myself, think that it is desirable to outlaw arranged marriage as such (though there may be a case for preventing its pathological form of forced marriage). There will be arguments amongst democrats about such points such as these. In the outcome, however, it has to be accepted that there is a common culture in a multicultural society which imposes some ethical limits, even though cultural variety is recognised.

The Problem of Political Loyalty

All those who come to live in a society owe it some political allegiance. Such individuals should not commit treasonable acts, or have another national allegiance taking precedence over their allegiance to their land of settlement. They should even be prepared to serve in its armed forces. This does not mean that they should be required to feel a strong emotional sense of patriotism, whether in war or in sport. What is required of minorities in a multicultural but unitary society is that they should accept a set of institutions as binding on themselves, not that they should have particular inward feelings.

Language in the Multicultural Society

The next point concerns the position of language in the public and private spheres. Clearly the public sphere has to have its own language, or limited range of languages, in which public business is transacted. Without this we should have a Babel. This implies that minorities will accept that however much they may justifiably claim their right to speak their mother tongue amongst themselves, there are public spaces in which they must try to communicate in the national language. Thus immigrants to the United States, at least until recently when there has been something of a Hispanic challenge, expect that public business will be transacted in English, immigrants to Belgium must learn to speak French or Dutch, and those to Canada, French or English. They may even be required to be bilingual in the national languages.

Of course, while participating in a society of settlement implies a willingness to accept such a public language, this does not mean that minority languages and their speakers should have no rights. Minority community members should be able to speak their own language amongst themselves, and public resources should be devoted to the maintenance of such languages. There is a case too, where there is a concentration of speakers of a minority language, for accepting that the minority language should be the medium of instruction in the early school years. Finally, there can and should be provision in the transaction of business in the social services and the courts for intepretation, to ensure that minority members have the fullest possible enjoyment of their rights.

The Claims of Majority Culture and Religion

A much more contentious area concerns the claims which are made for the majority culture and majority religion. Many people in the majority community will continue to believe that their own indigenous culture and religion should be regarded as having a stronger claim than that of being just one amongst many cultures and religions. I do not think that this claim has to be accepted. There is no reason why such cultural practices should be regarded as more than a private matter and there is no reason why the religion of the majority should be given precedence. Of course it is true that as immigrant minorities and their descendants remain settled for a long time many of them will move toward acceptance of majority culture and religion, but is of the essence of a multicultural society that they should not be forced to do so.

Schools and Multicultural Education

Many of the problems discussed above are particularly evident in relation to schools. Schools have a two-fold function. On the one hand, they prepare children for their participation in the public world of the market place and the polity. But in the earlier years at least they are concerned with moral education. The difficult question is whether such moral education should take account of cultural diversity. The French model of 'l'école laique' suggests that it should not. Some in Britain suggest that it should, and that religion should be taught on a multi-faith basis. It is also emphasised by the proponents of the multicultural society that multicultural education is essential for the achievement of the third, and least discussed, element of the Jenkins formula given above, namely, mutual tolerance between communities. (For a discussion of the whole question of multicultural education in schools, see Lord Swann's report entitled *Education for All*, Department of Education and Science, 1985.)

None of these are closed arguments by any means, and as well as those members of the majority community who oppose multi-culturalism in the schools, there are also those in the minority communities in Britain who have argued against multicultural education, for fear that it might conflict with the education which really matters as a preparation for life in the world of work (Stone, 1981). But this is an argument about whether cultural diversity is reflected in the school syllabus. What should not be at issue is whether minority cultures are encouraged and publicly supported in some place, even if outside the school.

The Role of Aesthetic or High Culture

A final question about the culture of the public domain concerns the place of literary culture, or, more generally, aesthetic culture. Clearly each separate culture should have within it such cultural achievements. But what about the aesthetic culture of the public domain? Is this not an important area of interpenetration of the different cultures? I can imagine a society in which attempts were made to protect and preserve indigenous cultural forms at the expense of all others. Such a culture would surely, however, become an archaic fossil. If one looks at the arts and the literature in nearly all modern countries, one find that the arts reflect on experience, and that not the least important of the experiences, on which they reflect is that of contact between group and group. Therefore, in a multicultural society, while all groups have their own internal cultural achievements and works of art, the arts should be a means through which the sensitivities between group and group in the public sphere are also explored.

THE LIMITS OF THE PRIVATE AND COMMUNAL DOMAIN

Everything said in the last section is concerned with the exploration of the range and the limitations of the shared public cultural and political domain. We must now turn to the equivalent question of the range and limits of the private and communal domain.

It should be clear that I am arguing that the private and communal domain has important functions. I have said that it fosters important cultural values, that it provides a psychological home for its members, and that it provides the basis in solidarity which is necessary in a collectively organised struggle for, and defence of, rights. In many European countries, however, this tends to be regarded as an unrealistic ideal. There are many today who fear ethnic minority cultures, particularly in the light of the notion of ethnic cleansing; there is a fear that granting the claims of minority communities would lead to a kind of 'apartheid' or, still worse to secessionist claims, to political disloyalty and to the undermining of democratic states; and there is a fear that the ethnicity which is encouraged will be regressive and reactionary. These claims I believe to be exaggerated, but they are not entirely without foundation, and it is therefore necessary that those who espouse multiculturalism should say something about its limits.

Multiculturalism and Ethnic Cleansing

The notion that the recognition of minority cultures in the private communal domain is in some way connected with ethnic cleansing is in fact wide of the mark. Theories more closely connected with ethnic cleansing are that minority groups should be excluded through immigration control, that the indigenous culture should dominate all others, or that assimilation should be so complete that it amounts to ethnocide of minority cultures. There is in fact little evidence of immigrant groups seeking to assert themselves against other immigrant groups in this way, though one does sometimes hear of groups who reject the concept of the two cultural domains, and insist that their own usually religiously based culture represents 'a whole way of life'. This is the case with some extreme Muslim groups in Britain, and it is necessary to distinguish between them and others who either recognise a shared secular political culture, or are willing to negotiate such a shared culture with other groups.

Apartheid and Secession

In a book dealing with recent arguments about multiculturalism Schlesinger suggests that some ethnic political movements, particularly amongst Black Americans, now reject the idea of belonging to a single society, and claim that their culture and society should be entirely separate (Schlesinger, 1992). Indeed some of them present racist arguments, arguing that Black and White Americans are psychologically different. Clearly, if this were to be generally claimed by multiculturalists it would be politically unacceptable. But it was not the claim which was formerly made by minorities in America, who did accept the idea of two cultural domains, and it is not widely accepted elsewhere.

What is more likely to be the case is that the politics of minority immigrant communities may remain strongly oriented to the homeland, and that they may cling to a myth of return there. Insofar as they are so oriented, they may well be inclined to accommodate themselves to 'gastarbeider' status. This is, however, as unacceptable in a democratic multicultural society when it is suggested by minority groups as when it is imposed by the national state. The democratic notion of the multicultural society necessarily involves the idea of a shared political order.

The Political Loyalty of Minority Groups

Involvement with the politics of the homeland may also involve political loyalties to the state or to parties in that homeland. The possibility then arises in international relations that these political affiliations will conflict with the interests of the nation state within which the minority is settled. This may also be a problem when there is an overriding loyalty to an outside religious or linguistic group. For instance, in Britain during the Gulf War, some Muslims felt that their loyalty to Islam required opposition to a war pursued by an alliance made up largely of non-Muslims against Iraq. In fact, however, such disloyalty did not gain majority support and most Muslims accepted at least pragmatically their political obligations to the British state. Since there was no conscription, moreover, the question of military service did not arise.

The Regressiveness of Minority Cultures

Some traditional leaders of minority communities, as well as the national state in societies of settlement, are sometimes inclined to see their culture in reified terms, as static and unchanging, and insist on maintaining cultural practices developed in their homelands. In this situation the ethnic minority communities may well be seen as regressive. Minority cultures do, however, undergo change as they face up to the challenges of immigration and relocation, and younger members of the community may well, while insisting that they do belong to an ethnic minority, none the less adhere to that culture in a flexible and developing form. The notion of democratic multiculturalism recognises this, and cannot be based upon the notion of reified and unchanging cultures led by traditional leaders.

SUMMARY: THE DEMOCRATIC AND PATHOLOGICAL FORMS OF MULTICULTURALISM

Clearly there are forms of multiculturalism which are pathological and unacceptable in a democratic society, but this does not mean, as some European democrats have assumed, that multiculturalism as such has to be rejected, and that enforced assimilation is the only answer compatible with democracy. Nor does it mean, as Schlesinger seems to suggest, that minorities should simply accept the superiority of the established or indigenous political culture. These forms of assimilationism have their own cost and involve the loss of those advantages which, I have suggested, a sensible form of multiculturalism might have to offer in a democracy. A society totally devoted to assimilationism could be riven by far greater conflicts than one which offers the breathing spaces of a genuine multiculturalism, and it might well provide a fertile breeding ground for a racism as obnoxious as minority cultures in their most regressive forms.

Sub-Nationalisms in a United Kingdom

So far I have dealt with immigrant minorities, and though I have suggested there is some possibility of extreme groups in these communities becoming disloyal to the state, none of them are in a position to threaten secession on a territorial basis. The so called United Kingdom, however, does also include geographically located minorities, which do have nationalist movements, which may be attracted to the idea of secession and hence threaten the unity of the state. Clearly this is the case in varying degrees of intensity in Wales, Scotland and Northern Ireland.

Wales presents the least serious problem. It is distinguished from England by the use in parts of the principality of a distinct language, and its religion is predominantly Non-Conformist rather than Anglican. Its nationalist movement therefore concentrates on language questions, on gaining a greater share of economic investment and on seeking to discourage the settlement of English people in holiday homes. The language question is relatively easily settled with the recognition of some Welsh-speaking schools, and through fostering the teaching of Welsh in all schools. The main constitutional political party, Plaid Cymru, concentrates on ensuring that investment is preserved at a level necessary to sustain the economy. The Anglican Church which is the national established church in England does not have a similar role in Wales.

Scotland aspires to and has achieved a greater measure of regional autonomy. Its religion is Presbyterian and Presbyterianism is the established church in Scotland, the monarch of the United Kingdom being expected to change her faith while in Scotland. Very few Scots actually speak a separate language although there are distinct Scots dialects. The school system is run separately from that in England, and a number of British government departments are replaced in Scotland by sections of a special Scottish Office, operating from the Scottish capital in Edinburgh. The idea of a separate Scottish political assembly with limited powers is also sometimes discussed by the main British parties, but has not yet been brought into existence. A Scottish Nationalist Party standing for independence wins a handful of seats in the United Kingdom elections, but is still far from enjoying majority support. Normally the majority of Scottish seats in the United Kingdom Parliament are won by the Labour Party, even when the Conservatives win the British elections. This reflects the fact that Scotland is economically disadvantaged. Thus Scotland remains politically part of the United Kingdom, although in many ways it has a distinct culture and is thought of proudly by many Scots as constituting a distinct society. There has been no significant violent resistance in Scotland to the Union.

It is in Ireland that the nationalist problem has not been completely resolved. The island of Ireland was partitioned in 1921, with the bulk of the island in the South being allowed to achieve independence. This Republic remained, or became, predominately Catholic in religion. In the six Northern Counties there was a majority descended largely from Scottish settlers three hundred years ago, who were Protestant in religion and who supported continuing union with the United Kingdom. This however was not acceptable to the minority who remained opposed to partition and the Union, and professed the Catholic religion. The political conflict in Northern Ireland is essentially a *political* one between Irish Nationalists and Unionists, but the two parties are usually referred to and see themselves as Protestants and Roman Catholics. The Republican and Catholic parties have been unable to win a majority in elections in the North, but their more militant and extreme members have sustained a programme of terrorism for more than twenty years through the Irish Republican Army and have created a situation of low-level civil war. At this time the governments of Britain and the Republic of Ireland and the United Kingdom have sought to give assurances to both communities in the North in order to sustain a cease-fire, but have yet to persuade them.

It has been necessary to add this brief review of the political situation in Wales, Scotland and Ireland in order to show that the problem of multiculturalism is not simply one of integrating ethnic minorities. It also has a political dimension which is concerned with nationalism. There is a similar overlapping of immigrant and national problems in several other European countries but most notably in France and Spain.

The Application of the Multicultural Model in Other Political Circumstances

The model we have set out in the earlier sections of this chapter is one which has been developed primarily to deal with the problem of the integration of immigrant ethnic minorities in Western Europe. That had to be extended to take account of the sub-nationalism of the Welsh, the Scots and the Irish. But whether we are talking about the integration of immigrant ethnic minorities or the accommodation of territorially based nationalisms, it is clear that there is no simple blueprint. There is in fact an *art* of multiculturalism in dealing with immigrant ethnic minorities which avoids its pathologies and develops it in a way which is compatible with democracy. Equally there is a political art in judging what degree of autonomy in what institutional areas is necessary to accommodate territorially based ethnic nationalism. What we now have to consider is the application of this art to other political circumstances, especially in cases like those of the new or restored Baltic republics, which had formed part of the Soviet Empire, and which have settler minorities who previously enjoyed a privileged status but are now looked upon in the new national communities as simply one amongst a number of minorities. It seems to me that there are lessons to be learned from the model of democratic multicultural societies as developed in the West, but that there are also crucial differences.

It is, of course, to be expected that in the circumstances of the liberation of the new nations there will be those who will wish to emphasise the restored national culture and insist upon the cultural, social and political assimilation of the former privileged minority. They may even wish to impose tests of language, length of residence, and descent, on this minority. This would involve an extreme case of assimilationism.

The problem here is complicated by the fact that, cross-cutting ethnic boundaries, under the Communist system, the local Soviet states were held together by the structure of the Communist Party. Some of those who came to settle were ordinary Russians, while others were Russian Communists. Similarly there were smaller numbers of settlers from Byelorus or the Ukraine who might either have been simple settlers or Communist settlers. There was also the possibility that some of them might have regarded themselves as

Soviet citizens coming to another part of the Soviet Union, and there would also have been some Lithuanians, Latvians or Estonians who regarded themselves as Communists or Soviet citizens. The achievement of independence meant that all came under the authority of new *national* governments. The overthrow of Soviet rule was combined with an overthrow of Communist rule, although within the Communist Party there were those who, while remaining Communists, identified themselves as communists within the new republics which provided them with their nationality. At first the problem of asserting national independence and achieving national integration was combined with the problem of abolishing Communist rule, but in time it was likely to be the case that the two issues became dissociated. National integration had to be achieved both outside the former party structure and within it.

Because of these complications it is not possible to look at these events simply in terms of a Lithuanian, Latvian or Estonian people now independent and confronting an alien settler minority. Some Russians and settlers from the other Soviet Republics would still be integrated through party structures and some would have voted for and would have supported independence. None the less a problem does remain, namely that of what rights and what degree of autonomy should be accorded to those who are culturally different. There would be problems of language and of religious difference sometimes involving concentrations of minorities on a regional basis, but sometimes involving interspersed populations.

I do not wish, however, to pretend to any expertise on the subtleties and complexities of the Baltic situation. I only wish to ask questions about this situation from the standpoint of the theory of multiculturalism, as it has been developed in the West. From this standpoint, the main problem would appear to be this: How far dare an independent government in one of the new states allow the perpetuation of minority cultures or any degree of autonomy on a regional basis? The dilemma is that not to recognise these forms of cultural diversity would be likely to promote resentment and resistance or even external intervention, but recognising them in even a mild cultural form might also provide the basis for the creation of a secessionist movement or one involving loyalty to another state. To illustrate this I will refer to another East European country, namely Slovakia. The Hungarian government, even though it may lack all expansionist ambitions may be concerned to ensure that the Hungarian minority has cultural and linguistic rights within Slovakia, and members of that minority might wish to enjoy those rights. From the point of view of the Slovakian government, however, this constitutes a problem, because it is likely to fear that even if the right to form only cultural associations were granted these could provide launching pads for political secessionist movements. Quite clearly if they did exist they would have to be policed.

Let us suppose that a government in a Baltic Republic accepted the idea of multiculturalism and actually encouraged a diversity of cultures. It would then have to decide what the limits of cultural activity were. I believe that these could be defined. They would include the right to speak and to foster minority languages and religions as well as the perpetuation on an informal basis of minority customs, particularly in family matters. This could be combined with an insistence that the minority should be committed to the maintenance of a shared public culture along the lines which I suggested in the case of Western societies. This insistence would be more possible if there were institutions guaranteeing equality in the public domain, so that it was worthwhile for minority people to make this commitment.

Naturally the governments of the Baltic countries would also have to take account of the development of nationalism in Russia itself. Recent developments there have not been reassuring. The worst option from the Baltic point of view would be that advocated by some extreme Russian nationalists, namely reconquest and reincorporation into a Russian empire. Understandably they would wish to prevent the establishment amongst the Russian minority of a kind of political fifth column. Slightly less dangerous, but none the less unacceptable to such governments, would be a situation in which Russia sought to establish autonomous regions owing an allegiance as much to Russia as to the countries in which they were situated. This would parallel the fear which Northern Ireland Unionists have of Catholics having an allegiance to the Republic of Ireland. But there is also another option which is discussed by moderates in Russia. This is that they should encourage the cultural development of Russians in the so-called 'near abroad'. It does seem to me that understandings could be developed with such Russian moderates on this question and a kind of cultural development envisaged which ensured the cultural rights of minorities, and did not involve any form of spying or policing. In terms of international relations, moreover, this might have advantages for the Baltic governments, in that it would undercut the appeal of extreme Russian nationalists, both in Russia itself and amongst Baltic Russian minorities. It could therefore be argued that the case for multiculturalism is even more compelling for these minorities than it is for those of Western Europe.

Let me repeat the formula which was put forward in Britain as the charter of multiculturalism: 'not a flattening process of uniformity, but cultural diversity coupled with equal opportunity in an atmosphere of mutual tolerance'. The art of democratic multiculturalism in the Baltic Republics would seem to lie not in seeking to create cultural uniformity but in developing a public political culture which is rewarding for all because it is based upon equality of opportunity and, at the same time, in encouraging the development of diverse cultures which are satisfying to those who adhere to them and yet not subversive of the essential unity of the society.

I believe that a socio-cultural system of this kind offers the best prospects of long-term stability for the new states though I do wonder whether it would be possible to persuade the indigenous population of this, when enforced assimilation appears less of a risk. Perhaps, however, there will be statesmen who can take the longer view, and perhaps the threat of externally inspired political unrest, if minorities are not offered a rewarding life in the new states, will weigh in favour of the multicultural alternative.

8 The Potentiality for Conflict between National and Minority Cultures

THE CONCEPT OF INTERCULTURAL CONFLICT

The problem facing European countries in dealing with ethnic minorities is oversimplified if it is stated as simply one of conflict between cultures, or at least it will be so oversimplified if the concept of culture is not analysed in a critical way.

According to what has come to be called an essentialist view of cultures, each culture contains a certain 'essence', and the problem is seen as the compatibility of these essences. Such a view rests upon little in the way of empirical study of the cultures involved, and, indeed, it is hard to see how it could, because the notion of a cultural essence is a philosophical, rather than an empirical social science concept.

More empirical in its orientation is a view that is often assumed in traditional anthropology which suggests that the population of the world can be divided into peoples and that each people's collective behaviour is controlled and directed by a closed, bounded, and relatively unchanging set of cultural rules. In this case the sole task of the social scientist is to describe these separate sets of cultural

---

*A paper delivered to a conference on Hostility to Foreigners – Conflict about Major Differences, organised by Art Service Research Management and the Austrian Ministry of Science and Research, Vienna, 28 October 1994.

rules and to explore the internal relations of meaning and function between them. Many anthropologists now see this view to be inconsistent with their own empirical observations. The cultural rules governing any people's behaviour turn out to be much less closed to outside influences; the boundaries of the groups whose culture is being studied vary in different situations; and the rules themselves have to be adapted and supplemented to deal with new situations.

In the study of ethnicity these problems are conveniently focused in the theories of ethnicity commonly referred to as primordial or situationist and associated with the earlier writing of Clifford Geertz (Geertz, 1963) and Frederick Barth (Barth, 1959, 1969). According to Geertz, there are certain types of social relations and rules which do not rest on what he calls 'personal attraction, tactical necessity, common interest or incurred moral obligation', but are simply the 'givens' of social existence. They include connections based on kinship and neighbourhood, on speaking a common language and sharing beliefs and some traditional customs. The bonds to which these give rise are said by Geertz to have an ineffable and inexplicable power over the individual. By contrast, Barth, in answering the question 'Who is and who is not a Pathan?' in his field studies in Swot, argues that who counts as being or not being in the group, and as sharing a culture, depends upon the situation. The individuals who count as members in one situation may not be the same as those who do so in another situation, even though the two groups involved may overlap in their membership. But while the boundaries of these purposively oriented groups may vary, Barth does not deny that they will use Pathan culture as a resource.

Barth, of course, was dealing with fairly simple societies, but his view of ethnic groups and boundaries has often been applied in a more radical way in the study of more complex societies. The polar extreme of this view is that which suggests that there really are no distinct cultures at all and that when one looks empirically at the individual members of ethnic groups, thought of as having separate cultures, one finds that these individuals are almost infinitely various in the social ties into which they enter and in the sets of cultural rules they follow. This concept is particularly popular with those who do not wish to recognise ethnic minority group cultures and assumes that their members can relatively easily be assimilated by dominant groups and cultures.

Sensible empirical studies reject both the extreme primordialist view and the notion of infinite individual cultural and social variability. What such studies assume is that there is a sense in which relatively bounded communities do exist, but that they are open to interaction with other groups and that their cultures change in the course of this interaction. The task of the social scientist is therefore seen as studying the actual structures of social relations and the situations which exist at any moment, as well as the complex and changing cultural rules which govern these structures. Such a view is very different from that of the cultural studies approach and of much contemporary anthropology which is based upon what Margaret Archer has called 'downward conflationism' which assumes that social structure is determined by culture (Archer, 1992). It also draws upon the Durkhemian and the Weberian traditions in sociological theory, looking both at social relations of the normative and integrated kind and at others based on conflict and conflict resolution (Durkheim, 1933; Weber, 1968).

The basic unit within migrant minority groups is the extended family. Such extended families will be concerned with improving and enhancing their estate, their property and their life-chances. In doing so, however, they will not be engaged in a process of total competition. They will know that there are wider networks in their homelands, in their present countries of settlement, and indeed across the world, to which they can look for protection and support. They will recognise who belongs and does not belong to these networks by markers such as physical appearance, shared language, shared religion and shared domestic customs. Quite commonly, moreover, they will look to their religious institutions for support in dealing with the crises of life, birth marriage and death. On the other hand, the recognition of the existence of an 'imagined community' of this kind, to use Anderson's term, by no means excludes the possibility of internal conflict and struggles for power.

The example I would use to illustrate this are the Punjabi Sikhs, who are an important and well-organised minority in Britain, but who are also spread across the world from Fiji to California. An individual Sikh in Britain is first of all a member of an extended family, some of whom may be with him/her in Britain, but others of whom may be at home in the Punjab or, say, in Canada. He/she will use this familial network to improve his/her life, but beyond such an immediate extended family will recognise potential allies amongst those who speak Punjabi or practise the Sikh religion. Within this they may feel particularly able to rely on the support of those from the same caste or village. Some, of course, may be in the process of moving away from these networks and culture, but, to a remarkable degree, even those who appear to be assimilated to the culture and society of their lands of settlement continue to turn to their gurdwara (Sikh temples) for ceremonies to mark births, deaths and marriages. Within the community so defined there are none the less struggles for power between political factions, between religious and secular leaders, between castes and classes, and between different economic interests.

There are also, of course, those who are moving away from their own community and culture in various countries of settlement, and some who become completely assimilated there, and any policy towards minorities must take account of these assimilators. None the less the total description of this or any other migrant community has to do justice both to the continuing communal elements which set the bounds of community and to a partial move towards assimilation. Another point to be noted here is that although members of the community may be conscious of traditional notions of appropriate gender relations, there are likely to be within the community those who are in the process of redefining the role of women.

Of course not all ethnic minority groups settling in relatively economically successful countries have the same structure. The case which I have mentioned above is one in which migrants develop their community structures, both in reference to their society of settlement, and in relation to a transnational community. They are also clearly committed to migration rather than seeing it as a temporary phase to be followed by return to the homeland. Other migrants may come from neighbouring countries and maintain their links with their homelands, whether or not they intend to return. Some will be refugees claiming asylum because they are in personal danger. Some will not be able to claim asylum but will be fleeing from situations of civil war or ecological disaster. Amongst these, some will look forward to possible return following a political change in their homelands, while others will have no such hope of return and must perforce settle permanently in a different society, thus becoming, in effect, immigrants. In all cases there will be variation between those whose culture, language and religion is very similar to the culture, language and religion of their society of settlement and those who feel themselves to be and are seen as culturally alien.

POSSIBLE RESPONSES TO IMMIGRANTS AND REFUGEES BY GOVERNMENTS

The problem of so-called multicultural societies is, like the definition of culture itself, oversimplified, if it is suggested that there are simply a number of equally powerful communities and cultures which are finding ways of co-existing. In fact the situation is usually one in which there is a long-established national culture and set of institutions to which incoming minorities have to adapt as a condition of their settlement, even if the longer-term historical record shows that this apparently unitary culture emerged from earlier migrations. Where this is the case there will be, *inter alia*, a national language or languages, there may be a national religion, an economic system based upon markets, criminal and civil law and a national education system.

Commonly such national cultures include conflicting class and status cultures as well as religious diversity, but by the twentieth century the conflicts to which these give rise have been resolved politically by the establishment of welfare states, by the peaceful co-existence of status cultures, and by the acceptance of religious tolerance at least between the more closely related religions (e.g. Catholicism and various forms of Protestantism). In this case the question arises as to whether the existing compromises and forms of tolerance can be extended to include not merely the existing range of classes, status groups or religions, but also incoming groups, having new different relations to the labour and other markets, new positions in the status order, and different religious beliefs.

It is to be expected that in established national systems there will be alternative reactions to the new groups. One will be based upon what we have come to call xenophobia (fear of the unknown) and racism (the attribution to new groups of what are regarded as 'natural' and unchangeable characteristics of an unacceptable kind).

This might also lead to demands for the repatriation or extermination of the new minorities. A second alternative is that incoming groups and their cultures are accepted as having a place within the system, but an inferior place, including that which involves the denial or restriction of rights of political citizenship. A third is that which demands that members of the incoming minorities should lose their culture and be assimilated to the host culture. The fourth alternative is that of a society which recognises cultural diversity and does not regard the incoming cultures and communities as inferior, yet which seeks to extend to all individuals, regardless of their group membership, equality of opportunity.

With regard to the first of these, overtly racist and xenophobic parties in Europe have not succeeded in gaining governmental power, though they have gained significant minority representation and have influenced the policies of the majority parties, persuading them to stop or restrict immigration and to limit not only political but social rights. The second alternative is represented by the guest-worker system of the German-speaking countries. Under this system it might still be possible, despite the denial of political rights, for those who are sympathetic to the immigrants to campaign for their being accorded social rights. The third alternative is the republican and Jacobin one, still evident in French thinking, under which there is strong pressure for incoming minority members to have equal rights, but very often at a cost of their abandoning their own cultures.

Any of these three alternatives represents a possible source of ethnic conflict arising from the host nation side. The first does so in that, even if it does not involve overt violence against the newcomers, it none the less sets itself against allowing what immigrants and refugees want, namely the right of residence and the right to seek work. The second does so in that it creates a kinds of estate system based upon what M. G. Smith has called 'differential political incorporation' (Smith, 1974) and thereby denies the incomers the peaceful means of fighting for rights which they seek. The third does so in denying them the possibility of the emotional, moral and political support which their communities and cultures would otherwise give them, and marks them as inferior by stigmatising their culture.

The alternative which is likely to involve least conflict is the fourth, namely that which seeks to ensure equal treatment in the sphere of political, economic and social rights for individuals from incoming groups, but none the less respects their separate cultures (see Rex, 1986b, 1991a). It is this alternative which accords most completely with immigrant needs and demands and which is therefore likely to lead to a peaceful process of integration.

To enunciate such an ideal, however, is not to suggest that it will be easy to realise in practice. The higher-status groups and classes may find it more difficult to accept the cultures and political demands of the incomers than those of the classes and status groups with which in the past they have achieved a *modus vivendi*. On the other hand, lower-status groups and wage-earners may well fear that the incoming groups will be used by the upper classes and status groups to undermine their own hard-won social rights. Both these groups would require considerable reassurance before fully accepting the ideal of a multicultural society. True, capitalist entrepreneurs might find it convenient to employ cheap immigrant labour, and to that extent might welcome immigration, but they would still hesitate to pursue policies which led to labour unrest amongst indigenous employees, and might, on the cultural level, fear the unknown element in minority cultures; and so far as the working classes were concerned they would need to be reassured that the level of immigration allowed was that which was necessary for economic growth without their own position being undermined.

These are assurances which could be given. The fear of alien cultures can be overcome if they are more fully understood. They might also be seen as having a positive role in strengthening the morality of these sections of the community and diverting it from crime. (The Turks in Germany like to quote Frederick the Great as saying, 'All religions are good and equal and, if the Turks come to Germany, we should build mosques for them'.) On the other hand, it can be argued that in the long run the use of cheap labour is damaging and that policies can be worked out which enlarge the labour force as necessary but which maintain the standards of skill and reward which have proven successful in the past. Giving this reassurance, however, is much more difficult in times of economic recession.

The setting up of political institutions of a multicultural kind can take differing forms. One possibility would be that of creating negotiating and liaison mechanisms in which male elders with highly traditional views are taken as representative. Where this has happened, there are many in the minority communities who are in the process of redefining their culture or who may have moved partially towards the culture of the host society or to developing syncretic links with other communities, who will resist this traditionally defined leadership (see Schierup and Alund, 1987, 1990). The difficult problem is that of establishing communication with the whole range of conflicting interests and definitions of culture represented in the minority communities. There are few examples to be found in Europe of the development of this more sensitive kind of multiculturalism.

Apart from the question of political liaison and multiculturalism, the other area in which multiculturalism has to be faced is in the educational system. There may be a variety of special needs which immigrant children have in schools, not least those relating to language, and there may be some demand in the immigrant communities that the schools should allow for education in their own culture and religion and that they should also seek to encourage respect for these cultures and religions amongst indigenous children. On the other hand it is very likely that indigenous parents will feel threatened if they think that their own culture or religion is being undermined by multicultural programmes.

The acceptance of refugees, of course, involves questions of a different order from those faced by immigrants. The first and difficult point for the majority of the population is that there is an international obligation. Such an international obligation is more likely to be accepted if it is clear that it is being dealt with internationally, that any one country is not bearing an undue share of the burden, and that there is also a well-understood process for both the temporary protection of some, and the long-term integration of other, refugees. If there is no such well-understood process, the danger is that refugees will be regarded as immigrants in disguise, getting in even after the immigration stop, and they will be attacked for doing this. Moreover, insofar as such attacks occur, they are likely to be extended to the established immigrant population, as has happened in Germany.

It should be clear from the above that there are many tendencies in European societies which make the acceptance of both immigrants and refugees difficult and that the most likely scenario is the growth of xenophobia and racist hostility to these groups. It was, however, the need for economic growth which led to immigration in the past and which will lead to its recurrence in the future, and there is every reason to suppose that the problem of refugees and of those fleeing from civil disorder (and sometimes ecological disaster) will increase rather than abate. Since these problems are inevitable, it is all the more necessary that governments should develop and gain acceptance for policies which ensure that those who will come are peacefully integrated and that their coming does not lead to the collapse of the post–1945 political order.

THE NATURE OF ETHNIC MINORITY MOBILISATION

Having dealt with the causes of conflict which arise from attitudes in the host society, I now wish to turn to the question of those causes which might arise from the incoming communities themselves.

There are three elements in the structure of ethnic minority communities and their culture (see Rex, 1994b). First of all they are affected by the interests of the individuals involved in the migration process. Secondly there will be a need to maintain the cultural and other markers which distinguish members from non-members, thereby providing a framework of economic, moral and social support and a basis for solidarity in collective political action. Thirdly there will be a continuing concern with the affairs of the homeland. We need to analyse the structure of such communities in terms of these three elements rather than seeing them as involving some kind of 'fundamentalist' commitment to alien traditional cultures.

Clearly immigrant ethnic communities and refugees have distinct interests in their societies of settlement. They are seeking to enter labour markets or to achieve political safety. They will be concerned to defend themselves against exploitation by employers and with fighting against exclusion by indigenous workers. Commonly they will find, moreover, that what they are offered is a compromise in which they are allowed to enter the least wanted jobs and prevented from entering the more secure and rewarding ones. One strategy for dealing with this situation is that of allying themselves with indigenous unions in their struggle against exploitation, yet also retaining their own organisations within the unions to ensure that they are not excluded by the monopolistic organisations of indigenous labour. The alternative is to take advantage of the fact that employers may want the cheap labour they are in a position to offer, and to compete with indigenous workers at all levels, even if this means undermining their position. Generally immigrant groups in Europe have adopted the first of these strategies, identifying themselves with the international trades union and socialist movement, but there is always a temptation for hard-pressed individual immigrants to follow the second, and the possibility of immigrant brokers emerging to facilitate the supply of cheap labour.

Refugees and quasi-refugees, of course, are in a somewhat different position. Some may, it is true, be immigrants in disguise, and acceptable to employers as providing a supply of cheap and rightless labour, but more serious problems arise for those who are not needed economically and whose acceptance rests purely on legal and moral considerations. For the latter much will depend upon the degree of sympathy felt in the indigenous community for their plight in the countries from which they have fled. In this respect, refugees to West Europe from the former Yugoslavia are most likely to be acceptable, and during the period of the Cold War refugees from Communism enjoyed considerable political support. This kind of sympathy has also been extended to a lesser extent to Iranians fleeing the Islamic revolution in their country; and Chileans fleeing from a right-wing tyranny have been able to appeal to socialist and communist allies in Europe. Others, like Tamils from Sri Lanka and refugees from the Horn of Africa, however, will lack political allies of any kind, and even in the case of Vietnamese, who like Eastern Europeans are actually refugees from Communism, it may be felt that they are too distant in terms of race, culture and geography for them to be able to call on any sense of moral obligation in the West.

From the point of view of West European governments which actually have internationally agreed obligations to all of these groups, the problem is to limit the numbers of those arriving, by arranging 'safe havens' in the countries from which they come, by insisting on visas and punishing these without documents, and by returning asylum applicants to their first countries of refuge. As against these policies, the refugees themselves have an interest in keeping open as many options as possible, sometimes living as illegal immigrants rather than seeking and risking refusal in asylum applications. They will also be concerned to increase their rights to obtain work and housing. At the same time they will do whatever they can with the aid of liberal indigenous lobbies on an international level to persuade governments to accept their international obligations.

In the case of both immigrants and refugees there are several other groups who should be mentioned. These include professionals with wanted skills, traders and entrepreneurs entering unfilled entrepreneurial niches, and serious foreign investors. The professionals with wanted skills have rarely constituted any problem for countries of settlement, and in the medical profession particularly they have done much to sustain West European medical services. Such immigrant professionals constitute more of a problem for their countries of origin, where they are seen as part of a brain-drain. So far as refugees are concerned, the existence of professionals within their ranks is an obvious bonus for the countries of settlement. There is also a place for entrepreneurs filling unwanted niches and for servicing the immigrant community, though they may well become scapegoats too easily blamed for the evils of capitalism and regarded as representing a lower order of economic morality than that which has been established in Western business. Their position is that traditionally occupied by the Jews in the past. They are seen as pariahs. Such traders, however, might well escape from this pariah position and many will seek to do so, by entering the economic mainstream. This is what is happening to Indian businessmen in Britain today. Many started as shopkeepers, working long hours with no holidays, and relying on family labour to make their businesses profitable. But some may start serving indigenous clients, employing indigenous labour, and investing in mainstream business. When this happens they may come to join the class of serious foreign investors to which I have referred. Such investors include, apart from Americans whose role has not been seriously questioned, Arabs and Japanese. But these are now joined by those from the Pacific rim (at the moment the British government is proud and delighted to have persuaded the Korean firm Samsung to invest in one of its development areas) as well as some Indian firms which may have grown out of pariah trade but are now seen as important international investors as well as trading partners in India itself.

The possibility exists, of course, that all these groups might draw to themselves the sort of resentment which was directed against Jews in the past and, along with the racism and xenophobia directed against immigrant workers, it may be expected that there will be another kind of racism and xenophobia, directed not against those who are poor, but against the apparently successful.

We now turn from the discussion of the pattern of immigrant economic interests generated by the experience of migration to the somewhat different question of culture maintenance. In doing so, however, it is necessary to repeat that the latter set of considerations should not be divorced from the former. It is too glibly asserted by many Western sociologists nowadays that ethnic minority community and culture is not based upon the pursuit of interests but upon a quest for identity. Touraine, for example, has suggested that whereas in the past people were defined in terms of their occupation (what they do) (Touraine, 1990), they now tend to be defined in terms of 'what they are'. The position taken here is that the two questions are intimately intertwined. Immigrant communities may be thought of as quasi-classes and their cultures as resources in the class and factional struggles in which they have to engage.

Since immigrants are social human beings, they will have the needs of social human beings. They face the problems which Durkheim described so well in his *The Division of Labour* (Durkheim, 1933). As he saw it, the danger in an individualist society was the collapse of any sort of moral order, and the creation of a state of anomie. For this to be avoided, he believed that it was necessary that there should be some kind of group standing between the individual family and the state. This is precisely what immigrant minority communities provide for their members. They provide the individual with an emotional and moral home to which he/she can feel attached and serve to mediate between the warmth of family ties and the impersonality of the modern nation state. It is also entirely consistent with Durkheim's thinking to suggest that individuals in the migrant situation will, if they are not to slip into anomie, need some way of interpreting the meaning of their lives. This is something which religion provides, and though this religion might itself change and develop in the face of new situations it will not be possible for the migrant simply to discard the religion learned in the homeland, since it is through its symbols and codes that he or she seeks to understand the meaning of life.

One special feature of this situation is that, from the point of view of Western individualism and secularism, the culture of immigrant ethnic minority groups often seems to be based upon a narrow-minded family and sexual morality. Indeed it is often so based, but this is surely not a peculiarity of immigrant groups. It is precisely the discipline of this morality which has prevented other exploited and disadvantaged groups in Western society from becoming demoralised in the past, and what is advocated in Britain, for instance, as a return to Victorian values for the indigenous population is not dissimilar to what is demanded by immigrant religious leaders. To say this is not to side with the plea for a return to Victorian values. It is merely to say that until individuals feel sufficiently secure to deal with society as moral individuals, this apparently narrow-minded community-based morality will sustain them, and prevent demoralisation and anomie. It should also be noted that one feature of immigrant cultures in the complex sense in which we have sought to define such cultures is that there will be ongoing arguments about the role of women and sometimes an internal feminist movement which has more significance than the indigenous feminist movement, which is often seen in immigrant communities as insensitive and lacking in understanding of minority values.

The last few paragraphs suggest that immigrant community and culture does have the primary function of providing the individual with a sense of identity. I would agree that it does have this function in the special sense I have outlined. But this quest for identity is not divorced from the pursuit of interests. The sense of identity which attachment to a community and a culture provides is also a resource which is called on in the mobilisation of a community to fight collectively for justice and equality in the conditions of a modern economy. While it may be true that the culture itself is changed by its use by ethnically mobilised groups fighting for social justice, it is also true that it does provide the basis for necessary political solidarity. Both elements in Barth's situational theory are true. The boundaries of the group do depend upon the situation in which it finds itself, but in that situation it calls upon the resource of a changing and developing ethnicity. There is thus a place for ethnic politics in a modern society both as a means of preventing demoralisation and anomie and as providing a basis for solidarity.

It is, however, to be expected that the different groups in indigenous society will be suspicious of minority cultures and the separate ethnic politics to which it leads and it will always be necessary for ethnic community leaders to counter this suspicion by demonstrating their commitment to normal egalitarian values. I would myself suggest that this is what happens when ethnic communities appeal, as they do, along with the assertion of traditional values, to a kind of pragmatic Marxism which they have learned in their homelands and which is reinforced in the migrant situation. The goals they pursue may be their own self-interested goals but they have a place in the political culture of a modern democratic society and welfare state.

Related to this question is the attitude taken by immigrant communities to the other institutions of the society in which they settle. They cannot determine the nature of these institutions and it is absurd, for example, for some Muslim leaders to suggest that they can turn established Western societies into Islamic states. What is necessary therefore is that immigrant communities should, as many do, accept that living in a society with its own, language, religion, economic system, law, folk customs and school system, means that they must pay a price for their chosen situation. What they have to do is to learn to be culturally bilingual, to be able to operate within the institutions of their society of settlement as well as maintaining their own solidary culture.

Learning to operate in this culturally bilingual way is not easy, and there will be those who retreat from its challenges, particularly if the rewards which the new modern society appeared at first to offer are not forthcoming, and where minority cultures and religions are subject to insult. In such circumstances one might well find movements based upon the notion of retreat and withdrawal, of institutional separation, of disloyalty to the society of settlement, and even of a hypothetical secession. This is what Arthur Schlesinger sees as happening amongst Blacks in the United States, in his book, *The Disuniting of America* (Schlesinger, 1992), and is also the position of a minority of Muslims in Britain (see Siddiqui, 1990b).

What one would expect in minority communities then is a struggle between those movements and leaderships which adopt the policy I have called cultural bilingualism and those which tend towards withdrawal and cultural and political secession. Clearly one of the tasks of statesmanship in the host societies is to encourage the former at the expense of the latter. Such a task is unlikely to be helped by the suppression of minority cultures or by denouncing any tendency towards ethnic politics as 'fundamentalist'.

More serious problems arise from the continuing interest of ethnic minority groups in homeland politics and their political commitments on a geopolitical level. Immigrants often come from countries in which there are unresolved political problems and in which there are violent and extremist political movements. Those who support these movements are therefore likely to see the transnational community of migrants as a base for mounting terrorist campaigns which cannot be pursued at home. A number of assassinations and hijackings have been organised in this way. There is, of course, no reason why members of immigrant communities should not, as citizens of their countries of settlement, seek to influence foreign policy towards their homelands, but they should accept that if they commit what are serious crimes in these societies they risk the punishment of long terms of imprisonment or deportation, because government policy in their country of settlement will be determined by national interests.

Before turning to the question of what has to be done to defuse political conflicts which follow immigration, it is worth noting that the above discussion involves a deconstruction of the notion of minority cultures. They are not seen here as essences or as bounded value systems. Rather what one has to deal with are changing community structures and complex, changing and developing value systems. It is certainly not the case that these structures and value systems will not lead to any conflict, but whereas the essentialist view regards such conflicts as not negotiable, our review shows that the sources of these conflicts on both the majority and the minority side can be understood and handled with political skill, so that they do not lead to violence and social and political breakdown.

A final word should be said in this section about the means available to immigrant minority groups to act politically. Most of what has been said above assumes a kind of communalism, in which immigrants have to act through special institutions set up outside the framework of the mainstream political system. In some countries like Britain, however, a majority of immigrants have the vote, and in other countries there are likely to be increasing numbers of those who acquire it through naturalisation. When this happens, these immigrants will be able to act not merely through liaison and consultative mechanisms but through their own members of parliament and local councillors usually elected on the ticket of one or other of the mainstream parties, and there may be some conflict between the communal type of representation and that through the political system. The eventual outcome of this is unclear, but one may guess that what will happen over a number of generations is that the descendants of immigrants will rely less on the communal forms of representation, which may become increasingly depoliticised, and more upon direct participation in the democratic mainstream.

THE RESOLUTION OF ETHNIC CONFLICT

In the light of all that has been said above, we are now in a position to recommend the kind of politics, institutional arrangements and policies which will be necessary in dealing with immigrant minorities in European societies in the future. In doing this we reject the possibility that there will simply be no more immigrants or refugees because they have been excluded. As we have seen, there is likely to be a future demand for immigrant labour and there will be an increasing refugee problem. The problem, therefore, is to make arrangements for the peaceful integration of those who have already settled and for those who will come in the future.

First, the governments of countries receiving immigrants and refugees should make quite clear to their electorates what the needs of the economic system and the international obligations towards refugees actually are. So far as the demands of the economic system are concerned, this is a matter which should be discussed with indigenous trades unions so that they can explain to their members that what is being advocated is not a cheap labour policy, but one which is necessary for the filling of otherwise unfillable jobs and for economic growth. So far as refugees and quasi-refugees fleeing from civil wars are concerned, it is essential that the problem be discussed and policies developed on an international level, so that there is not a sense of a particular country carrying an unfair burden.

Second, the problem of political citizenship has to be faced. Continuing to pretend that those who are clearly immigrants are actually only guest-workers can only mean that a section of the labour force is marked out as a potential target for scapegoating and attack. One particular problem in this area is that of both receiving and sending societies recognising dual citizenship, but once the fact of immigration is acknowledged, the emphasis should be on the naturalisation of those who are settled and in regular employment.

Third, some arrangements must be made to ensure that those who are distinguished by their colour, culture, religion and national origin are not marked out for unequal and inferior treatment. This should at least involve laws enforceable in the courts against racial and ethnic discrimination in employment and in the delivery of social services. And beyond this there is a need for monitoring discrimination and assisting complainants to obtain their legal rights. There also has to be a clear policy for the protection of some refugees and quasi-refugees and the integration of others into the national economy and the national community.

Fourth, while it is certainly undesirable that separate ethnic political parties should develop, members of these minorities should be encouraged to participate in the political mainstream. Since, however, they have specific interests to defend during the period of settlement, there should be some provision for consultation and liaison with community-based organisations.

The establishment of such forms of community consultation raises the fifth point, namely that of the type of consultative mechanism to be set up. What has to be avoided is consultation only with those who are acceptable to the government or those who can easily be manipulated, but there is no simple way in which really effective representation of diverse individuals in these communities can be established. In part there must be some element of election, but even if there is, since election might easily lead to the community being represented only by a minority faction, a government committed to just and peaceful relations with all the members of these communities might to some extent have to make its own decisions so as to ensure the representation of minorities within minorities.

Sixth, consideration has to be given to how far and for how long ethnic community organisations and ethnic minority culture is to be encouraged. Many reasons have been given above as to why a policy of assimilationism and the suppression of minority cultures should not be pursued. What is necessary is that over a period of three or four generations immigrants should have the moral and emotional support of their own community and culture and the possibility of collective political action. In the longer run what may survive is only a symbolic ethnicity which will not be regarded as a political threat and may even be regarded as a means of enrichment of the national culture.

Finally, against this background, it should be possible and would be necessary that the government should counter the activities and propaganda of racist and xenophobic indigenous parties. This is not something which can be done simply by denying that problems exist. It has to be done within the context of the whole range of policies designed to deal with these problems.

In short, the conclusion of this chapter would be that: immigration and the acceptance of refugees does undoubtedly create a potentiality for conflict and it is misleading to pretend that they do not. From what has been said, however, these are not problems which it is beyond the capacity of governments to resolve in consultation with their own indigenous electorates and with the minority communities themselves. Resolving them should in fact be one of the primary goals of statesmanship.

THE CASE OF AUSTRIA

In many ways the main purpose of this chapter has been to deal with the problems posed by immigration and refugee settlement and the necessary policies for dealing with them in general terms, rather than suggesting specific *ad hoc* solutions for Austria. It is, moreover, unlikely that an outsider would have the necessary knowledge to deal specifically with the Austrian situation. None the less it may be useful to list some of the questions which Austrians might ask. Perhaps the main point is to consider the peculiarities of Austrian immigration compared with Western European countries. This would involve looking at, first, the older type of immigration arising from Austria's position as the centre of the Hapsburg empire; second, the need of a successful economy to recruit labour and the adoption of the guest-worker system; and, third, Austria's geographical position which made it a neutral in the Cold War, but which now places it on the border across which many refugees and quasi-refugees are likely to come, and for whom Austria is the country of first refuge.

A further set of questions arises from Austria's position in a larger international community. It is part of the German-speaking world and its citizens will have privileged access to other parts of that world. It is also now to become part of the European union and may have to participate in policy formation on questions of migration within the EU. Membership of the EU will greatly enlarge the opportunities of indigenous Austrians as it will of all settled European citizens as they acquire the right of the free movement of labour. But decisions still have to be taken of the rights of free movement of non-EU residents and there will still be a question regarding the Austrian response to guest-workers from other European countries seeking work in Austria.

In a guest-worker situation, or one in which there is a problem of refugee and quasi-refugee settlement, it is unlikely that there will be any major effort devoted to set up institutions to promote equality of opportunity or multiculturalism in either political or educational terms, although it is likely that there will be some concern to protect the social rights of those who are denizens rather than citizens.

Finally, any political decisions which are taken will have to be taken in a situation in which a populist third party has gained increasing support on an anti-immigrant programme. The question is whether a policy of integrating ethnic minorities can none the less be pursued which, because it creates greater conditions of internal peace and security, also helps to undermine tendencies towards xenophobia and racism.

9 Anti-Racism and Ethnic Mobilisation in Europe[*]

ANTI-RACISM AND ETHNIC MOBILISATION IN EUROPE
WITH SPECIAL REFERENCE TO GERMANY

The Political Context

There is considerable concern in Germany, and more widely in Europe, today, about the significance of recent violent attacks on refugees, foreigners and immigrants, and the relative gains made by parties of the extreme right espousing 'racist' policies. Such developments are not unique to Germany. There have been outbreaks of violence directed against Maghrebians in France, and there the National Front under Le Pen has achieved greater electoral success than any other party of the far right in Europe. In Britain there is a record of racist attacks particularly directed against Bangladeshis in East London, which is actually far greater than anything equivalent in Germany, and the Fascist British National Party has recently gained local government representation and could possibly increase it. There are also equivalent political developments in Austria and in Flanders. In Germany, however, the question has been posed in a particularly sharp form, and there are fears that recent racist attacks might presage the re-emergence of Nazism as a political force.

It is against this background that the political integration of different kinds of minorities has to be considered. Are they to remain non-citizens? Are the problems which they face themselves

---

[*]A paper delivered to the XII Europaische Kulturtage der Stadt Karlsruhe 1994 – 'Widerstand', 6 May 1994.

168

and pose to the national society capable of being handled within the normal political system, or are special institutional arrangements necessary for dealing with them? If they retain their own culture, will this mark them for unequal treatment and for physical attack, or make them available as scapegoats? Is the very fact of mobilisation on an ethnic basis not regressive and dangerous, as the recent history of Yugoslavia has shown? Alternatively is there a possibility that ethnic mobilisation could occur in ways which protect minority rights and actually contribute to the strength of democracy in a welfare state?

The Fear of Ethnic Mobilisation

The existence of organisations and the maintenance of distinct patterns of culture amongst immigrant ethnic minority groups have made these groups targets for physical attack. But anxiety about, and hostility to, these groups is by no means confined to young groups of skinheads and neo-Nazis. Unlike other countries in West Europe, there is a traditional notion in Germany of ethnic nationalism amongst the majority population. Germanness, according to this view, is regarded as a cultural matter, rather than merely a matter of citizenship, and 'ethnic Germans' are recognised even when they do not live within the national boundaries, while, at the same time, several millions who actually live and work in Germany are thought of neither as citizens nor as Germans. This produces an even stronger sense of ethnocentrism than that which exists in other countries in which the main bond between residents is thought of, in part at least, in terms of a common citizenship. The cultures of minority groups are also likely to be considered as alien and regressive, particularly if they involve differences of religion, as may be the case with some of the Turkish residents. Xenophobic and racist parties now make a small but significant electoral showing, and perhaps even more significantly the mainstream parties have adjusted their policies on such matters as asylum in response to racist attacks.

Fear of the outsiders is by no means confined to those who subscribe to right-wing ideologies. A common view on the left of politics is that ethnic consciousness is a form of false consciousness which divides the working class and prevents it from taking collective action. More than this, there is a liberal view that citizenship rather than ethnicity should be the basis for collective action, and many social democrats have an ideal of a pluralistic welfare state, in which people are thought of in terms of the interest groups to which they belong and between whom potential conflicts can be resolved by bargaining and compromise, and which they see as threatened by special multicultural arrangements. Thus radical socialists, liberals and social democrats all tend to be suspicious of the idea of ethnic mobilisation and ethnically based politics.

It is very difficult in these circumstances to promote discussion amongst German social scientists of the possibility or the desirability of a multicultural society, in which ethnicity and ethnic politics play a part, but, believing, as I do, that such ethnic politics do deserve recognition and may have a positive role to play in a democracy, I want to devote this chapter to a discussion of the nature of ethnic mobilisation and the ways in which a democratic society might respond to it.

Primordial Ethnicity

Recent events in Yugoslavia have led to a widespread negative view of ethnicity as such. It is commonly thought that, with the collapse of empires, and more recently with the collapse of the Communist system, which cut across both ethnicity and nationalism with a bureaucratic party structure, men and women were likely to cling together and act together in terms of a mysterious bond of ethnicity which was irrational and incomprehensible This was usually expressed by saying that ethnicity was 'primordial'. Our starting point in any discussion of ethnic mobilisation, therefore, must be the unpacking of this notion of primordiality.

On the level of theoretical anthropology the notion of the primordiality of ethnicity was defended in his early work by Clifford Geertz (Geertz, 1963), and it is useful to begin our discussion by considering what is unacceptable and acceptable in what he has to say. His definition of primordiality is given as follows:

> By a primordial attachment is meant one that stems from the 'givens', or, more precisely, since culture is inevitably involved in

such matters, the assumed 'givens' of social existence: immediate contiguity and live connection mainly, but beyond them the givenness that stems from being born into a particular religious community, speaking a particular language, or even a dialect of a language, and following particular social practices. These congruities of blood, speech, custom and so on, are seen to have an ineffable, and at times, overpowering, coerciveness in and of themselves. One is bound to one's kinsman, one's neighbour, one's fellow believer, *ipso facto*, as a result, not merely of personal attraction, tactical necessity, common interest, or incurred moral obligation, but, at least in great part, by some unaccountable absolute import attributed to the very tie itself. (p. 109)

What is not acceptable in this definition are all the mysterious terms which Geertz uses: 'givens', 'ineffable', 'in and of themselves', *'ipso facto'* and 'unaccountable absolute import'. One cannot make a serious sociological analysis using such terms. In fact they erect barriers to sociological investigation.

What Geertz does do, however, and this is theoretically valuable, is to distinguish between two types of bonds. On the one hand, there are those which arise from kinship, neighbourhood, common language, common religious beliefs and cultural practices. On the other, there are those which rest upon personal attraction, tactical necessity, common interest or incurred moral obligation.

The first of these sets of bonds are certainly inevitable in that every infant must find himself or herself caught up in them. This is what I have sometimes called the 'infantile ethnic trap'. More precisely it refers to the set of social relations within which primary socialisation takes place. This also has certain psychological correlates. Because these social relations are learned about, and joined within, the context of the family, they are experienced with a sense of emotional warmth and they are even likely to be thought of, as Durkheim suggested, as 'sacred' (Durkheim, 1964). They are thus quite unlike impersonal exchange relationships.

To admit that such a social and cultural network is inevitable in infancy, however, by no means implies that it will necessarily be projected into adult life. What happens, of course, is that from this network there is constructed the personality of the individual. The infantile network becomes projected into his or her head, and thereafter it is possible for socialised moral individuals to confront one another in more impersonal ways.

When Aristotle said that 'man is a creature destined by nature to live in the polis' he was referring to a community of this kind. He thought of it as a more rational form of association rather than as one based upon ethnicity and kinship. The Stoics, moreover, sought to transcend even the limitations of the polis and envisaged an international community of the wise. It is, however, not simply that there is a transition historically from simple ethnic bonding to political units of a more rationalistic kind. The fact is that most individuals do move in their own lives from the world of infantile ethnicity to new forms of association based, to use Geertz's terms, on 'personal attraction, tactical necessity and incurred moral obligation'. As Tonnies might have put it, we are born into a world of *gemeinschaft*, but move on to the world of *gesellschaft* (Tonnies, 1955).

The Extension and Sustaining of Ethnicity

The real problem of ethnicity, however, lies in the fact that not all individuals grow up in this way, and that even those who do, might also develop, along with their participation in an individualistic world, a continuing sense of emotional belonging to a group larger than that based upon simple kinship. Ethnic leaders emerge who create a larger ethnicity. They invite their followers to believe that a larger group has something of the same sacred and emotionally warming appeal that the infantile ethnic group had. They may appeal to co-religionists, to those sharing a common language, to those who live in, or aspire to live in, a particular territory, or to those who share a common history or myth of origin, but, however the bounds of the group are drawn, what is created is more than simply another association. It is a community and it has sacred qualities.

The Situational Basis of Ethnicity

In contrast to Geertz's notion of primordial ethnicity, Barth suggested that the boundaries of the ethnic group depended on the situation or the purpose in hand (Barth, 1969). Someone who was seen as a fellow Pathan in one situation would not be seen as such in another. If, however, this is true in a relatively simple tribal ethnic society, it is much more true in larger-scale situations when leaders seek to attach the emotional warmth and sacredness of ethnicity to a larger group. They do so in accordance with the needs of their project.

An extreme version of this view is based upon the notion of ethnogenesis which suggests that such ethnicity is cynically created (Roosens, 1989), but even if we do not take this view we do have to notice that the bounding of the group depends upon the project in hand. Thus, in looking at complex societies we have to notice that they may be thought of not merely as the result of the interaction, conflict and compromise which takes place between individuals, but also as the result of such interaction conflict and compromise between groups with projects. I now want to suggest that there are two such important projects in European history. One is the project of nationalism; the other, with which we shall be more concerned here, is the project of migration.

The Project of Nationalism

There seem to be two theories of nationalism. One is that the principle on which the nation is organised is entirely at odds with ethnicity. The nation is thought of as a community of individuals. It comes into being, as Gellner has suggested (Gellner, 1983), as a part of a modernising project, and cannot tolerate the special loyalties which ethnicity involves. The best example of nationalism of this kind is provided by the French Republican and Jacobin tradition. Paradoxically, however, those who espouse this type of nationalism do also commonly claim that this new constructed group has many of the sacred and emotionally warming characteristics which ethnic groups have. Moreover these positive feelings towards the nation to which one is called to belong are coupled with negative feelings towards other nations.

As against this modernising theory of nationalism, an alternative view is that nations actually have ethnic origins. What is called an 'ethnie' exists in the first place, but it becomes a nation when it seeks to assert its sovereignty over a territory. Moreover, once it has established such sovereignty, it may subordinate competing ethnies living in the same territory. One may then have a situation in which there is a ruling ethnic nation, and subordinate ethnic nations, either accepting their subordination, or developing their own ethnonationalism and seeking independence, secession, or autonomy. The German ideology of nationalism is an ethnic nationalism of this kind.

The Project of Migration

The particular concern of this chapter, however, is not with nationalism, which is always concerned with claims to a territory, but with the business of migration. In this case, some individuals from a group whose members may share a common territory and be united in terms of kinship, language religion and myth, and who may or may not be a recalcitrant ethnic nation in their country of origin, find it necessary to move to another sovereign national territory, most commonly for economic reasons but sometimes as a result of political persecution.

A group which engages in migration of this kind will have two major points of reference. On the one hand, its members will still retain links of kinship, culture and territory with the homeland. On the other, its immediate purpose will be the establishment of rights in the country of settlement for its members. In the course of this latter struggle, the maintenance of the group's culture will serve as a valuable resource in creating solidarity amongst the group's members.

Class Conflict, Status Systems and Minority Groups

In some ways migrating groups in this situation become quasi-classes. Of course it is true that classes, in an ideal-typical Marxist sense, should be based solely on what Geertz calls 'tactical necessity and common interest', and any sense of solidarity based upon purely cultural or ethnic grounds constitutes a form of false consciousness. Yet if we look at actual working-class history rather than at this ideal type, we find that the European working class has always drawn on the solidarity and strengths which come from regional cultures. In this sense we may say that the indigenous working class draws on its own ethnicity.

So far as immigrant ethnic minority groups are concerned their entry into the process of class struggle is complicated by the fact that they often enter divided labour markets. The jobs which are at first available to them are those which involve the greatest insecurity and the most arduous conditions. They are often jobs which are not wanted by members of the indigenous working class, and which involve for those who occupy them, in a quite literal sense, a different relation to the means of production. Those who enter them will, while having something in common with all other workers, also have their own class or factional struggle to pursue. Similarly, those who enter the system not as workers but as small-scale entrepreneurs find themselves at first confined to 'pariah' business roles, with specific interests of their own to pursue.

Another way in which the immigrant ethnic minority has to fit into the structure of the social system of the country of settlement is in terms of its status system rather than in terms of class struggle. What we loosely call class, involves, as Weber saw, considerable overlap between class, in a more Marxian sense, and status (Weber, 1967, p. 963). Ruling groups do not merely unite in the market place to exploit inferior groups ; they also develop their own 'way of life' and techniques of closure to keep out those who have inferior ways of life. The inferior groups, on the other hand, have their distinct cultures and ways of life, and while some members may seek to enter the upper groups despite their closure practices, many will value their own culture and way of life, both in itself and as a source of solidarity in collective bargaining. These processes were classically documented in the United States in Lloyd Warner's Yankee City studies (Warner and Lunt, 1947).

An immigrant ethnic minority group may be seen, therefore, not merely as a quasi-class but as a quasi-status group. From the point of view of both dominant and subordinate indigenous status groups with their distinct ways of life, it appears as a new status group against whom the barriers of closure need to be set up. The incoming ethnic group, on the other hand, will be concerned with establishing a place for itself in the status order, even though some of its members will seek entry into the indigenous status system by way of social and cultural assimilation. The questions of status and status closure involved here have been well discussed by the British sociologist, Parkin (1979), who deals both with the status struggles of the indigenous working classes and the way in which they exclude incoming groups through their own practices of closure.

Many of the problems of ethnic minority groups in Europe can be understood in these terms. It should, however, be added that their conflicts, whether of a quasi-class or a quasi-status kind, are always likely to be more severe. For all the fact that they are often confined to jobs which indigenous workers do not wish to enter, they are none the less seen as competitors, and so far as their way of life is concerned this may often be seen as far more alien and threatening than the way of life of subordinate indigenous groups appears to upper-status groups. In the labour market immigrant workers are cheap labour, and in the hierarchy of ways of life they may have cultures and religions varying in their degree of remoteness and alienness from indigenous culture, but nearly always more remote and more alien than those of any indigenous status groups.

In this situation of severe class and status conflict, when their class position and their way of life appears under threat, it is to be expected that immigrant ethnic minority groups will do two things. One is that they will unite and fight as quasi-classes to win or defend their right to equality in the society of settlement; the other is that they will wish to defend their own way of life, their religion, and the solidarity which these offer them. They will also be more inclined and better able to do this because their culture has another lively point of reference in the homeland. By the same token, however, they are likely to become even more suspect in the eyes of the indigenous community in that they might be suspected not merely of having alien values but of being politically disloyal. There is thus ambiguity in the attitude of members of minority groups to the purpose of their mobilisation in ethnic terms, and also in the attitude of the indigenous classes towards such mobilisation. Ethnic minority organisations express and reflect both the process of getting into the social system of the country of settlement, and the need to maintain the group's own culture. The members of indigenous classes, however, see them, on the one hand, as a quasi-class which is part of their own society, but on the other hand as having regressive and alien cultures and as being potentially disloyal. Taken together these attitudes provide the basis for what may be called ethnic/class conflict.

THE ARGUMENT ABOUT MULTICULTURALISM

Germany and the other German-speaking countries have particular problems in dealing with ethnic minorities in that they continue to regard incoming groups not as citizens or potential citizens, but only as 'Gastarbeiders'. As Hammar puts it, they are regarded as denizens rather than as citizens (Hammar, 1983). While Germany has developed policies to ensure social rights for denizens and has, even in some cities, like Frankfurt, developed elaborate multicultural policies, it does necessarily face peculiar problems because of the Gastarbeider system and ideology.

The ideal of a democratic multicultural society has been more fully and adequately developed in other countries, most notably in Britain, the Netherlands and Sweden, and it may be of value here to spell out what that would mean as a general policy in structural terms before going on to look at the criticisms of it which have been made by European social scientists.

In Britain the argument began with the recognition that the fight for equality for immigrant groups needed to be coupled with a recognition of cultural diversity. The Home Secretary of 1968, Roy Jenkins, called for this when he defined 'integration', not as 'a flattening process of uniformity, but as cultural diversity, coupled with equal opportunity in an atmosphere of mutual tolerance' (Rex and Tomlinson, 1979). This seemed to emphasise that the pursuit of equality was not incompatible with the recognition of cultural diversity, but, equally, that cultural diversity should not be pursued if it meant inequality between culturally distinguished groups.

In seeking to spell this out, I have suggested that it involved the notion of two cultural domains (Rex, 1986b). On the one hand it was thought that there should be a shared public political culture, which all should be called upon to accept, and which was based upon the notion of equality between individuals. The notion of this shared public political culture was reflected in Marshall's notion of minimum social rights which the working class had won in the welfare state, over and above their right to legal and political equality (Marshall, 1950). On the other hand, the ideal of the democratic multicultural society suggested that there should be private communal cultures within the different communities based upon differences of language, religion and family and other cultural practices. I also argued later that since governments could not be expected to carry out such a policy through a generalised benevolence, minority groups should be allowed and even encouraged to mobilise themselves for political action in pursuit of their own rights (Rex, 1994a).

This idea of multiculturalism and ethnic mobilisation was not readily accepted amongst European social scientists, and, perhaps least of all, in Germany. There a powerful critique of the theory and practice of multiculturalism was put forward by Radtke, who had in mind particularly the way in which multicultural policy had been developed in the city of Frankfurt (Radtke, 1994).

Radtke sees the theory and practice of multiculturalism as based upon a dissociation of immigrant ethnic minority affairs from the political theories which had been developed in the social democratic welfare state. The theory of the social democratic welfare state recognised the existence of a pluralist society, in which different interest groups negotiated with each other, and reached the set of compromises which we call the welfare state. The protection of the rights of ethnic minority groups was then assigned either to the Churches, so far as Christian immigrants were concerned, or to organisations based on the trades unions in the case of non-Christian immigrants. Finally, while the political interests of indigenous interest groups were defended by the mainstream political parties, a Multicultural Office was established to deal with ethnic minority communities through their own organisations and through those church and trades union organisations which had been set up to protect them.

According to Radtke, this policy has meant in practice a radical dissociation of immigrant problems from those, normal in the welfare state, which arise out of conflicts of interest. Those from the immigrant ethnic communities were forced in this situation to define any problems they faced as being due to cultural difference, and the most reified notions of minority cultures were used as a basis for dealing with them. Very often this meant the encouragement of the most reactionary and regressive features of immigrant culture.

Strong opposition to the notion of multiculturalism has also been expressed by other social scientists in France, the Netherlands and Sweden. In France, Wieviorka (1994) has suggested that the very term 'ethnicity' is one which is only applied to inferiors. As he sees it, 'they' are thought to have ethnicity, while we indigenous people are thought of as being merely normal. In the Netherlands, Rath (1991) has argued that the recognition of ethnic minorities under official policies of multiculturalism involves their 'minorisation' and, necessarily, their treatment as inferiors. Finally, in Sweden, Schierup and Alund (Schierup and Alund, 1987, 1990; Schierup, 1994) see minority and multicultural policy in Sweden as being based upon a reification of minority culture, leading to consultations with minority elders, which take no account of the new syncretic links and cultures being developed by minority youth, on a cross-ethnic basis, both with youth from other ethnic minority groups and with young Swedes.

These critics have made important criticisms of multicultural practice and even suggest that such multicultural policies might only have served to make matters worse. They do seem to me, however, to be dealing with caricatures of the multicultural ideal, and I therefore now find it necessary to further clarify some of the issues involved, in order to preserve what is important in it, because I believe that assimilationist policies, which in one form or another are the alternative, might lead to still worse conflicts.

In my original formulation, following Jenkins, I had insisted that the recognition of cultural diversity must be linked to the pursuit of equality between all individuals. I would now want to say that there should be no political or institutional arrangements which prevent the entry of members of immigrant minorities into the mainstream and that it should be recognised that, in the second and third generation especially, there will be many who pursue strategies alternative to that of collective organisation through a tightly organised ethnic group. I would also recognise that if minority cultures are reified and looked upon as unchanging, they are likely to involve reactionary and regressive elements, which are at best irrelevant to and possibly dangerous in a modern democratic society. But if these concessions are made to the critics, what remains of the case for recognising cultural diversity?

There are, I think, four important reasons for still recognising and encouraging such diversity. First, it may simply be that the values pursued by these communities have something to contribute to our understanding of the human condition, and that we should all lose by ignoring or destroying them. Second, is what I call the Durkheimian point (Durkheim, 1933), that in a complex industrial society individuals need the protection and security of belonging to a group which stands between the individual family and the state, and that ethnic groups have more than any others provided this, at least during the first few generations after settlement. Third, if groups are not to be treated unequally, they need to be able to defend themselves through independent organisations based in their own communities. Finally, this ability of communities to defend themselves will serve to counterbalance the racist and inferiorising view of them which might be held by indigenous groups. Thus, even when the malign and manipulative forms of multiculturalism have been dismissed, there remains the case for encouraging an ethnicity which is self-chosen rather than ascribed.

What I am concerned with is the creation of appropriate institutional arrangements which will ensure the rights of minorities and give them a sense of psychological security during a period of three or four generations, while at the same time not threatening the security of indigenous groups. The two conflict scenarios which I believe we have to avoid are, on the one hand, that in which we fail to recognise the rights and the cultures of minorities and force them into the position of an alien underclass, and, on the other, that of making special provision for minorities in an inept way, which prevents their members attaining their rights and, worse than that, marks them for unequal treatment.

ETHNIC MOBILISATION IN THE BRITISH EXPERIENCE

Britain, as elsewhere, has certainly experienced manipulative forms of multiculturalism, but if we look at the ways in which ethnic minority communities have mobilised themselves, there is no reason to believe that they are likely to become reactionary and regressive. I have sought to show this for British minorities as a whole in several recent publications (Rex, 1991b, 1994a). Here I would like to take as an example the case of the Punjabi community.

The Punjab is one of the more prosperous areas of India. Many of those who migrate aspire to holding land in their home country. Most are Sikhs, but there are also some Hindus, and in the Punjab the differences in religious belief and practice between these two groups are less marked than is commonly imagined. Politically, however, there is a Sikh political party, the Akali Dal, which campaigns for greater autonomy, and a more extreme group seeking an independent Sikh state of Khalistan. While this nationalist movement focuses the attention of a majority of Sikhs, others, Sikhs and Hindus alike, are members of the Communist and the Congress party. Sikh community organisation is also complicated by caste differences. The majority are Jats, who are agriculturalists, but there are other castes as well, most notably the Ramgarias, who, though they were thought of as inferior to the Jats in the Punjab, often arrived in England after a period of settlement in East Africa, where they were a highly successful group and were therefore able to claim a higher status than they would have had in the Punjab itself.

On settlement in England, the Sikhs have established gurdwara or temples which provide a focus for local communities. At their religious services there are readings from the Sikh holy books, and communal meals with special provision for the poor from a communal kitchen. Nearly all Sikhs, even those who appear to have become Anglicised, turn to these gurdwara for the celebration of births, marriages and deaths, which are marked in traditional religious terms. This is also a very visible minority, because many Sikhs continue to wear the five symbols of Sikhism as well as turbans.

All of these things would appear to suggest a closed and traditional community, but it is very far from being the case that Sikhs are not concerned with entry into and playing a role in British society. In work, in education, in business and in politics, both the Sikh and the wider Punjabi community are very instrumentally oriented. They are concerned with obtaining jobs and defending their rights as workers, often through the Indian Workers Associations, which, although they are Marxist organisations with strong links with the various Communist parties in India, actually adopt very pragmatic policies and serve the interests of a wide range of Punjabi workers, including, especially, Sikhs. They see the English educational system as providing opportunities for mobility for their children, and many of these children have done well at school, and have gone on to higher education and the professions. Many combine employment as waged workers with entrepreneurship, first in small businesses servicing the Indian community and, at a later stage, entering the business mainstream. In politics they have joined the mainstream political parties, especially the Labour Party, and have usually played an important role in the trades unions. In the major cities a number have been elected as councillors (usually Labour) and they have played a leading role in developing an anti-racist movement amongst both the various ethnic minorities and the indigenous people.

What this record seems to show is that maintaining a distinct and supportive cultural identity by no means implies a negative attitude to the society of settlement and making its democratic institutions work. It also seems to be the case that, so far as the younger generation are concerned, the combination of having a strong home culture with an instrumental attitude towards education is a very good recipe for educational success. Finally, it should be noted that in the second and third generation many young Punjabis, Sikhs and non-Sikhs alike, develop associations with their English peers and either move easily out of the minority culture and community, or interpret that culture in a new way.

I have chosen to use the example of the Punjabis and the Sikhs here because they provide a very good example of a community which maintains a strong and visible cultural identity with a very positive attitude towards participation in democratic institutions. Other communities have different problems and in some groups there is a greater tendency to look backwards to the assertion of traditional culture and less in the way of adaptive attitudes. Yet I think the traditionalism of minority groups can be exaggerated. All of them, including the vast majority of Muslims, who are sometimes thought of as the least adaptive, do actually become involved in modern British institutions. In Birmingham, for example, there are some 20 Labour councillors (out of a total council membership of 117) drawn from minority groups, and no less than twelve of these are Muslims. They are concerned not merely with defending special minority interests, but with making democracy and the welfare state work. This would seem to be a very different situation from that which Radtke describes.

A final point to be made here concerns the forms of consultation which have been set up in Britain to deal with minorities and their problems apart from their direct participation in elections and government. Nationally there is now a considerable apparatus set up to combat discrimination and promote what is referred to as 'racial' equality. But local councils are also called upon in the 1976 Race Relations Act to make provision for 'equal opportunity and good race relations'; ethnic minority organisations are now frequently funded by these councils; and there is often some sort of consultative apparatus for a consideration of minority needs and problems. The existence of such top-down organisation, of course, does raise the possibility of a sort of manipulative multiculturalism, criticism of which I have accepted above, and my own view would be that it is essential that ethnic minority organisations should retain their independence. None the less, while many of the minority organisations are conscious of this danger, a situation has now been reached in which most of them would say that it is better to fight for rights within these apparatuses than trying to deploy what are actually rather weak sanctions against them from the outside.

FUTURE IMMIGRATION AND REFUGEE POLICY

It is, of course, far from being the case that the ideal form of multiculturalism for which I have been arguing is actually fully operative in Britain. Ethnic minorities have not yet achieved equality of opportunity, nor is their right to maintain their own culture or to have their own organisations fully accepted. Minorities are still subject to physical attack. But processes are developing which will make possible the operation of a multicultural society, leading on to a situation in which there is equality of rights for all, and where only what has been called 'symbolic ethnicity', which no-one regards as threatening, remains. Through this process the immigrants who arrived before the immigration stop of the 1960s, together with their families, will be integrated into British society. It is a process which involves both the continued mobilisation of the separate minorities and the operation of state and local state institutions to control and reduce discrimination and racist attack. For all its present imperfections in practice, I believe that this British model is relevant to other European countries. It stands in contrast to the Gastarbeiter model, the assimilationist model, and any form of purely manipulative multiculturalism.

This, however, is a policy only for the integration of those immigrant communities whose family heads became established before the immigration stop, which occurred for New Commonwealth people in Britain in the mid-1960s and for immigrants to continental European countries in the 1970s. Further problems are likely to arise with possible new immigrants in the future, with refugees, and with those fleeing from politically disturbed circumstances, from ecological disasters or from intolerable poverty.

There does seem to be some consensus that there will be a future need in West Europe for further immigration, both because of the low fertility rates in West European countries, and because, with present levels of education, there are likely to be jobs which educated indigenous workers will not accept. To some extent, this need may be met from the other two categories mentioned in the previous paragraph.

Refugees, of course, come not in response to labour market needs but out of a need for asylum. The inevitability of their coming arises from international obligations under the existing international conventions. It is to be expected that there will be a margin of discretion in fulfilling these obligations, and most countries, including those with a reputation for generosity, will make application for and the granting of asylum more difficult. In the German case, relatively generous provision made to deal with the applications of refugees from Communism has now been considerably modified.

Not all those granted asylum, or those refused asylum but none the less allowed to remain, will actually wish to remain in their country of refuge. Many will look forward to the possibility of return to their own countries if or when political circumstances change, and if they are not to be kept permanently in camps they will require special policies to enable them to be housed and to work. Many others, however, will seek to remain, and their problems will be similar to those of immigrants. They will also need to have some hope of obtaining citizenship. In dealing with them, governments will need to have clear policies and will have to explain to their voters exactly what the inescapable international obligations are which make the reception of these refugees inevitable.

A much larger category are those who are not refugees at all, but who have been allowed by their governments to migrate, or who have fled from conditions of civil war and social disintegration.

They are likely to be seen by receiving societies as 'bogus refugees' who are really disguised economic migrants. In dealing with these flows the receiving societies will have to recognise that they have an interest in developing foreign policies to bring stability to politically disturbed areas, and they will have to be concerned with economic development and reconstruction in the sending societies. But some of those in these categories will still remain, and they will have either to be treated as refugees who may return in the shorter or the longer term, or as immigrants. If they are seen as immigrants, they will need to be treated in the ways suggested in the previous section.

RESPONSES TO THE IMMIGRATION AND REFUGEE CRISIS

Clearly these problems will not be easily dealt with in the present situation of economic recession and it may be that the flow of incomers of all kinds will exceed the need for labour in the receiving society. If that is the case, the problem of immigrants and asylum-seekers can only be dealt with by increasing the demand for labour in conditions of economic recovery. But even if economic recovery does not occur quickly, these new refugee and immigrant flows might not involve all the negative consequences which are sometimes assumed. There will still be jobs which indigenous workers are unwilling to fulfil, and it is likely that many of the new incomers will be people who constitute a 'brain drain' for their own countries and a positive asset for the receiving societies. Governments should be clear as to what their obligations are, should understand the scale of the problem with which they have to deal, and should explain this to their voters. This would be a very different scenario from that in which such governments simply respond to panics about limitless flows of immigrants and foreigners.

THE MOBILISATION OF INDIGENOUS DISADVANTAGED MINORITIES

The present problems of Germany are particularly acute because of the disruption of normal economic life by the process of unification, compounded by the onset of recession. It would be surprising in these circumstances if there were not those citizens whose own futures looked very bleak and who looked for easy scapegoats and for simplistic ideologies. Such problems are very evident today throughout the former Communist world and are much more acute in Russia than they are in the West. In both cases, however, they provide fertile ground for recruitment by parties of a nationalist kind, who offer a myth of a pure ethnic nation, and are quite prepared to encourage violence.

It seems to me that in these circumstances there are only three things that governments can do. They can address themselves to the real problems faced by indigenous disadvantaged minorities; they have to see to it that violence against minorities is effectively outlawed and to do so must ensure that their own police do actually enforce their policies fully in this regard; and they must see to it that their own programme of political education is more effective than that of nationalist and neo-Nazi groups.

Such policies, however, depend upon prior understanding of what is involved in the absorption of immigrant communities and foreign-born residents of all kinds. What I have tried to show in the main part of this chapter is that this process of absorption can and should be a part of the routine business of government. When we have shown that immigrants do contribute to national well-being and that their collective action can actually contribute to the workings of democracy, we shall be better able to ensure that they do not become scapegoats and the object of violent attack.

My final point, in addressing a German audience, however, would be this. Problems are much more difficult in Germany because of a situation in which several million residents, including 1.6 million Turks, are seen as less than citizens. There seems to be a real danger that even though these Turks are actually to all intents and purposes becoming German, their legal and political status makes them easy scapegoats who will be blamed and attacked as a false way of responding to the country's current severe economic and political problems. What seems to be needed is a new kind of nationalism based upon the notion of the common and equal citizenship of all those who contribute to the economy.

10 Ethnic and Class Conflict in Europe*

ETHNIC CONFLICT AS A POLITICAL ISSUE

Ethnic conflict has moved to the top of Europe's political agenda, and if sociology is to make any contribution to the analysis of Europe's contemporary political problems, its very first task must surely be to clarify the concept of ethnicity and of the structures to which, in combination with other factors, ethnicity gives rise.

Unfortunately sociological discourse on the question of ethnicity hardly rises above the level of popular ideological understanding. Thus it is widely believed that with the collapse of the Communist political order a new regressive and dangerous ideology of 'ethnic nationalism' has come in to fill the vacuum. In the West, on the other hand, it is suggested that in a 'post-modern' world ethnicity is the new form of social bonding and that this has nothing to do with the traditional concepts used in the study of class conflict and social stratification. Everywhere the emergence of ethnic politics is seen as a danger against which a rational society must safeguard itself. I want to suggest in this chapter that it should be the task of sociologists to adopt a less hysterical approach to this problem and to seek to define and describe the various phenomena which go under the ethnic label.

THE ALLEGEDLY PRIMORDIAL NATURE OF ETHNICITY

A good starting point for the development of adequate conceptualisation of ethnicity could be found in a careful analysis of the

---

*A paper presented to the meeting of the European Sociological Association, Vienna, August 1992. Published in 1993 in *Society and Economic Quarterly*, Journal of the Budapest University of Economic Sciences, vol. XIV, no. 3, Budapest.

classic definition of Clifford Geertz (Geertz, 1963). This is not because Geertz is right, but precisely because it is in the use of his definition that relatively precise sociological conceptualisation is mixed with ideological mystification. Geertz tells us that ethnicity is 'primordial' and defines primordiality as follows:

> By a primordial attachment is meant one that stems from the 'givens' of existence, or, more precisely, since culture is inevitably involved in such matters, the assumed 'givens' of social existence: immediate contiguity and live connection mainly, but beyond them the givenness that stems from being born into a particular religious community, speaking a particular language or even dialect of a language, and following particular social practices. These contiguities of blood, speech, custom and so on are seen to have an ineffable, and at times, overpowering, coerciveness in and of themselves. One is bound to one's kinsman, one's neighbour, one's fellow believer, *ipso facto*, as a result not merely of personal attraction, tactical necessity, common interest or incurred moral obligation, but, at least in great part, by virtue of some unaccountable import attributed to the very tie itself.

Part of this is sociologically clear and important. Part of it seems almost deliberately to mystify the concept of ethnicity and to remove it from any serious sociological analysis.

The sociologically clear part of the definition is to be found in what is given in the very nature of human social existence and what is not. What is 'given' includes biological relatedness, territorial proximity and shared religion, language and culture. What is not given and should therefore be excluded from the pure concept of primordial ethnicity and ethnic ties are those ties which arise from 'personal attraction, tactical necessity, common interest or incurred moral obligation'.

Now clearly one must accept this. The few recorded cases of 'feral' children, brought up in isolation from other human beings, show that these children cannot survive. Children who do survive are inevitably caught up, as a condition of their survival, in a network of social relations. Thus any human infant anywhere finds himself or herself with biological relatives, with neighbours, with those who share religious beliefs with his/her parents, with those who speak the same language and with those with whom he/she

shares rules governing his/her behaviour. Perhaps there may be
some argument about the inclusion of shared religious belief here,
but it would surely be accepted that, as a matter of empirical fact,
there is a set of social ties which is an inevitable part of the human
condition. All of us face this fate and it is therefore true to say that
we all have ethnicity.

Such 'primordial' ethnic bonding can and should also be
distinguished for analytical purposes from the bonding with others
which results from personal liking, from having to act together in a
deliberate way to pursue interests and achieve goals, or from owing
someone duties as a condition or a result of services rendered. Such
ties are not 'given' in the terms of human existence but result from
having to take account of the behaviour of others in the course of
affective or purposive action (Weber, 1968).

If, however, all this is conceded, there is nothing mysterious
about the ties involved. They can be comprehended and described
sociologically. What is questionable is the suggestion that these ties
bind us together with particular others in an unalterable way for
life. We do not in fact remain infants all our lives. We may replace
the ties which are given to us in our families of birth by others which
we choose. In doing so we may identify with an increasingly wide
range of chosen others, ties with whom may supplement and may
displace those with our immediate community of birth. This is
another fact about the human condition. Arguably, indeed, what
has to be explained is the extension of the feeling of original ethnic
bondedness to a wider range of persons and into adult life. Since
this is an alternative line of development the task of the sociologist
should be to describe and explain the processes by which it happens.

The first point to be noted here is that religious, linguistic and
cultural communities are much wider in scope than the kin and
village based community of birth. Thus a child may be born into a
particular family and village in Egypt, but may also be a Muslim,
speak Arabic and share the guidance of cultural rules with wide
national and international communities. Each of these offers an
identity analytically distinguishable from that provided by the kin
and village community. What is to be expected is the emergence of
leaders and spokesmen for each of these communities who press the
claims of this or that identity for primacy. What we usually call an
ethnic group is one in which the primacy of one of these identities

has been established and the others arranged in a subordinate hierarchy.

When we speak of a group we suggest that some individuals may act as representatives of others or take decisions which bind others. Their role may be more or less rationally determined. That is to say they may be thought of as communal or associative leaders in Tonnies' terms (Tonnies, 1955). In groups which are called ethnic, however, it is the communal type of leader who is most significant. His/her authority is of the traditional sort.

An ethnic group, or, as it is sometimes called, an 'ethny', will also be to some extent stratified. Such stratification might rest on property or on status closure or simply on the emergence of elites. Where there is such stratification, dominant classes and elites will appeal to one of the criteria of primordial ethnicity, very often referring to the simple criteria of kinship but extending this to cover wider groups based on religion, language culture and territory. Thus, when the ethny is located in a territory reference may be made to the motherland or fatherland. In this way the simple communities of kin and village become extended to constitute much wider ethnic communities.

A final point to be noted here is that there is a difference between self-claimed ethnicity and the ethnicity which is attributed to a group by other out-groups. Very often such a concept of ethnicity and ethnic minorities is used by dominant against inferior groups. The dominant group does not see itself as having ethnicity but sees it as a feature of the life of subordinate groups. Understandably this has led members of such groups to reject the very terms 'ethnicity' and 'ethnic minority'. This should not, however, prevent us from recognising that ethnicity is a fact of life for all groups, dominant and subordinate alike, in the sense of both self-claimed and attributed ethnicity.

SITUATIONAL ETHNICITY AND THE BREAKDOWN OF PRIMORDIALITY

Returning to the specific question of self-claimed ethnicity, the work of Frederick Barth has led to the questioning of the closed communal nature of ethnic groups or ethnies (Barth, 1959, 1969).

What Barth suggests is that the question of who and who is not a group member varies according to the situation and according to the interests pursued. Thus, instead of there being one clearly bounded ethny, there is a *concept* of ethnicity but a number of overlapping *groups* each of which claims to be the ethny. The *raison d'être* of the group is what Geertz calls 'tactical necessity', yet each group formed for purposes of tactical necessity calls on primordial ethnicity as a resource in the building up of its organisation.

On the other hand, from the point of view of attributed ethnicity, being called a member of an ethnic group may be a stigma which ensures that the inferior position of a group is maintained.

A more fundamental reason for the undermining of ethnicity, however, can be simply put. It is that human beings grow up. They do not stay forever cocooned in ethnicity. They have interests to pursue and they develop ideas about their own identity and the groups to which they belong which go far beyond the bounds of the ethnic group either as a primordial community or as a situational group using ethnic resources. The real problem is the relation of surviving ethnies to structures and groupings based upon these other analytically distinct criteria. Most importantly we have to consider the relationship of ethnicity to class and nation.

ETHNICITY AND THE CONCEPT OF CLASS

The factor which is most corrosive of ethnicity is the emergence of markets as a major structuring factor in modern society. Markets generate shared and conflicting interests and, in principle, give rise to groups united solely for the purpose of pursuing shared interests, that is groups arising, to use Geertz' term, from tactical necessity. This is what Weber means when he defines class-situation as market-situation and this is why Marxism is inclined to see any form of bonding which arises other than from the pursuit of interests as resting upon false consciousness.

In fact, of course, the notion of a pure class understood in these terms is at best an analytic abstraction and at worst a Utopian illusion. Those who are united by shared interests never build up their group structures *ab initio*. They employ the cultural tools which are available. Thus the solidarity of the working class in a modern industrial country actually rests upon pre-existing bonds of shared local and regional cultures. What Marx speaks of as a class-in-itself becoming a class-for-itself may find that the possibility of forming new bonds based purely on tactical necessity is pre-empted by the existence of pre-existing bonds of regional ethnicity.

If, however, class in an advanced market-based society is inevitably involved with ethnicity of this kind, both regional ethnics and ethnic minorities entering the society may have a class position. If class is seen as arising from the relation of individuals to the means of production, then the fact that ethnic and regional discrimination places ethnic groups in positions of varying strength and weakness in relation to the means of production, bears the consequence that regional and ethnic groups become quasi-classes or, as some like to say, 'class-fractions' (Miles, 1982). If class is inevitably involved with ethnicity, therefore, ethnicity amongst regional and immigrant minorities expresses itself in class terms.

A further fact to be considered here is that of the relation between class structure and class conflict on the one hand and the status order on the other. Status groups involve three elements. The first is that they are based upon a shared 'way of life'. The second is that dominant status groups see different ways of life as meriting different degrees of esteem so that they are seen as arranged in a hierarchy. The third is that upper-status groups employ strategies of closure to exclude members of lower groups (Parkin, 1979). As Lloyd Warner put it, they make 'ever more exquisite distinctions' to distinguish themselves from the lower orders (Warner and Lunt, 1947).

The first of these criteria of status groups means that such groups share many of the characteristics of ethnies. It is not difficult therefore for those who arrange status groups in a hierarchy to place immigrant ethnies along with other indigenous status groups in a hierarchy of esteem. Thus ethnies are not simply quasi-classes in an advanced society. They also have a place within a status order.

The distinction made here between classes, status groups and ethnies is an analytic one. Classes such as the bourgeoisie may also operate as status groups and status groups may use their superior position to defend economic interests and hence behave as classes. Ethnies, therefore, have to enter a complex pre-existing order involving both class and status.

A final distinction which needs to be made here is that status groups may be differentiated legally. When they are so differentiated we refer to them as estates. In M. G. Smith's terms (Smith, 1974) they are differentially incorporated. As he saw, however, the ethnic segments of a plural society often shared this characteristic of estates, and even where there was formal legal equality there might be *de facto* differential incorporation. Thus, when one looks at the position of immigrant ethnic minorities in complex feudal or market-based societies, they are not merely quasi-classes and quasi-status groups, but also often quasi-estates. This is particularly true if immigrant groups are denied citizenship.

ETHNIES AND NATIONS

The terms 'nation' and 'nationalism' are variously and loosely used. Often the concept of the nation is taken to refer to something like an extensive and numerous ethny. It is important, therefore, to recognise that, just as Marxism envisaged classes as a pure type based solely on the pursuit of interests, so the ideology of nationalism in Europe at least envisaged nations as rational modernising groups *divorced* from any sort of communal ethnic ties. As Gellner puts it,

> the economy needs both the new type of central culture and the central state; the culture needs the state and the state probably needs the homogeneous cultural branding of its flock, in a situation in which it cannot rely on largely eroded subgroups either to police its citizens, or to inspire them with that minimum of moral zeal and social identification without which social life becomes very difficult. (Gellner, 1983)

In its complete and ideal typical form this concept of the nation is based upon the notion that all *individuals* enter into a direct relationship with the state, whether in a democratic form in which all share the same liberty, equality and fraternity or in an authoritarian form in which all are subject to the same authority of a traditional or charismatic leader.

Nations, in this sense, of course exist in a world of nations and the authority of any one state exists only for its citizens. Relations with other states are based upon wars and other power contests. One of the reasons why the state demands loyalty of all of its citizens is that it should be prepared to pursue their shared interests against those of the citizens of other states. As in the case of ethnies confronting each other, therefore, the world of the citizen of any state consists of in-groups and out-groups, and the symbolism of ethnicity, including references to the mother or fatherland, may be used in mobilising the nation. This does not mean that nations are ethnies, simply that international and inter-ethnic conflict may share a basic common language.

Pure nations in this sense, however, rarely exist. Usually the nation is stratified in terms of classes, nations, and ethnic groups. Often, indeed, a dominant ethnic group claims to speak on behalf of the nation. It may suppress other ethnic groups, but it actually seeks to strengthen its own ethnicity and claim that its particular ethnic culture is the culture of the nation.

Because dominant ethnic groups are often less than completely successful in this enterprise, other ethnic groups continue to exist and to resist the dominant group. They may seek secession of part of the state's territory or union with fellow ethnics who are part of other nations, or, while accepting the unity of the nation state may strive for the preservation of their own language, for cultural autonomy or for religious freedom. All such movements mean that if the central state's power is weakened the new modernising nation may break up, leading to the formation of more homogeneous ethnic nation states.

Nations of the modernising European sort are therefore less than stable and unitary, but still wider problems arise when one nation creates an empire which includes a number of other nations. Such were the Austro-Hungarian Empire, the Ottoman Empire and the Tsarist and Communist Empires. When these broke up there was renewed national conflict. With the break-up of empire, the pre-existing nation states themselves sometimes broke up, leading to the existence of simple ethnic conflict, but it would be absurd to regard the conflict between, say, Ukraine and Russia as an ethnic conflict, since the Ukrainians are themselves a nation of more than fifty million people and by no means just an ethnic group. What is true is that with the break-up of empire old nations will be revived and that, internally, each of these may have to deal with ethnic minorities. On the other hand there will also be a new problem when settlers from the dominant nation find themselves deserted by their own nation state and having to fight for minority rights within one of the formerly subordinate nations. This is the problem facing Russian settlers in Moldova or Serbian settlers in Croatia or Bosnia.

If empires and nation states break up, their constituent elements may look to a variety of criteria to define the boundaries of group membership. This may rest on the revival of old nation states or the creation of new ones, but it may involve the positing of new political entities based upon commonalities of language, religion and culture. Thus within the former Ottoman Empire and the Communist Empire one finds the emergence of movements for Muslim and Arab Unity transcending national boundaries, and within these new entities considerable internal differentiation sometimes based upon national differences, but sometimes simply on differences of doctrine or dialect. The task of the new nationalisms is to hold these multifarious groups together within particular territories.

All these kinds of problems exist in the territories formerly ruled by the Austro-Hungarian, the Ottoman and the Tsarist and Communist Empires. It does not clarify them, however, to refer to them all as ethnic conflicts. Some are based on the reassertion of old nationalism, some on the continuation of conflict between nations, some on the struggle for secession and autonomy of ethnic nations, and some on pure ethnic conflict. The task of sociology should be to define these differences precisely rather than simply adopting common ideological language which merges them all together.

Special problems of nationalism and ethnic nationalism emerge in what were relatively stable nation states in Western Europe when they seek to unite. The existing nationalism of the separate nation states asserts itself against the attempt to impose an international order, albeit a negotiated rather than an imperial one. Moreover their own stability is threatened as the ethnic and cultural nations within their borders take advantage of the new situation to do a separate deal with the new centre from that negotiated by their former masters. Even the quasi-classes amongst immigrant ethnic minorities may form transnational networks across national boundaries to pursue their ethnic and class conflicts in a wider arena. It is interesting to note that, while the Eastern European countries face problems resulting from the break-up of wider imperial unities, nations in West Europe have to overcome problems of nationalism and ethnicity in seeking to create a larger international unity.

Finally, it should be mentioned that amongst immigrant ethnic minorities another kind of nationalism flourishes. The immigrant minority becomes concerned not simply with pursuing its economic and political interests in the land of settlement but with providing a base for ethnic, national and religious struggles in the homeland. Thus Sikh immigrants in Britain remain much concerned with the struggle for an independent state of Khalistan in the Punjab.

ETHNIC CLASS-STRUGGLE AND MULTICULTURALISM IN EUROPE

It is commonly suggested that Western Europe at least has entered a post-modern age in which the problems of the sociological and, particularly, the Marxist agenda are no longer relevant; that we now have societies which are based upon the control of information rather than on manufacture and in which individuals are mobilised in terms of consumption styles rather than in terms of class interests. Individuals are mobilised, it is said, not in terms of what they do, but in terms of what they are. Ethnic mobilisation, amongst other things, is then interpreted in these terms. It is seen solely as the expression of a way of life, divorced from economic and political conflicts.

From the point of view of this chapter such post-modernist speculation must be seen to be premature. Individuals in the new society still have to earn a living, and members of the poorer sections of society, who have little choice of consumption styles, are often concerned with the pursuit of interests necessary for their survival. Thus immigrant ethnic minorities above all have class-like interests to pursue.

The pursuit of these interests is not something which national societies are willing to acknowledge. What they are more likely to do is to interpret the differences between ethnic minorities and the mainstream as being purely ethnic or cultural and, coupling this understanding with the notion of a hierarchical cultural and status order, to see the minorities as suffering from some kind of cultural deficit. Alternatively they may seek to control the minorities through some process of multicultural consultation in which suitably compliant minority leaders are selected to facilitate the process.

As against such policies pursued by dominant groups, democratic, working-class and socialist organisations seek to incorporate ethnic struggles in their own. They decry ethnic politics and call upon minority workers to fight with them for the liberty and equality of all citizens. Very often this involves the dismissal of ethnic minority cultures as necessarily regressive. What this position ignores is that because of their specially disadvantaged position in the labour, housing and other markets the ethnic minorities do have particular interests to defend, and that given the failure of mainstream organisations to defend them they do need to sustain their own organisations and culture.

The democratic response to this situation has been to posit the idea of a multicultural society which does justice both to the importance of equal rights for all and to the respect for minority cultures. As I have suggested elsewhere (Rex, 1986b), this democratic ideal should involve the recognition of a public sphere in the economy and the polity in which all individuals have equal rights and liberties, as the democratic version of nationalism would suggest, but also a private or communal domain in which each group is allowed to practise its own religion, to talk its own language and to follow its own cultural and family practices. Of course it is true that this an ideal which is far from realised in practice (Rex, 1991a), but this does not mean that it is not a valid one and it is certainly one which in practice most immigrant groups accept. They do want the equal rights of citizens and much of the activity of their associations is devoted to this end; but they also need to act collectively and for this purpose they need to sustain their own culture and organisations. Beyond this, moreover, they would wish to participate in the existing sort of multicultural dispensation which has enabled Roman Catholics and Protestants to co-exist in Europe.

It does seem possible that a new kind of nationalism based upon this democratic ideal of multiculturalism will be worked out in

Western Europe, though it will have to be fought for, both against those who seek to discriminate against minorities and against those who would demand their total assimilation. This type of struggle will, I believe, be central to the political sociology of Europe in the next decade.

It remains to be seen whether such an ideal could be applied and made the basis of social and political peace in East Europe. Given the present Yugoslavian war and all the unresolved national and ethnic conflicts of the former Soviet Union, it may appear unreal to suggest it. But in the longer run there will emerge new nation states which have to come to terms with their minorities, and it could be that when the shooting stops there will be no other way forward than that which is based upon a democratic multicultural ideal.

CONCLUSIONS AND SUMMARY

By way of conclusion we may say:

(1) Ethnicity is part of the human condition and all people at birth enter an ethnically structured world.

(2) The creation of ethnic groups or ethnies depends on the use of symbolism by elites and leaders to counter the tendency of human beings to grow out of them and to form other groups and alliances based on choice rather than on primordiality. None the less the continued existence of such ethnies is a resilient fact even in modernising societies and polities.

(3) Analytically distinct from ethnies or ethnic groups are classes, status groups, estates, and nations. Such sociological entities generate their own forms of conflict which should not be thought of as ethnic conflicts. Immigration of ethnic minorities as well as the conflicts generated by the break-up of nation states and empires, and the attempts to unite nation states, means that ethnic minority groups enter complex pre-existing situations of conflict.

(4) Normally the entry of ethnies into such conflict situations means that they will be incorporated as exploited quasi-classes, as inferior status groups or estates, or as national minorities. It is, however, possible to conceive of the ideal of a multicultural

society in which all groups have equality in the public sphere of the polity and economy, but retain their rights to maintain their own cultures in the private or communal sphere and their own organisations to defend their rights. This ideal of the multi-cultural society will emerge in Western European societies as the result of the struggles of ethnic minority groups. It may yet also have some application as new nations emerge from the welter of confusion which has followed the break-up of East European empires.

11 Religion in the Theory of Ethnicity*

THE POLITICAL CONTEXT OF THIS DISCUSSION

There are many, no doubt, who would feel that talking about the theory of ethnicity in a country like Ireland, in which several thousand people have been killed in what some see as a low-level civil war, is simply fiddling while Rome is burning. Yet if this Irish conflict is to be resolved, it is necessary to have some idea as to what kind of conflict it is. Some would say that it is ethnic or national, but it is also a feature of this situation, as it is of that in Bosnia, that many see it as a religious or sectarian one, and sometimes the different faiths stand accused of being at least serious exacerbators of the conflict, or even, its primary cause. My aim in this chapter is to disentangle some of the threads of this problem by discussing the way in which religion is related to ethnicity, political conflict and nationalism. What I shall argue is that the conflict must be understood as a political one based upon competing nationalisms and what I shall call 'unionisms' which also occur in other places in the history of multi-national states, and that religion as such is not a cause of these conflicts, but that it is also difficult to see it as transcending them. I shall do this by considering, first, the nature of ethnicity and nationalism, and then the inner dialectic of religious development in terms of its social teachings and organisation and the way in which it becomes involved with political developments.

---

*A paper to a conference on Religion and Conflict organised by the Department of Conflict Studies, University of Ulster, Armagh, Northern Ireland, May 1994.

THE ALLEGED PRIMORDIALITY OF ETHNICITY

Northern Ireland apart, a common view amongst political commentators since the end of the Cold War is that with the break-up of empires, and of centralised and international control by the Communist party in the Eastern countries, men and women who had been held together as citizens or party members in nation states or colonies, have lost their focus for identification and collective political action. In these circumstances, they fall back on ethnicity, and ethnicity is a mysterious force which, while it is beyond explanation, none the less inspires men and women to uncontrolled violence against ethnic out-groups, as well as to great acts of heroism on behalf of ethnic in-groups. This idea has been rationalised by a number of anthropologists and sociologists who claim that ethnicity, unlike other forms of bonding, is 'primordial'. It is convenient, therefore, to begin our discussion of religion and ethnicity by considering a particularly clear formulation of the concept of primordiality as it appears in the earlier work of the American anthropologist, Clifford Geertz.What social scientists should not accept in Geertz' definition discussed in chapter 10 are all the mysterious terms which he uses such as 'givens', 'ineffable', 'in and of themselves', '*ipso facto*', and 'unaccountable absolute import'. The task of social scientists seems to me to be precisely to make the nature of these ties accountable.

What Geertz does do, however, and this is theoretically important, is to distinguish between two types of bonding. On the one hand, there are those bonds which arise from kinship, common language, common religious belief and social practices. On the other, there are those which rest upon personal attraction, tactical necessity, common interest and incurred moral obligation. The first of these sets of bonds is certainly inevitable in that every infant, apart from the few 'feral' children brought up by animals, must find himself or herself caught up in them. This is what I have sometimes called the 'infantile ethnic trap'. More precisely it refers to the set of social relations and practices within which primary socialisation takes place. Such a context also has certain psychological correlates. Because these social relations are learned about, and joined within, the context of the family, they are experienced with a sense of emotional warmth and are even likely to be thought of, as

Durkheim suggested, as 'sacred' (Durkheim, 1964). They are quite unlike impersonal exchange relationships.

The 'sacredness' which is involved in these primordial relations should lead us to ask our first question in relation to the role of religion in ethnicity. There is little problem about the adherence of infants to the simplest form of religious belief. Such religion merely asserts that the social practices and culture of the infantile group have a supernatural quality and cannot be questioned, though one should also note that deceased ancestors are thought not to have left the system but still to be part of it.

There are, however, very few parts of the world today in which the religious beliefs learned by infants are as simple as this. They usually enter sub-communities of the world religions and are brought up as Catholic, Protestant or Orthodox Christians, Sunni or Shia Muslims, Hindus, Sikhs, or Buddhists, and, if this is the case, it would seem, *prima facie*, that they necessarily enter faith communities much larger than the simple ones based upon kinship and neighbourhood. This may be true, yet two other things are also clear. One is that there are an almost infinite number of sub-varieties to choose from within these religions; the other is that, whatever theological subtleties the world religions may raise, their beliefs and rituals are quite commonly appropriated for the purposes of a much more localised and ethnic religion, as when simple Catholic communities parade images of the Virgin Mary as part of their local festivals. Thus religion, while it may point to a wider community, remains part and parcel of primordial ethnicity.

THE EXTENSION OF ETHNIC BELONGING

Before I return to a discussion of the role of the world religions in shaping political communities, it is necessary to consider the more general problem of the extension of the feeling of belonging from the infantile stage to larger communities.

Important though the infantile community is for primary socialisation, when that process is complete it does not have to be continually sustained in adult life. A well-socialised adult will have all the elements of the early community, as it were, in his or her head (though, of course, as Freudian or Meadian social psychology have taught us, the process is not a simple one, and not all adults will be successfully socialised and without pathological problems on the psychological level). Assuming successful socialisation, however, we may envisage a mature adult as then capable of entering social relations with newly encountered others on a different basis. When Aristotle said that 'Man is a creature designed by nature to live in the polis' he was speaking not of simple ethnic belonging but of social relations of a larger more rational civic kind; or, to go back to Geertz's other alternative, the mature individual would form new relationships based upon 'personal attraction, tactical necessity, common interest or incurred moral obligation'. Again, using Tonnies' terms, we might say that the individual comes out of the simple world of *Gemeinschaft* to enter the world of *Gesellchaft* (Tonnies, 1955).

The real problem of ethnicity, however, lies in the fact that not all individuals grow up in this way, and that even those who do might also have, along with their participation in an individualistic world, a continuing sense of emotional belonging to a group larger than that based upon the simple community of kinship. Ethnic leaders emerge who create a larger ethnicity. They invite their followers to believe that a larger group has something of the same sacred and emotionally warming appeal that the infantile ethnic group had. They may appeal to co-religionists, to those sharing a common language, to those who live in a particular territory, or those who share a common history or myth of origin, but however the bounds of the group are drawn, what is created is more than simply another association. It is a community and it has sacred qualities. Such a group is often called by sociologists an 'ethnie'.

THE SITUATIONAL DETERMINATION OF ETHNIC BOUNDARIES

As is well known, Frederick Barth (1969) offered a different account of ethnicity, or at least of ethnic boundary formation, from that of Geertz. In his study of Pathans in the north-west Frontier Province of Pakistan, he suggested that who was, and was not, a Pathan was not determined by fixed relations of an unalterable primordial kind, but that the answer varied with the situation or context. Thus, in one situation, A, B and C would count as Pathans, while D, E and F would not, but in another situation, say, A, D and F would do so, while B, C and E would not. This same observation would apply not merely to small-scale groups in relatively simple societies, but to the large-scale groups which I have referred to as ethnies. An even more extreme version of this view is provided by the theory of ethnogenesis which suggests that ethnicity has little in the way of traditional, let alone primordial substance, but that it is more or less cynically created by leaders with a particular project in hand (see, for example, Roosens, 1989). The two most important such projects, I now want to suggest, are nationalism and migration.

NATIONS AND NATIONALISM

There are two main theories of nationalism, as we have seen in Chapter 9.

One is that nationalism involves a modernising project, and is at odds with ethnicity. But this is to oversimplify. There is the further question of the boundaries that the nation state draws around networks of social relations and institutions which by their very nature reach across the territorial boundaries the state seeks to draw, and within which it claims sovereignty. Market relations are, in principle, universal in scope, left to themselves. Those who trade will seek out whatever trading partners they can where there is opportunity for profitable exchange. The language communities to which citizens belong may well stretch far beyond the nation's borders. Finally, what is of greatest importance in relation to our present concerns, is that religious groups may be members of faith communities of an international kind. The nation state, therefore, claims the sovereign right not merely to undermine local ethnies, but also to exercise control over the market, over language and over religion. Even a liberal market-supporting state seeks to establish a national economy; languages have a different role when they become the language of government business; and, as far as religious organisations are concerned, their authority structures within the state must be, at least in some measure, subordinated to the state, and the social and political ideas which they propagate must not undermine political loyalty. The nation state is thus inherently a boundary-creating organisation. It brings together institutions which, whatever their transnational ramifications, are required to play a functional role within the national social system. As against this modernising theory of nationalism, an alternative view is that nations actually have ethnic origins. What is called an ethnie exists in the first place, but it becomes a nation when it seeks to assert its sovereignty over a territory. Moreover, once it has established such sovereignty, it may seek to subordinate competing ethnies living in the same territory. One may then have a situation in which there is a ruling ethnic nation and subordinate ethnic nations, living either dispersed or in a particular part of the territory, and either accepting their own subordination or developing their own ethno-nationalism and seeking independence, secession or autonomy. Furthermore, where a dominant ethnie has some members living outside the territory which it controls, it may develop an irredentist movement seeking to recover control of and to incorporate its lost members. A political entity like the so-called United Kingdom involves all these problems. A dominant ethnic nation exercises its rule over territorially located and culturally distinct ethnies; it seeks to reclaim, or at least to defend, its own members living in subordinated territories; and the subordinated ethnic minorities fight for autonomy or secession and seek to reclaim their own members living under the authority of the dominant ethnic nation.

Imperial Systems and Post-Imperial Nationalism

Nations and ethnies also both become organised in multinational and imperial systems. As a result of conquest, a dominant nation asserts its control over defeated nations, and in the case of empires the whole empire comes under the control of an imperial army and an imperial bureaucracy. A simple form of such an imperial structure exists within some political systems which are commonly thought of as nation states, but which actually involve the subordination of several nations to a dominant one. This is what has occurred historically in the creation of the United Kingdom. But most of the nations of Europe were for several hundred years either controlled by imperial centres or exercised imperial control over other nations. Europe was ruled by the Hapsburg, Ottoman and Tsarist empires, and Britain, France, Portugal, Spain, the Netherlands and Belgium divided up Latin America, Africa and South and South East Asia between them. The Tsarist empire was, of course, succeeded by the international rule of the Communist Party, but this system produced the essential organisation of the Tsarist empire. Sometimes the dominant nations ruled directly through their armies and bureaucracies, while opening up all the subordinate territories under their control to their own traders and entrepreneurs; sometimes members of the dominant nation went as settlers to the colonies. When such empires collapsed there were a number of consequences. One was that settlers were left in newly independent territories, and were either forced to return to the metropolis, or to seek the protection of the formerly dominant nation.

Some of these problems have been placed at the top of the world's political agenda since 1989 after the collapse of Communism. The Russian empire collapsed and left behind a whole group of independent nations, many of which had not yet sorted out their relations with earlier collapsed systems. Bosnia, which had first been under Ottoman control and then incorporated into the Russian-dominated Communist Empire had the most obvious problems as it sought to establish itself as a nation state. Equally, when the European empires in Latin America, Africa and Asia collapsed, there were many newly independent states within which a new kind of post-imperial nationalism arose. Very often, moreover, the new and relatively weak nation states had to assert their authority over ethnies and minority ethnic nationalisms within their borders.

Nationalism or nationalisms within Ireland have to be understood within this context. Ireland, with its distinct ethnicity and with a religion whose authority had been overthrown in England, was none the less ruled by England. Part of its territory had been settled by Scottish Presbyterian settlers, and when the nationalist movement won independence for a republic in the South, it could not assert its sovereignty over the six counties of the North, where the descendants of settlers were in the majority. These settlers did not develop a separate nationalist movement, seeking independence from the new Republic and from England, but a Unionist movement insisting on their continuing connection with England.

The very core of political conflict in the island of Ireland then became that between Irish republican nationalists and Unionists. At the same time the minority in the North developed its own 'Unionist' movement seeking to unite with the Republic.

None of this will, of course, be news to Irish people, and it would be absurd for an outsider to tell them what they know well enough already. It is, however, useful to draw attention to the fact that this type of situation is by no means unique. It is one complex variant of the sort of problem which is occurring in many places with the break-up of empires and multinational states. Sakharov saw the connection when the issue of Nagorno Karabak exploded in what was still the Soviet Union. Noting that Nagorno Karabak was an Armenian outpost in the Muslim territory of Azerbaijan, he is said to have commented, when the fighting started, 'That's all we need, Northern Ireland!'

A final complexity has been introduced into the Irish situation in that, running in the opposite direction to the process of the disintegration of empires and multinational states, existing European nation states including Ireland and what we still call the United Kingdom despite evidence to the contrary, are seeking to unite in a larger international union. Thus, while the United Kingdom government in England struggles to hold together its constituent nations, it is itself losing its sovereignty to a new international political union, and inevitably developing its own recalcitrant nationalism en route.

MIGRANT MINORITIES

Quite different from an ethnie which aspires to nationhood is that which comes into existence in the project of migration. In this case, some individuals from a group whose members may share a common territory and be united in terms of kinship, language, religion and myth, and who may or may not be a recalcitrant nation within their country of origin, find it necessary to move to another sovereign national territory, most commonly for economic reasons, but sometimes because of political persecution and oppression.

A group which engages in migration of this kind will have two major points of reference. On the one hand, its members will still retain links of kinship, religion, culture and territory with the homeland. On the other, its immediate purpose will be the establishment of rights in the country of settlement for its members. In the course of this latter struggle, the maintenance of the group's culture will serve as a valuable resource in creating solidarity amongst its members. In these respects the immigrant group often replicates the struggles which have previously been carried on by subordinate indigenous classes. Ethnic groups, indeed, may be said become quasi-classes, often entering inferior positions in divided labour markets.

The vast majority of Irishmen and Irishwomen do not live in the island of Ireland. They have migrated to England, Scotland, the United States, and the old White Commonwealth. Emigrants from the Republic, like emigrants from other sending societies, are likely for several generations to form ethnic minority communities with a twofold political and cultural orientation. On the one hand they will act together in their country of settlement to fight their way into that country's system; on the other they will retain their connection with Ireland, their country of origin, through continuing kinship links, through remittances, through maintaining their culture and religion (both the American and British Catholic churches have many strongly Irish parishes and Irish clergy) and by giving support to political movements in their homeland. Though not the most important emigrant Irish community, the working-class Irish Catholics of Scotland are of some interest. They identify themselves with the Glasgow Celtic football team, and a recent study I have seen shows that Celtic supporters support not only their football team but a whole number of republican political positions and causes. Unable to fight these out in political terms, they do so in their support for a football team, since this is an area of life where relatively violent contestation is permitted, at least on a symbolic level.

RELIGION AND THE PROJECTS OF ETHNICITY

My thesis in this chapter is that the major conflicts in Ireland, and those in which Irish people are involved, are political conflicts arising out of nationalist, ethnic nationalist and quasi-class conflicts, but it is now necessary to turn to the role which religion plays in these conflicts. In order to understand this, it is necessary to look, first, at the inner dialectic of the development of religious thought, and then at the way in which religious ideas and organisations interact with ideas and organisations of a political kind. So far as the inner dialectic of religion is concerned, I find it useful to refer to the ideas of Max Weber (1968), Ernst Troeltsch (1931) and Richard Niebuhr (1975).

As Weber saw it, the world religions, with the exception of Confucianism, were salvation religions. That is to say, far from endorsing the economic and political institutions of 'the world' and giving them a supernatural sanction, they were led by charismatic prophets who, like Jesus, told their followers 'it has been said to you of old times, but I say unto you'. They were then required to deal with the world, either by fleeing from it, or by mastering it. Clearly such teaching would be of value to any group such as a nation or a class as it sought to transform the existing order.

Of course this was not the sole theme of the salvation religions, nor was relating the institutions of the world to the social notions like that of the Kingdom of God, the sole meaning of salvation; but they did have this social dimension and it is this which has to be considered, if we are to understand the relation between religious beliefs and organisation, on the one hand, and political conflicts on the other.

Some of the world religions, Weber believed, were based upon what he called ethical, as distinct from exemplary prophecy. They proposed a set of institutions and a way of life to which their members were required to adhere. Islam and Judaism do this, and in the case of Christianity, though it seeks to emphasise the spirit rather than the letter of the law, it does have forms similar to what we loosely call Puritanism which insist upon a rigidly defined social morality. Weber himself recognised, however, that purely ethical religions were rare and that the message of most prophets was 'Do as I do' rather than 'Do as I say'. This was also the important theme of Troeltsch's great book, *The Social Teachings of the Christian Churches*. His provocative thesis was that Jesus had no social teachings as such, but that in creating a radical distinction between the Kingdom of God and the institutions of the world he had challenged his followers to work out what the relationship between the Kingdom and the world should be. What Troeltsch then went on to show was that Christians had at various times given all the logically possible answers to these questions. St Paul's position was essentially conservative, holding that 'the powers that be are ordained by God'; St Augustine distinguished sharply between the Kingdom of God and that of Man. St Thomas Aquinas saw the state as governed by relative natural law, and as being a schoolmaster, who would discipline fallen man, and make him once again capable of the vision of God. Thomas Muntzer and the Anabaptists sought to bring about Christ's Kingdom in this world by revolution; and Calvinists, according to Weber's interpretation (Weber, 1964), assuming that the long-term destiny of man was determined by God, called upon those who might see themselves as chosen to impose on themselves a personal discipline so that they might be tools for his purposes, though outside bourgeois Geneva there were always many Calvinists who, ignoring the notion of the new Israel, simply saw their own nations or ethnies as chosen.

Christianity, according to this view, was extremely flexible, and far from having a single clear moral position could find a version of its doctrine which would serve either dominant ethnies and classes or those who sought to overthrow them. As Richard Niebuhr, having the relation between religion and class struggle in England in mind, put it, the sources of denominationalism were not so much religious as social. Troeltsch also saw that Christianity sometimes produced an organisation called a Church, which claimed to minister to all citizens, and which collaborated with, even as it sought to control, the state, while at other times it produced Sects which were not open to all members of the nation but only to believers. According to such views of the sociologists of Christian religion, then, Christianity was fertile with possibilities of its doctrines being open to political exploitation. A similar account could be given of the relation between various branches of Islam and the political world, since Islam shares with Christianity what Weber called a world-mastering approach.

In the case of Ireland, two distinct religious traditions selected from the total range of possibilities have come to have predominant influence. One is that of Catholicism in which a hierarchically organised Church seeks a close relationship with the state and, indeed, seeks to control the state. The other is the tradition of Scottish Calvinism which places a high value on the conscience of the individual and on democratic religious organisations, but whose members are also encouraged to see themselves as God's chosen people, whether as individuals or as a chosen nation. Having a Presbyterian upbringing myself, I would draw attention to a general rule that the more democratic a church is, the more closely it is likely to reflect the political views of its congregations, and the less likely to play an independent role. *Per contra*, a Catholic Church with a more hierarchical structure is more likely to be associated with the state in the country in which it operates.

The interaction of two groups such as these, however, does not follow from their simply having different religious views or forms of organisation which are incompatible. That one group is Church-based and one more sectarian is largely a product of historic accident, having been developed originally in other times and places and in other political contexts. They are not, therefore, likely to be resolvable by theological debate. What actually matters is that two groups which are, in any case, engaged in political conflict, find their differences of religious belief and practice the most convenient markers for the boundaries of their groups. Unionists are then referred to as Protestants and Republicans as Catholics. In other societies other markers like 'race' or phenotypical appearance fulfil the same function. In the Irish case, the struggle is essentially a political struggle based upon conflicting nationalisms and union-isms, but the invocation of religious terminology strengthens group solidarity and gives it a supernatural sanction. Protestants thus choose what are in effect tribal songs as their favourite hymns. Such are 'O God Our Help in Ages Past' or the metrical psalm which begins 'Now Israel may say and that truly, "If that the Lord had not been on our side when cruel men against us furiously rose up in wrath to make of us their prey . . . etc".' They sing these today in Ballymena, and we British sang them with great fervour at the time of Dunkirk. Catholicism is not so easily used for nationalistic purposes in that the church itself claims to be supranational, but within the island of Ireland it exerts an authority over its members in two separate states, and naturally lends itself to use by those in the Catholic state who seek their unification. In the other version of Church religion, namely that of the Church of Ireland, the fact that it is in communion with the established Church of England means that it also reflects Unionist thinking.

Similar problems exist in the former Yugoslavia and in parts of the former Soviet Union. There the separate ethnic nations may follow Catholic or Orthodox Christianity or Islam and may be thought of as Catholics, Orthodox or Muslims. The difference is made more sharp in the case of the Christian–Muslim divide by the fact that people in the Muslim communities have distinct Muslim names. None the less the conflicts in these countries are really nationalist conflicts. They are not fought about theological questions, but about the rights of nations to territories.

RELIGION AND CONFLICT RESOLUTION

It is, of course, difficult for clergy and religious leaders in these situations to know what to do, if they feel an obligation to assert some of the more universal values of Christianity. They are often forced to identify with their own congregations, because they draw their membership from distinct political groups, and the aspirations of these groups are often expressed in religious terms. The most they can do is to condemn overt violence, though, even here, there have always been clergy who, if not actually supporting violence by their own members, more readily condemn the violence of the other group. So far as the overall political conflict itself is concerned, however, they commonly avoid comment on the justice or injustice of the various political causes, preferring to confine themselves to urging neighbourliness between people of different religious faiths at local level, and to educating the younger generation in the schools to greater tolerance.

I am sure that what I have said in the previous paragraph will offend those from the various Christian churches in Ireland, who would like to believe that they stand for a universal Christianity, and that they are preaching a gospel which should bring men and women together in love and co-operation, regardless of their political affiliations. They might argue with John Wesley that the way to make a good society is to make good people first. But the world is not as simple as this. We are not just dealing with isolated people; we are dealing with people whose very identity is bound up with group memberships, and who will not and cannot give up that identity, and it is the relation between groups which is the real issue. So far as this is concerned what we face in the island of Ireland is a situation in which national groups fight for territory; they may do this through open warfare, or they may seek to make truces and compromises which make at least temporary co-existence possible. The task of politicians in each group is to pursue the interests of their own group in the most effective way. They really need mediators if they are to rise above the pursuit of group interests to the pursuit of inter-group justice.

At this point Christians might argue that they wish to play a more serious political role and to offer such mediation. Unfortunately, however, if religion is bound up with, and helps to give endorsement to, the goals of the two sides, it is hard to see how it can play this independent role. The most that can be said is that insofar as the various kinds of Christianity have something in common, they might jointly address themselves to questions of intergroup justice, and that they could be helped in doing this by working together with other non-Irish, non-British, Christians who have no vested interests in the situation. When they do this they will find themselves in the same position as other non-religious international mediators seeking to promote peace with justice.

Christians in South Africa have faced similar problems to those of Christians in Ireland. It is not the case that there has been a sustained Christian witness against apartheid and White supremacy, although such a pious retrospective claim is often made. In fact the churches lent themselves to supporting the 'tribal' aspirations of the various ethnic and racial groups, and were always able to bend theology to give endorsement and justification to these aspirations. Eventually, therefore, some of those opposed to racial oppression sought the help of the World Council of Churches in trying to find a just solution. But it cannot be said that it was the World Council of Churches which alone provided the mediation which led to the present power-sharing compromise. Its work was in fact quickly denounced by the South African government and disowned by most of the White churches as a Communist/ANC conspiracy, and it was also penetrated by the South African security services. If it had any effect at all, it was by giving a religious endorsement to other mediating efforts. The lesson this offers is that while religion might give endorsement to the programmes of groups in conflict it is also capable, when organised internationally, of giving endorsement to the cause of conflict resolution.

CONCLUSION: THE INTERACTING ELEMENTS IN ETHNIC CONFLICT

What the theory of ethnicity shows us is that there are a number of separate elements involved in ethnic conflict. Wherever groups are formed to pursue conflicts of interest, whether over political, economic or cultural matters, they are likely to become the focus of emotional identification. This is true of all ethnies, of nations, of ethnic nations, and classes. Religions are likely to give a supernatural backing to the bonding which exists in such groups, and whatever their more universal claims and programmes the world religions are likely to be perverted and used for the same purpose in their localised forms. But conflicts of interest do come to be resolved when the parties recognise that they have more to gain by compromise than by pursuing the conflict. More than this they may come to accept what they would call a just solution. Such compromises are more likely to be promoted as the result of a mediation process and this process will have its own sociology. Just as religion plays a part in the creation of ethnicity, so it may play a part in the development of the mediation process. The real problem is that of conflict resolution, of achieving peace with justice, a problem which those in religious groups have to face equally with others.

What I have sought to assert throughout this chapter is that religion is part and parcel of a process of group formation. It plays its part in the simple ethnicity of the 'infantile ethnic trap'; it has its role in the extension of ethnicity involved in the creation of ethnies; it is used by the nation state, by empires and by ethnic nations; and, finally, as empires collapse and disintegrate, it plays its part in the formation of resurgent ethnies. The conflicts between groups which occur at any of these stages are political conflicts which will either be fought out, or resolved in terms of compromise, peaceful coexistence and justice. The problem which we all face, whether in secular politics or religion, is that of moving beyond the group attachments in terms of which our present world is structured. It is a problem which was faced by the Stoics in Ancient Greece who, seeing the collapse of the polis, posited the idea of an international community of the wise. Even they may, however, have been simply providing new rationalisations for the Macedonian Empire. The all-important political question is how to find forms of social organisation which transcend the limitations of ethnicity and nationalism. At the end of the twentieth century we still seem to be stuck with them, and with the violence, wars, and killing which they seem inevitably to involve.

12 The Integration of Muslim Immigrants in Britain*

THE PROBLEM OF BRITAIN'S MUSLIM POPULATION IN A WIDER SETTING

The question of the integration of Muslim immigrant communities in Britain has to be understood as part of two much wider problems. The first of these is the increasingly sharp confrontation between countries seeing themselves as Islamic on the one hand and the Christian and secular West on the other. The second is that of Muslim immigration into the European Community and other European countries. Muslim immigration in Britain has to be seen as partly reflecting these larger problems, but has also to be differentiated from them.

Some Christian and Secular Westerners and some Muslims see the general drift of world history as being towards eventual confrontation between the West and Islamic countries. So far, however, this state of polarisation and confrontation has not been realised. Most predominantly Muslim countries have patrimonial, feudal, military or democratic regimes which operate through secular state institutions. Of the countries which claim to have established Islamic states, moreover, one, Saudi Arabia, is economically and militarily allied with the West, while the other, Iran, sees itself as opposed both to Western capitalism and to the former Communist regimes.

Neither are complete Islamic states. Saudi Arabia has adapted its institutions in ways which make its alliance with the West workable,

---

*First published in *Innovation*, vol. 5, no. 3, Carfax, Oxford (1992).

and even Iran's government now pursues more pragmatic policies than would have been permitted by Ayatollah Khomeini. What is the case, however, is that the ideology of what we may call Islamism is widespread, with revolutionary parties projecting the idea of the Islamic state, and the oil-rich countries, particularly Saudi Arabia and Iran, using their resources to mobilise such Islamicist ideas in ways which are compatible with their own interests.

Muslim migration to Britain is part of a wider migration of immigrants from former colonial territories to the metropolis and originates directly or indirectly from the Indian subcontinent. It is, however, paralleled by Muslim migrations which are part of the labour migrations to other West European countries, especially migration from the Maghreb to France and the Benelux countries and Turkish migration to Germany. So far, the most important ideological influences have been those deriving from Pakistan in Great Britain and those deriving from Algeria in France. Pakistan, although it officially calls itself an Islamic country, is very far from having achieved an Islamic state. The principle Islamicist organisation, Jamaat-i-Islami, has never been electorally significant, though it does have some ideological influence in the present governing coalition of Islamic parties. Algeria has been far more thoroughly westernised than has Pakistan, and has since independence been governed by a secular Nationalist Party. The rule of this party has, however, been challenged by an alliance of Islamic groups known as the FIS, which would clearly command majority support in a free election. There is no equally strong Islamicist tendency amongst Europe's Turkish guest-workers and no sign in Turkey itself of a significant Islamicist bid for power.

Islamicist groups in Britain have drawn their ideological notions from Pakistan but have looked most especially to Saudi Arabia for financial support. It is by no means equally clear what the sources of ideological and financial resources are for Islamicist Algerians, Moroccans and Tunisians in Western Europe and these may well change as the FIS exercises more influence in Algeria. Broadly speaking, the Pakistani-based Jamaat-i-Islami, which bases its policies on the teachings of Sayyid Abul Acla Mawdudi, has parallels in the more radical sections of the Muslim Brotherhood in Egypt, and some of the leading groups in the Algerian FIS are also close to the Brotherhood. There is therefore some potential for the development of ideological unity amongst South Asian Muslims in Britain and Maghrebian Muslims in Western Europe, but whether this is realised in practice may well depend on the alliances which these groups make in order to obtain financial support. It could be that the struggle for influence within world Islam between the political regimes of Saudi Arabia, Iran and perhaps Libya will be a more important factor in mobilising and dividing the Islamic diaspora than simple doctrinal differences.

THE NUMBER OF MUSLIMS IN GREAT BRITAIN

The are no useful statistics of the number of Muslims in Britain. There is no religious question in the census and such figures as are quoted in public debate usually reflect the fears and aspirations of interested parties. Strangely both of the principal opposed parties are inclined to exaggerate the numbers: many British people who fear Islam exaggerate the extent of what they see as 'the danger', while militant Muslim leaders seek to keep up the morale of their followers by claiming large numbers. Thus the suggested number is quite often said to be two million, while more sober estimates by social scientists put the number as low as 750,000.

In fact the most we can do in order to guess at this is to look at the numbers living in families originating from Pakistan and Bangladesh, assuming that the vast majority of them are Muslims, and add to this a proportion of those originating in India and East Africa as well as a relatively small number of Arab workers and professionals from the Middle East, Africa and Asia, known to be Muslims, and a minuscule number of indigenous British converts.

The total number of those living in households with a Pakistani or Bangladeshi head at the time of the 1981 census was about 360,000. The equivalent figure for those of Indian origin was 674,000 and for those from East Africa 181,000: a crude guess of the proportion of Muslims in the Indian and African groups might be that it was 25 per cent and it might therefore be assumed that Indian and East African Muslims together numbered about 216,000. If one allows for about 100,000 Muslims of other origins the total 1981 figure would be about 676,000.

Numbers have undoubtedly risen since 1981 owing to a continuing process of family completion in immigration as well as high Muslim fertility, but the only figures available in 1991 are those from the Labour Force Survey based on a sample of individuals being asked to choose one of a number of ethnicities listed on a showcard. According to these figures, 2.5 million people in Britain claimed to belong to these ethnic minorities, which did not include White immigrants from Ireland, the old Commonwealth, the United States or those from the Mediterranean countries. Of this 2.5 million, 20 per cent or 500,000 were from Pakistan or Bangladesh and 31 per cent from India. Since the showcard referred to ethnic groups and offered a choice of Indian, Pakistani, Bangladeshi or African, it may be assumed that many East African Asians chose 'Indian' or 'Pakistani' to describe themselves and the number choosing African was tiny. We may perhaps assume that, say, 30 per cent of the Indian number would give us a figure for South Asian Muslims other than those not coming from Pakistan or Bangladesh of about 300,000. If therefore we add to the 500,000 possible Muslims from Pakistan and Bangladesh and the 300,000 from India and East Africa, a rather generous figure of 200,000 other Muslims, the total number of possible Muslims would be about one million.

But since we are especially concerned with the integration of Muslims rather than the foreigners from various countries into British society, we cannot automatically assume that all of these million 'possible Muslims' look to Islam as the primary basis of their orientation to social and political life. Many will choose 'Pakistani', 'Indian', 'Bangladeshi' or 'Punjabi', 'Gujerati' or 'Bengali' as their primary identity and may not be much concerned with or influenced by religion. Some may even see themselves as primarily 'Asian' or 'Black'. In this case the number of Muslims would have to be reckoned as considerably less than a million.

A further point has also to be noted. Of those who do claim to be Muslims, most would say that they are 'plain and simple' Muslims. They say their prayers, try to follow the teachings of the Qu'ran, try to give their children a Muslim education and with varying degrees of frequency attend a mosque. It is not therefore to be assumed that if there are, say, 750,000 in Britain, that there is a number of people to whom the narrower and more specific teaching of the major

Muslim sects may be attributed. The problems of counting 'Muslims' therefore are very similar to those involved in counting Christians.

The above paragraphs could easily be taken to suggest that the influence of Islam in Britain was insignificant. It is important to insist that it is not. The number of mosques in Birmingham, or at least the number of places of public prayer, is more than fifty, and there are similar numbers in Bradford and West Yorkshire areas. Moreover, as we shall see later, there are some public issues on which a Muslim view has had to be stated, and the emergent Muslim spokesmen serve to reactivate and mobilise the latent Islam of many Pakistanis and other South Asians as well as uniting them with other Muslims nationally and internationally. It would therefore be true to say that there is a significant Muslim voice in Britain today which speaks for up to a million people and which perhaps has a greater resonance and elicits a deeper response than the public voices of other religions and cultures.

With all this said, we can begin to consider the processes through which Muslims become integrated in British society. But first, we need to look at the doctrinal influences which are brought to bear on Muslims by various Islamic sects and teachers, and second, at the non-religious factors involved in the mobilisation of the Muslim community.

DOCTRINAL INFLUENCES IN BRITISH ISLAM

Numerically, the vast majority of British Muslims are poor people in lower working-class jobs or, since the recession, unemployed. The version of Islam which influences them, therefore, is of a highly traditional kind. Their imams reflect the traditional teachings of South Asian villages. The main division is that between groups who are trying to purify Islam through the elimination of Hindu and pagan practices which have been adopted by the inhabitants of those villages, and groups who although they would deny being anything but pure Muslim do in fact introduce into their version of Islam other doctrines deriving from Sufism. The conservative and traditionalist elements here are represented by the Deobandis, the Jamiat-Ahl-E-Hadith and the Jamaat Tabligh. These groups are opposed in some aspects of their teaching to the Barelwis who are led and influenced by Sufis.

All the groups referred to in the previous paragraphs are Sunnis and, within Sunni Islam, most of them are the followers of the Hanafi Law School. This means that they are amongst the most pragmatic of Muslims when compared as Sunnis with the Shias or as Hanafis with the followers of the other law schools, particularly when it comes to dealing with secular political administrations. What differentiates the Deobandis and the other traditionalist groups is not their political extremism but their rigidity in theological matters. They suspect the Barelwis of adopting non-Muslim ideas through their cult of 'pirs' or saintly leaders, in particular through the belief that pirs can intercede with Allah on behalf of their followers. Such ideas they believe are not justifiable in terms of the teachings of the Qu'ran, the Hadith or the law schools.

Practically, however, Deobandi teaching is directed not simply at questions of theological beliefs but at questions of daily communal and family life. This does not bring them into conflict with the state unless the state or its local representatives follow policies which undermine that way of life. Mostly therefore they are encouraging a way of life which most Westerners would call, using the word in a loose sense, 'puritanical', and they see themselves as having to stand up to and to oppose the corruption and promiscuity of Western urban life, particularly sexual life. They are supportive of local government and the social services insofar as they represent the carrying-out of the Islamic injunction to charity, but deplore the liberalism of British political parties, particularly those of the Left in dealing with sexual matters. 'They give money to gays,' my colleague and I have often been told, 'but they don't support us in our educational work even though we have done so much to stop young people from rioting.' Such attitudes mean that Deobandi teaching is a socially conservative force in Britain, even though their teachings of compassion and charity, as well as their working-class following, mean that they remain closer to the Labour than the Conservative Party. They would not be drawn to Conservatism by John Major's espousal of what he calls 'the right to choose and the right to own', since Islam for them involves a much more compassionate view of human beings.

The Jamiat-Ahl-E-Hadith is more radically conservative on the doctrinal front than the Deobandis. Theologically, it bases its beliefs on the Qu'ran and the Hadith only, by-passing the law schools. With that said, its practical teachings are as conservative as the Deobandis. Apart from this, however, Jamiat-Ahl-E-Hadith has significant international connections. It is strongly connected with the Wahhabi movement in Saudi Arabia which led to the installation of the Saudi monarchy, and its leaders have a particularly close intellectual as well as financial relationship with the Saudis. It has also taken a strong stand on the Kashmir issue, since many of the British members come from Mirpur, in what Pakistanis call Azad (Liberated) Kashmir.

The other great influence amongst Deobandi communities is the work of the Jamaat Tabligh. Tabligh is actually in origin a Gujerati Indian organisation and its leaders in its British headquarters in Dewsbury, Yorkshire are principally Gujeratis. None the less, Tabligh works on an international scale across Europe and in Africa and works not merely with Pakistanis but with Maghrebians and other Muslim ethnics in Europe, as well as with Indians. In Birmingham they have their own mosque, financed partly by Iraqi money and called the Saddam Hussein mosque. The director of this mosque is actually a South African Gujerati. Their teams of evangelists also visit and work within Deobandi mosques amongst Punjabi and Pushtu speaking people. At their headquarters in Dewsbury again most of the leaders are Gujerati, but they are concerned with the training of imams from all ethnic groups and train missionary teams to visit all parts of Britain and Europe. These missionary teams are concerned not with the conversion of non-Muslims to Islam, but rather with reinforcing the faith and the purity of the Islamic lives of people who already call themselves Muslims. None of this activity, however, involves political matters, except insofar as the encouragement of a 'puritanical' way of life leads to political quietism. It should also be added that Tabligh missionaries bring to their work the sort of joyful enthusiasm which one sometimes finds among evangelical Christians.

The overwhelming majority of British Muslims belong to either Deobandi or Barelwi groups, but the largest proportion of these are Barelwis. Interestingly the Barelwis in the West Midlands are united in what they call a federation of Sunni mosques, which does not include Deobandis. What distinguishes them is not so much their Sunni Islam as their Sufi leadership and their Sufi ideas. The Sufis who lead them are holy men who have undergone a long spiritual discipline in conjunction with their 'pirs' in Pakistan or elsewhere. Though they take the puritanical way of life preached by the Deobandis for granted, they go beyond this to advocate a quest for liberation from the flesh and man's animal nature. Such teaching is mystical and involves withdrawal from the world rather than a political stance within it. Its ideas are derived by its British teachers from their pirs in Pakistan who in turn are members of Sufi orders, such as the Naqshbandi order which stretches across the Middle East and Asia. However, there is great similarity between the position of a Sufi and his pirs in Islam and that between believers and their gurus in later Hinduism. Sufism, of course, has in many parts of the world led to considerable developments in philosophy and science and Sufis have often been outstanding intellectuals. There is, however, also another end of the scale, in which the Sufi appears to be little more than a village magician, dispensing magical cures. What my colleagues and I have encountered in Birmingham is a Sufi leadership connected with pirs in Pakistan who are members of the Naqshbandi order, who in their pastoral work with their congregations do appear as kindly village magicians, but who in their educational work have well-developed doctrines about spiritual discipline. They bring to the life of an industrial city a peculiar sense of spirituality and sanctity, which was well expressed recently when the most important local Sufi, Sufi Abdulla, led a march from his own mosque to the Central mosque in Birmingham which he described as 'beating the earth for Allah' and which an anthropological observer described as 'the sacralisation of space in Birmingham' (Werbner, unpublished).

The common feature of the doctrines mentioned above is that they are oriented to the past. They are sometimes criticised for advocating and specifying a way of life appropriate to Mecca in the sixth century rather than modern urban conditions. Naturally therefore there will be alternative forms of Islam which address themselves to the problems of the modern world.

The crucial difference between such modernising trends in Islam and the doctrines of the traditionalists is that they emphasise, not a literal interpretation of the scriptures, but interpretation (ijtihad) of those scriptures to make them relevant to modern problems. This meant for some who called themselves 'modernists' in Pakistan adaptation to Western styles of government and administration and the encouragement of Western science and technology, but for others it meant seeing the possibility of Islam providing the spiritual basis for a universal modern civilisation. The latter tendency, that is to say claiming the modern world for Islam rather than modifying Islam to fit in with Western ways, is the basis of many radical forms of Islam in the modern world. It is best to refer to such Islamic teaching as Islamicist, and here we should mention one of the most widely respected Islamicist teachers, Sayyid Abul Acla Mawdudi, who began his life in a united India but died in Pakistan.

Mawdudi was significant not merely for being a prolific writer and teacher and a considerable commentator on the Qu'ran, but as the founder of a religious and political movement, Jamaat-i-Islami (Mawdudi, 1955). This movement, which Mawdudi insisted was essential for the development of Islam, had what might be called a Leninist structure. Mawdudi would have understood Lenin's remark that he wanted as Communists those who would give to the revolution not merely their spare evenings but their whole lives. He expected an equivalent devotion to Islam from his members. But there was to be only a small elite of full members, whose task was to give intellectual and political leadership to a wider group of associate members and supporters.

Mawdudi had not originally supported the movement for a separate state of Pakistan, but when partition occurred he wanted Pakistan to become a fully Islamic state, which would be conceived of as a theocracy in which the ulema or learned men of Islam would have a predominant voice. In order to achieve this, Jamaat-i-Islami offered its own candidates in elections, but when they received little support it sought to persuade the elected and the military governments to turn Pakistan into an Islamic state. It has not been particularly successful in achieving this, though the present government based on a loose alliance of Muslim parties is committed in principle to introducing the Muslim sharia law.

In Britain, Jamaat-i-Islami is represented by the UK Islamic Mission. This body has established some of its own mosques, but also has a wider influence exercised through the control of mostly Deobandi mosques and other Muslim organisations by a tight-knit and disciplined membership. There are, however, constraints which stand in the way of the Islamicisation of Britain in the manner which Jamaat-i-Islami might wish. One is that it is not dealing in Britain with a society that has the potentiality of becoming an Islamic state, but with an immigrant minority of little more than 1 per cent of the population which has to live in a non-Muslim society. The other is that much of its financial support now comes from Saudi Arabia and the development would be constrained by this fact.

Numerically Jamaat-i-Islami is relatively small in Britain, but potentially its influence may well be out of proportion to its size. It does have contacts amongst the Pakistani middle classes, and through its association with bodies like the Islamic Foundation carries out an impressive body of intellectual work. It will also increasingly produce an educated elite of members with the organisational skills to influence many other Muslim organisations.

Although South Asian Islam is overwhelmingly Sunni there is a minority of about 10 per cent in Pakistan who are Shias. These are divided between the Twelvers and the Seveners. The Twelvers believe that there were twelve legitimate Caliphs entitled to rule Islam of whom the last occulted or disappeared and is expected one day to return miraculously as the Mahdi or the Imam. The Seveners on the other hand believe that there are only seven legitimate Caliphs and that thereafter the leadership of Islam passed to the family of the Aga Khan. Both Twelvers and Seveners venerate as a martyr, Hussein, who resisted the imposition of the rule of the Ummayad dynasty and was killed in battle. This identification with Hussein expresses a strong tendency in Shia Islam towards the idea and martyrdom.

Shias in Britain are divided between Twelvers and Seveners. Both are more likely than Sunnis to follow the leadership of Iran, but whereas the Twelvers are quite radical in their Islamicist beliefs, the Seveners, represented by the Ismaelis, are very far from radical, drawing their membership from the successful business classes, many of whom have come to Britain via East Africa. Generally Shias have not been influential in British Islam but there is a tendency for the leaders of Muslim youth to be drawn from Shias as well as Sunnis and for young Muslims indeed to deny the difference between Shias and Sunnis. Naturally too the apparent success of

Ayatollah Khomeini in standing up to the West and to Neo-colonialism appeals to radical Muslims beyond the bounds of Shiism.

One last note which may be made about Islam in Britain is that there are also sects which seek a closer relationship with Christianity, and the idea of the Second Coming of Christ is easily seen as analogous to the return of the Mahdi. The most important group following such ideas in Britain are the Ahmadiyyas. Ahmad, the Punjabi founder of this group, claimed not merely to be the Mahdi but the reincarnation of Jesus and a manifestation of the Hindu god, Krishna, thus laying the basis for a new eclectic religion. Unfortunately for the Ahmaddiyyas, their success in winning non-Muslim friends has been won at a cost of being denounced as non-Muslim in Pakistan. None the less it is important to note that amongst Muslims there is an attempt on the part of some of them to relate their beliefs more closely to those of other religions. A new opening occurs for this in Britain in the form of attempts to promote interfaith activities, which many mainstream Muslims regard with suspicion even though those who promote them would insist that they are not seeking to undermine or incorporate Islam.

'FUNDAMENTALISM', ISLAMICISM AND RADICALISM

The rich diversity of Islamic doctrine which has been described is rarely understood by British people and any such understanding is prevented by the now common and widespread use of the term 'fundamentalist'. This term attributes to Muslims the characteristics of right-wing, 'moral majority' Christians in the United States who believe in the literal truth of the scriptures, together with those of political extremists and terrorists in the Middle Eastern countries. It imputes political irrationality to those to whom the term is attached and has some of the characteristics of a 'racist' term.

In the sects described above we see the following distinct elements: (1) the belief in literal adherence to the teachings of the scriptures to be found in such groups as the Deobandis, (2) the mysticism and devotional intensity of the Barelwis, (3) the commitment to creating an Islamic society in the modern world represented by Jamaat-i-Islami, and (4) the awaiting amongst Shias of the coming of the Mahdi coupled with preparation for his coming.

(1) and (2) do not have much political significance other than that of encouraging political quietism, and there is little evidence of (4) in Britain, partly because of the role occupied by Ismaelis amongst the Shias. The main political challenge comes from Jamaat-i-Islami, which does not have the characteristics of fundamentalism as it is usually described. The best thing therefore would be to define and separate the different characteristics which are usually bundled together under the term 'fundamentalism' and respond to them separately. Undoubtedly the most important of these would be the islamicist political militancy of Jamaat-i-Islami.

Even if attention is focused on Jamaat-i-Islami, it should not be thought that in its English incarnation, the UK Islamic Mission, it reproduces the militant characteristics of the Jamaat in Pakistan. It may, indeed, be the case that the UK Islamic Mission will work out a new doctrine regarding the appropriate attitude of Muslims to the state when they are a small minority in a non-Muslim society, just as Mawdudi at an earlier period changed his notion of the state after the partition and the creation of the state of Pakistan.

Looking at the sociology of Islam in a wider setting, it is perhaps worth pursuing a question which I raised in an earlier paper (Rex, 1988), namely that of the analogy between the position of Muslim sects in British society at present and that of Christian sects in the past. Here the crucial classifications of types of sects and doctrine are those of Weber (1968) and Troeltsch (1931). As Weber saw it, the world salvation religions (excluding Confucianism which according to him involved adaptation to the world rather than salvation from it) were either Mystical or Ascetic and either Other Worldly or Inner Worldly, with the Judaeo-Christian tradition representing the polar case of Inner Worldly Asceticism. Troeltsch on the other hand saw all Christian churches and sects as having to give an answer to the question of the relationship which should exist between the Kingdom of God and the institutions of 'The World'.

In Weberian terms, the religion of the Sufis represents the Mystical alternative, although it might well be counted amongst Mystical doctrines as a case of Inner-Worldly Mysticism. The religion of the Deobandis and other traditionalist groups expresses not so much a desire to escape from the world but to submit to the natural order of things which Allah would desire. This may count as Inner Worldly Asceticism, but it surely has more of the characteristics of adaptation which Weber sees in the non-salvation religion of Confucianism. Finally, Jamaat-i-Islami and Shiism can both be seen as forms of Inner Worldly Asceticism with the Jamaat committing itself to the creation of an Islamic world here and now and Shiism preparing for the coming of the Mahdi.

Looking at these matters in Troeltschean terms, it would seem that the teaching of Sufism parallels that of Christian sects which saw God's Kingdom as not being of this world; the Deobandi alternative paralleled a whole number of conservative Christian adaptations to the world understood as God's world; Jamaat-i-Islami represents the most militant alternative of creating God's Kingdom or the Islamic state in this world and now; and, finally, Shiism, provides an emotional basis for the preparation of revolution in its concept of martyrdom, and at the same time an expectation that the existing order 'will be overthrown 'with the coming of the Mahdi.

In trying to develop a political sociology of Islam, however, we do not simply have to consider possible relationships between a religious community and 'the world'. We would also have to consider the question of the relation between Islam and Christianity. Muslims often still regard the issues posed by the Crusades as living ones and Orientalist scholarship has perpetuated the attitudes of the Crusades towards Islam. Thus even though there are moderate sects which reach out for co-operation with Christianity, probably the predominant view is that Islam has to be protected from attack by Christians.

The actual problems which have confronted Muslims in Britain have not taken the form of demanding a clear and total stand on the whole of the existing order, or on relations with Christianity as a whole. Rather they have arisen in relation to quite specific problems, and we shall examine how the different Muslim groups handled these problems, which include the attitude to violence and rioting, the education of Muslim children, the question of blasphemy as exemplified by the Rushdie affair, and problems relating to Muslim political loyalties at a time when Britain became involved in a war between two predominantly Muslim countries.

Before we do this, however, we should note that the mobilisation of the Muslim community is not solely in terms of different sects and denominations represented by the mosque. There are other non-religious bases for division and co-operation, and before we can understand the reaction of Muslims on the contentious issues mentioned we must consider these other forms of mobilisation and the way in which they interact with the various doctrinally based groups.

Non-Religious Factors in Muslim Mobilisation

Neither the Muslim nor the Pakistani and Bangladeshi communities are organised only on doctrinal religious grounds and not all religiously oriented groups are organised within or around mosques. The sense of Muslim identity is often merged with or expressed through ethnic, cultural, regional, linguistic and national identity and what is taken to be the Muslim voice is often of a complex interlocking network of associations. Moreover community organisation is not always spontaneous and independent. British society and the British state at national and local level finds it necessary to communicate with ethnic and with religious minorities, selects leaders with whom it is willing to talk, and sometimes itself creates ethnic minority organisations to represent the community.

The primary basis of social organisation in the Pakistani community is the extended kin group known as a biraderi. The senior kinsman speaks for this group. Even in Pakistani villages, however, individuals need to look beyond the biraderi to patrons at village level who can help them in dealing with the outside world. These relationships are reproduced and modified after migration to Britain. The old kin and village leaders still operate but individuals will now necessarily turn to those who speak English or who have access to or connections with British society. There is likely to be a significant struggle for leadership involved in the performance of this broker's role and a claim to community leadership might well rest upon having performed it.

Those who are involved in networks of this kind might well also be involved in organising a place for prayer and for the Qu'ranic education of children. This will mean forming a committee and appointing an imam to conduct prayers. The committee may itself be based on village connections in Pakistan and consist of individuals with shared doctrinal views. But there may also be conflicts, and when an imam is appointed some of those at first involved may leave.

Generally in this process conflicts are sorted out and particular mosques come into being with congregations who share the same language, the same broad kind of village background and the same view of doctrine. But perhaps those who simply attend the mosque for prayers or use its Qu'ranic schools for their children will do so without attending too much to the doctrinal tendency of the imam or of those who hold power in the committee.

Apart from these natural and religious groupings, more formal associations may be formed, including social work and advice centres, business and workers' associations, cultural organisations, sports clubs, parents' groups, and youth associations and movements. The mosque itself might also carry out its functions through specialised associations. Each of these associations is a source of power and generates claims to community leadership by individuals.

The last three paragraphs assume independent organisation by the Muslim community, but part of the role of the various associations will be concerned with handling dealings with British society. At national as well as local level Community Relations Committees come into being and it becomes important for the leaders of the different associations that they should sit on these bodies. While there may sometimes be a feeling that those who sit on these bodies have 'sold out' and are doing the bidding of national and local government, such feelings have not been particularly strong in the Muslim community in Britain and, on the whole, the community has regarded membership of such consultative committees as an important form of political representation. In any case, city councils have taken an active part in bringing the different mosques together. Several of the so-called Councils of Mosques have actually been created by city councils and there is now usually some sort of special Muslim liaison committee set up independently of the more general Community Relations Councils.

There is of course the possibility in Britain, given that most Muslim settlers have the vote, that they might be represented not merely through the election of their own councillors. In fact Muslims have been particularly adept at local politics and have more councillors than any other religious minority, and being a councillor, or even an important figure in a local Labour Party management committee, may become one of the most important bases of a claim to community leadership.

Very important to the operation of the Community Relations Councils and to the political parties is the availability of individuals who are attracted to them. Thus, while it may be true that there are councillors and members of Community Relation Committees who see themselves as acting to protect Muslim interests, there are many British Muslims who are simply interested in politics or in their own political careers. Just how important involvement in Labour politics can be in the life of a Muslim community is shown by studies of Bangladeshis in Tower Hamlets by John Eade (1989) and of Pakistanis in Manchester by Pnina Werbner (1989), although Werbner's subtle study also shows the reverse, namely the way in which community issues are played out in the context of ordinary British politics.

There is a similar interaction between indigenous British and Muslim personnel and themes to be found at a more intellectual level. It is surprising how many of the Muslim intellectuals in the migrant Muslim community in Britain have come to affirm Islamicist ideas only after some contact with British and Christian intellectual life, particularly in the universities. To give but one example, Shebir Akhtar, who wrote an important and controversial book, *Be Careful with Mohammed* (Akhtar, 1989) during the Rushdie crisis, had a theological training at a Canadian university and has written 'with considerable insight about Christian theology (Akhtar, 1988). Thus, whether at a pragmatic political level, or at a more academic and intellectual level, a new group is emerging distinct from the humble traditional leadership, the political brokers and the imams: a group of individuals whose work for Islam occurs as part of a very complex involvement with British society. It would be a mistake therefore to think of contemporary Muslim leaders simply as representatives of an alien culture. Their Islamic ideas and their political strategies actually belong to a very British and Western context.

Another facet of the Muslim community organisation, however, turns on the role of the middle classes. Britain is a deeply class-divided society in terms of income and education especially, and there is now, mostly in London, a professional and business Muslim bourgeoisie who have little knowledge of or relationship with the humble Muslims and their imams who are to be found in inner-city cottages and mosques in the provinces. They have a direct relationship with the British bourgeoisie and ruling elites and are much concerned to strengthen that relationship. They are often contemptuous of the simple and, as they see them, largely superstitious Muslims in the poor inner city areas and the provinces, and they represent their own Islam as a not very troublesome matter for the British. While such contacts may be an important part of the total picture of Islam in Britain, there is no connection between them and the life of the overwhelming majority of Muslims in Britain. Unfortunately there are many British people in public life who will assume that the problem of Muslim integration has been solved because of the gracious interaction of metropolitan bourgeois elites, whereas in fact the working-class majority of Muslim continue to feel ghettoised, alienated and hated.

We should note that Muslim groups, whether religious or secular, are made capable of more effective organisation insofar as they have financial resources. To some extent such funds are provided by members' subscriptions or, in the case of the mosques, by religious dues of the faithful. But it is a peculiarity of the situation of the Muslim immigrant community that it can look to another rich source of funding in the governments and religious foundations in the oil-rich states of the Middle East. Such funding has been generously given but it would be unrealistic to suppose that it comes entirely without strings. Middle Eastern governments and religious groups in the Middle Eastern countries feel that it is important to build up their support across the Muslim world and, not least, amongst Muslim immigrants in Britain. Saudi Arabia, Iran, Iraq and Libya thus all become important players in the British situation acting through the groups which they finance. Which country finances which group cannot be entirely clear since the accounts of Muslim organisations are understandably not available to researchers, but it is probably true that Saudi Arabia is the major source of funding for most groups though the Barelwis enjoy less of this kind of financial support than other groups.

Some of the money which comes into Britain from these external sources is not directed to the doctrinal groups as such but to a plethora of new cultural centres, religious groups and colleges. One such body which has received much publicity recently is the Muslim Institute founded by a Muslim who had previously been a journalist on the *Guardian* newspaper. This body is believed to have originally been financed from Saudi Arabia and its Director was a Sunni. When its Saudi support ceased it was able to obtain alternative funding from Iran. Shortly after this change, the Director, Khalid Siddiqi issued a *Muslim Manifesto* (Muslim Institute, 1990); he said he was ashamed to have brought his family to Britain and that Muslims should establish their own Parliament and should direct their political loyalties to Iran. There clearly was political space within the context of British Islam for the statement of this position, but it was also equally clearly in Iran's interest that it should be stated. By the same token the Saudis could be expected to do everything possible to undermine Siddiqi and to deny that he had a significant following.

One last form of mobilisation beyond the scale of the individual mosque is that of the Central Mosques which exist in some of the major cities like Birmingham. Since these are open to and used by members of all the Sunni sects as well as by Shias, it is of some importance who controls them. From our own limited knowledge of these mosques we can only say that there are conflicts between all the various sects and between representatives of organisations which are not primarily religious for control of these mosques. None the less it is to the spokesman who emerge from them that British people often look for a Muslim opinion.

MUSLIM POLITICAL MOBILISATION IN BRADFORD

The way in which a Muslim community mobilises for action may be better understood by looking at events in Bradford, a large woollen textile town in Yorkshire, where Pakistanis succeeded East Europeans as textile workers in the 1950s and where Pakistanis make up about a quarter of the local population.

As Pakistani settlement grew, both political parties in Bradford actively sought the Pakistani vote, and during the 1970s there was a surprising degree of inter-party consensus between the Conservatives and the Labour Party about the importance of multicultural education. At the same time there was increasing political militancy amongst Pakistani youth, and in the early 1980s twelve Pakistani youths were arrested for possessing petrol bombs, but were actually acquitted when they argued in court that the bombs were for self-defence.

Organisation in defence of the 'Bradford Twelve' prepared the way for further militant youth activity which was further expressed in connection with the so-called Honeyford affair. Honeyford was a secondary-school headmaster of working-class origin but strong Conservative beliefs. He was unwilling to accept the city council's multicultural education policy and wrote several articles in the Conservative journal, *The Salisbury Review*, in which he referred contemptuously to Asian parents and to Pakistani life and culture (Honeyford, 1983, 1989). Parents and teachers demanded his dismissal and eventually, after prolonged demonstrations, he was given a handsome financial settlement by the council and offered early retirement which he accepted.

The Honeyford affair made the council aware that it was not sufficiently in touch with Pakistani or Muslim opinion and, amongst other things, organised a Council of Mosques, through which the religious leaders rather than militant youth could express their opinion. Interestingly, although the majority of Bradford's Muslims are Barelwis, there appears to have been no difficulty about co-operation between Deobandis and Barelwis in the council. Some of its leading spokesmen were Barelwis; others were Deobandis.

More important than the divisions between the sects, however, was the relationship of the Council of Mosques to the Asian youth movement. If it was set up to provide a buffer between militant Muslim youth it clearly failed. Very soon its statements appeared as militant as those of the youth organisations. Crucially this came to a head over the Rushdie affair.

Before we turn to the response of Bradford Muslims to *The Satanic Verses* it should be noted that on a wide front young people of Pakistani origin in Bradford suffered racial attacks and racial abuse as well as very high levels of unemployment. Also, despite their clear Yorkshire accents, these young people were still regarded as 'Pakis' (which became one of the most common racist terms in Britain). It was not without significance that the Yorkshire county cricket team which only accepted players born in Yorkshire extended this exclusion *de facto* to Yorkshire-born Pakistanis, even though many of them were excellent cricketers.

It is extremely unlikely that many of these young people in Bradford had read Rushdie's book or had any knowledge of the centuries' old use of the notion of the *Satanic Verses* as part of anti-Muslim attacks on the Muslim religion. But when a Jamaat-i-Islami journal drew attention to the book's appalling blasphemy, the ordinary Barelwi and Deobandi imams and teachers picked up the message and began to organise demonstrations against it.

Jamaat-i-Islami, after drawing attention to the book, in fact, played little part in the subsequent demonstrations, not least because they then found themselves outbid by the Ayatollah's fatwa calling for Rushdie's execution and had no wish to be seen marching under his banner. In many other parts of the world, including India and Pakistan, the demonstrations died down but they did not stop in Bradford. There were some who supported the fatwa, but nearly everyone demanded the banning of the book. The fact of its not being seen as blasphemy even though there was a law to protect the Christian religion against blasphemy, confirmed for many young Pakistanis that British society treated them and their religion with contempt. Their political militancy, in fact, far from involving a drift away from religion, now involved an assertion of a specifically Muslim identity. It is hard to imagine any issue more capable of uniting Shia and Sunni and all the Sunni sects.

It is perhaps too early to judge the true significance of the Rushdie affair in Bradford. Some would say that it shows incompatibility between Islam and its religious intensity and a liberal and secular society in which freedom of speech includes freedom to blaspheme. Others, however, would argue that the fact that the protests died down in other places but not in cities like Bradford showed that there were other non-religious factors in the Bradford situation for which the tolerance of Rushdie's blasphemy served only as a symbol.

Another issue which divided Muslim and non-Muslim in Bradford was the question of separate Muslim schools. The move for separate state-funded Muslim schools paralleling those provided for Catholics was never a majority movement in Bradford, but there is no doubt that the demand was expressed more strongly in Bradford and West Yorkshire than elsewhere. Muslims who supported such schools argued that it was quite possible to give children a thoroughly good education in mainstream subjects and yet to combine this with a Muslim moral education and, more generally, with a Muslim vision of the world. But to some Muslims as well as non-Muslims such schools appeared to aim at preparing children not for full participation in secular British society, but for an Islamic society which they would create. Interestingly, Honeyford and some other White leaders appeared to support this demand, preferring to have separate Muslim schools to having the mainstream school modified in the direction of multiculturalism (Honeyford, 1988).

A final issue which focused the political attention of Bradford's Pakistanis was the war against Saddam Hussein. This created grave dilemmas for young alienated Muslims. Clearly the Americans and their allies were going to war against a country with a predominantly Sunni Muslim population, and if this was the case some felt that their loyalty to Islam challenged their loyalty to Britain, even though this latter loyalty was something on which many Muslim leaders insisted. Things became particularly difficult when Saddam called together Muslim leaders and sought to pronounce a jihad. Not surprisingly there were different views in the Muslim community on the issue. The immediate reaction was to offer support to Saddam, but despite the fact that two statements to this effect were issued nationally by *ad hoc* groups claiming to represent the British Muslim community, little more was heard of the issue. This was because this was manifestly not simply a war of the Western powers against Islam, but a war being fought on behalf of one of the most important Islamic states, Saudi Arabia. Apart from the political judgements which had to be made, moreover, the Saudis were much the most important financial backers of Islam in Britain.

The Integration of Muslims in a Multicultural Society

In 1968 the then Home Secretary, Roy Jenkins, declared himself in favour of the integration of ethnic minorities and defined integration as 'not a process of flattering uniformity but of cultural diversity, coupled with equal opportunity in an atmosphere of mutual tolerance'. We must now ask how far it is possible for Muslims to be integrated in terms of this definition.

It should be noted that Jenkins does insist on one political value which should be part of a shared culture, namely that of 'equal opportunity'. I have suggested subsequently in a number of papers that this seems to suggest the notion of a culture in two separate 'domains', that of the public political domain which is shared and should not be questioned by any group, the other the private domain of the family and the community. The question then is how far British people and their politicians on the one hand and Muslim minorities on the other are willing to accept this 'two domains' thesis and what they would see as falling within each of the domains. In this final section we will first state what appear to be the major difficulties which exist at present and then go on to discuss the possibility of resolving them.

On the British side it is clear that most British politicians and probably most British people would make far sharper demands in the sphere of the 'shared public culture' than simply 'equal opportunity'. They would probably demand loyalty to the British state, acceptance of the notion of political democracy and, at the same time, the privileged position of aspects of British culture, including the role of the Established Church and of primarily Christian education in schools. They might also question whether some Muslim practices, particularly those affecting the rights of women, should be tolerated in contemporary Britain.

There are, however, also difficulties on the Muslim side. Most Muslims if asked would in the first place reject the whole 'two domains' idea. Islam, they would say, is a whole way of life. They might argue that there are some international situations in which they would have a prior loyalty to Islam: they would see their own family and communal ways not merely as a matter of private choice but as ways which should be upheld in a wider society; they would demand the right not merely to practise their religion and to have that practice taught in schools, but to have it protected against blasphemous attack; some also would argue for the ideal of an Islamic state.

In fact these difficulties are considerably less far-reaching than they appear to be. Let us deal with them in turn.

The first question is that of political loyalty. On this there seems to be plenty of evidence that Muslims do in principle accept that Muslim citizens have a duty to the British state, including the duty to perform military service. Of course problems might arise if Britain went to war against an Islamic state, but in any clear-cut case of this kind the state would have the right to deport or detain those who were manifestly disloyal as well as the duty to extend to conscientious objectors the same right to a hearing as has been extended to other individuals opposed to wars for religious reasons.

The idea of democracy, too, would have to be defended. If there were an Islamic party which announced that if victorious it would suspend further elections, that party would have to be banned as other anti-democratic parties have been. In the case of Jamaat-i-Islami there might well be cause for concern if what they proposed was some sort of theocracy or theo-democracy with the ulema or learned Muslim men taking the place of the people in determining government policy. This should be a matter for serious discussion with groups like Jamaat-i-Islami. My own belief is that, faced with the need to make their views clear in the British situation they would be very pragmatic, as they have been in dealing with political situations in other democratic countries.

A more difficult but related issue is that of the secular state. The difficulty in defending the present British position is, of course, that Britain is not a secular state. It has an Established Church whose Archbishop crowns the Queen. The Queen is declared to be the 'Supreme Governor' of that church, and Christianity has a privileged place in the schools. The recently appointed Archbishop of Canterbury, in his enthronement speech insisted on the duty of his church to evangelise and convert people of other faiths. And finally, it became apparent in the discussion of the Rushdie affair that the Church of England was uniquely defended by a law of blasphemy. It is hard to see how Britain could fully claim to be a multicultural society so long as the Anglican Church enjoys these privileges. It might also be added that the position of the Anglican Church is really only a theoretical one and that in the past two hundred years it has come to be expected that other religions will, in fact, be tolerated.

One question which might well be discussed here is how far the institutions of the public domain should be described as 'secular'.

Some, it is true, would see the notion of equal opportunity as implying nothing more than a set of convenient 'rules of game' of no moral significance. Others, however, would see such rules as morally important, and certainly in our own research interviews with Muslims we have found that our subjects are willing to accept not only the minimal notion of equal opportunity but the whole notion of a welfare state, which is seen as exemplifying Muslim ideals. In fact, if we were to confront most Muslims not with the question 'Do you accept the secular state?' but rather with the alternative 'What do you think about our social and political institutions?' we should find that we shared many common values. Equally it is not the case that the education which we offer our children is morally neutral and it might well emerge in discussion that many of the values we are trying to achieve are in fact shared between religions.

Looking at the Muslim side of the equation the prospects of agreement on the nature of the two domains would at first appear bleak because of Muslim insistence that Islam is a whole way of life. Many people believe that this implies a kind of theocracy in which government enforces the narrow way of life required by the sharia law. If, however, one looks at the adaptations which Muslims have made in other countries one need not be too pessimistic about this. What is necessary is that there should be a willingness on both sides to discuss the issues involved.

Similar considerations arise in connection with the strong notion of the Islamic State. In fact, Mawdudi is unusual amongst Muslim teachers in arguing for this (Ahmed, 1987), and even Jamaat-i-Islami has had in practice to come to terms with secular government. The fact is that there are many necessary actions and institutions in the modern state which are really neutral from the point of view of efficiency. Moreover, theories which have been developed to cope with the problems of Pakistan or Saudi Arabia clearly need rethinking if they are to be applied to the problems of an immigrant Muslim minority. Another important area of argument concerns women's rights. It is generally thought by Western feminists that the Islamic way of life involves the exploitation and oppression of women. Muslim thinkers and leaders on the other hand see Western sexual life as wholly corrupt and promiscuous. But in fact there is much in the Qu'ranic and

Muslim tradition which is based upon the idea of an enhanced status for women, and Muslim leaders would find in dialogue with Western feminists that they were very far from simply defending sexual promiscuity.

Lastly there is the question posed by the Rushdie affair: 'Has anyone the right in a multicultural society to denigrate and blaspheme against the religion of another group?' Here the first reaction of many British intellectuals has been to say that freedom of speech is an absolute value. Yet clearly it is not. Racial incitement in Britain is illegal. Could it not be argued that incitement against a religion is equally so? The argument against Rushdie is not that the Muslim religion should enjoy a privileged place as a religion. Many would agree that even the Anglican Church should not have that protection. What Rushdie's book does infringe is the not often considered third principle involved in Jenkins's definition of integration, namely that of mutual tolerance. No doubt, had he been prosecuted under an extended Race Relations Act, Rushdie would have made a vigorous defence, but Muslims might well have had the satisfaction that the courts did at least offer them a hearing.

All in all one cannot be optimistic that the integration of Muslims in Britain will be easy. What this chapter would suggest, however, is that there is still considerable scope for dialogue which is prevented by prejudices on both sides. On the British side there is the widespread dismissal of all Muslims as fundamentalists, and on the side of Muslims there has been an unwillingness to extend their thinking to deal realistically with the problems of Muslims living as a minority in a non-Muslim society.

Bibliography

ACUPA (1985) *Faith in the City*, Report to the Archbishop's Committee on Urban Priority Areas London.

Ahmed, I. (1987) *The Concept of an Islamic State*, Pinter, London.

Akhtar, S. (1988) *The Light of Enlightenment: Christianity and the Secular Heritage*, Grey Seal, London.

Akhtar, S. (1989) *Be Careful with Mohammed*, Bellew Publishing, London.

Althusser, L. (1969) *For Marx*, Allen Lane, London.

Anderson, B. (1991) *Imagined Communities*, Verso, London.

Archer, M. (1992) *Culture and Agency*, Sage, London.

Barth, F. (1959) *Political Leadership Among The Swat Pathans*, London School of Economics Monographs on Anthropology, No. 19.

Barth, F. (1969) *Ethnic Groups and Boundaries*, Allen & Unwin, London.

Brown, A. Radcliffe (1952) *Structure and Function in Primitive Society*, Cohen & West, London.

Brown, C. (1984) *Black and White Britain*, Policy Studies Institute.

Chivers, T. (1987) *Race and Culture in Education*, Nelson-National Foundation for Educational Research London.

Commonwealth Immigrants Advisory Council (1964) *Third Report*, Cmnd 2458, HMSO, London.

Daniel, W. (1968) *Racial Discrimination in England*, Penguin, Harmondsworth.

Department of Education and Science (1981) *Report of the Committee of Enquiry into the Education of Children from Minority Groups – Interim Report: West Indian Children in our Schools* (Chairman Mr Anthony Rampton), Cmnd 8273, HMSO, London.

Department of Education and Science (1985) *Education for All: Report of the Committee of Enquiry into the Education of Children from Ethnic Minorities*, The Swann Report, Cmnd 9453, HMSO, London.

Durkheim, E. (1933) *The Division of Labour in Society*, Free Press, Glencoe, Illinois.

Durkheim, E. (1952) *Suicide*, Routledge & Kegan Paul, London.

Durkheim, E. (1964) *The Elementary Forms of Religious Life*, Allen & Unwin, London.

Eade, J. (1989) *The Politics of Community: The Bangladeshi Community in East London*, Gower, Aldershot.

Eliot, T. S. (1948) *Notes Towards a Definition of Culture*, Faber, London.

Fletcher, R. (1966) *The Family and Marriage in Britain*, Penguin, Harmondsworth.

Furnivall, J. (1939) *Netherlands India*, Cambridge University Press, Cambridge.

241

Geertz, C. (1963) *Old Societies and New States: The Quest for Modernity in Asia and Africa*, Free Press, Glencoe, Illinois.

Gellner, E. (1983) *Nations and Nationalism*, Blackwell, Oxford.

Glazer, N. (1983a) *Ethnic Dilemmas 1964–82*, Harvard University Press, Cambridge, Massachussets.

Glazer, N. (1983b) *Ethnic Pluralism and Public Policy*, Heinemann Educational Books, London.

Glazer, N. (1988) *The Limits of Social Policy*, Harvard University Press, Cambridge, Massachussets.

Hacker, A. (1992) *Two Nations: Black and White: Separate, Hostile and Unequal*, Scribner's, New York.

Hall, S. (1992) 'The Question of Cultural Identity', in S. Hall, D. Held and T. McGrew (eds), *Modernism and its Futures*, Polity Press, Cambridge.

Hammar, T. (1983) *European Immigration Policy*, Cambridge University Press, Cambridge.

Hoggart, R. (1957) *The Uses of Literacy*, Penguin, London.

Honeyford, R. (1983 & 1984) articles in *The Salisbury Review*, Summer and Winter, Claridge Press, London.

Honeyford, R. (1988) *Integration or Disintegration*, Claridge Press, London.

Layton-Henry, Z. (1984) *The Politics of Race in Britain*, Allen & Unwin, London.

Layton-Henry, Z. (1992) *The Politics of Immigration*, Blackwell, Oxford.

Lockwood, D. (1964) 'Social Integration and System Integration', in G. K. Zollschan and W. Hirsch (eds), *Explorations in Social Change*, Houghton Mifflin, Boston.

Malinowski, B. (1952) *A Scientific Theory of Culture*, University of North Carolina Press, Chapel Hill.

Marshall, T. H. (1950) *Citizenship and Social Class*, Cambridge University Press, Cambridge.

Mawdudi, S. (1955) *Islamic Law and the Constitution* (translated by Kurshid Ahmed), Islamic Publications Ltd, Lahore.

Mawdudi, S. (1981) *Towards Understanding Islam*, Islamic Foundation, Leicester.

Melucci, A. (1989) *Nomads of the Present*, Hutchinson, London.

Miles, R. (1982) *Racism and Migrant Labour*, Routledge & Kegan Paul, London.

Miles, R. (1993) *Racism after 'Race Relations'*, Routledge & Kegan Paul, London.

Modgil, S., Verma, G., Mallick, K. and Modgil, C. (1987) *Multi-cultural Education – The Interminable Debate*, Falmer, Brighton.

Modood, T. (1994) 'The End of Hegemony: The Concept of Blacks and British Asians', in Rex and Drury (1994).

Montagu, A. (1972) *Statements on Race*, Oxford University Press, Oxford.

Muslim Institute (1990) *The Muslim Manifesto*, London.

Myrdal, G. (1944) *An American Dilemma*, Harper, New York.

Netherlands Scientific Council for Government Policy (1979) *Ethnic Minorities, B. Towards an Overall Ethnic Minority Policy*, The Hague, Netherlands.

Netherlands Scientific Council for Government Policy (1990) *Immigrant Policy*, NSCGP, The Hague.

Neveu, C. (1994) 'Is "Black" an Exportable Category to Mainland Europe? Race and Citizenship in a European Context', in Rex and Drury (1994).

Niebuhr, R. (1975) *The Social Sources of Denominationalism*, Meridian Books, New York.

Parkin, F. (1969) *Middle Class Radicalism*, Heinemann, London.

Parkin, F. (1979) *Marxism and Class Theory: A Bourgeois Critique*, Tavistock, London.

Parsons, T. (1952) *The Social System*, Tavistock, London.

Parsons T., Shils, E. and Bales, R. (1953) *Working Papers in the Theory of Actions*, Free Press, New York.

Patterson, S. (1968) *Immigrants in Industry*, Oxford University Press, London.

Radtke, F-O. (1994) 'The Formation of Ethnic Minorities and the Transformation of Social into Ethnic Conflicts in a So-Called Multi-cultural Society: The Case of Germany', in Rex and Drury (1994).

Rath, J. (1991) 'Minorisering: De Sociale constructe ven Ethnische minderheden', PhD thesis, University of Utrecht.

Rex, J. (1961) *Key Problems of Sociological Theory*, Routledge & Kegan Paul, London.

Rex, J. (1973) *Race Colonialism and the City*, Routledge & Kegan Paul, London.

Rex, J. (1983) *Race Relations in Sociological Theory*, Routledge & Kegan Paul, London.

Rex, J. (1986a) *Race and Ethnicity*, Open University Press, Milton Keynes.

Rex, J. (1986b) *The Concept of a Multi-cultural Society*, Occasional Papers, Centre for Research in Ethnic Relations, University of Warwick, Coventry.

Rex, J. (1986c) 'The Role of Class Analysis in the Study of Race Relations – a Weberian Perspective', in J. Rex and D. Mason (eds), *Theories of Race and Ethnic Relations*, Cambridge University Press, Cambridge.

Rex, J. (1988) 'Urban Sociology of Religion and the Study of Islam', in Thomas Gerholm and Yngye Litham (eds), *The New Islamic Presence in Western Europe*, Mansell, London.

Rex, J. (1991a) 'The Political Sociology of a Multi-cultural Society', *European Journal for Intercultural Studies*, vol. 2, no. 1, Trentham Books, Stoke.

Rex, J. (1991b) *Ethnic Identity and Ethnic Mobilisation in Britain*, Research Monograph no. 5, Centre for Research in Ethnic Relations, University of Warwick, Coventry.

Rex, J. (1992) 'The Integration of Muslim Immigrants in Britain', *Innovation*, vol. 5, no. 3, Carfax, Oxford.

Rex, J. (1993) 'Ethnic and Class Conflict in Europe', *Society and Economy,* Journal of the Budapest University of Economic Sciences, vol. XIV, no. 3.

Rex, J. (1994a) 'Ethnic Mobilisation in a Multi-cultural Europe: Introduction: The Problem Stated', in Rex and Drury (1994).

Rex, J. (1994b) 'The Second Project of Ethnicity: Transnational Migrant Communities and Ethnic Minorities in Modern Multi-cultural Societies', *Innovation,* vol. 7, no. 3, Carfax, Oxford.

Rex, J. (1994c) 'Ethnic Mobilisation in Britain', *Revue Europeene des Migrations Internationales,* vol. 10, no. 1, Paris.

Rex, J. (1995) 'Ethnic Identity and the Nation State: The Political Sociology of Multi-cultural Societies', *Social Identities: Journal for the Study of Race, Nationality and Culture,* vol. 1, no. 1, Carfax, Oxford.

Rex, J. and Drury, B. (1994) *Ethnic Mobilisation in a Multi-cultural Europe,* Avebury, Aldeshot.

Rex, J. and Moore, R. (1967) *Race, Community and Conflict,* Oxford University Press, London.

Rex, J. and Tomlinson, S. (1979) *Colonial Immigrants in a British City: A Class Analysis,* Routledge & Kegan Paul, London.

Ringer, B. (1983) *We the People (and Others),* Tavistock, London.

Robinson, F. (1988) *Varieties of South Asian Islam,* Centre for Research in Ethnic Relations, University of Warwick, Coventry, Research Papers in Ethnic Relations no. 8

Roeland, T. and Schuster, J. (eds), (1990) *Een Ethnische Onderclass in Nederland,* Migrationstudies, Anthropology/Sociology Centre, University of Amsterdam.

Roosens, E. (1989) *Creating Ethnicity,* Sage, London.

Rushdie, S. (1988) *The Satanic Verses,* Viking, London.

Schierup, C-U. (1994) '"Culture" or "Agency": Ethnic Mobilisation as a Swedish Model', in Rex and Drury (1994).

Schierup, C-U. and Alund, A. (1987) *Will They Still be Dancing? Integration and Ethnic Transformation Amongst Yugoslav Immigrants in Sweden,* Almqvist & Wiksell, Stockholm.

Schierup, C-U. and Alund, A. (1990) *Paradoxes of Multi-culturalism,* Avebury, Aldershot.

Schlesinger, A. (1992) *The Disuniting of America,* Norton, New York.

Scott, A. (1992) 'Political Culture and Social Movements', in S. Allen, P, Braham and P. Lewis (eds), *Political and Economic Forms of Modernity,* Polity Press, Cambridge.

Siddiqui, K. (1990a) *The Muslim Manifesto,* Muslim Institute, London.

Siddiqui, K. (1990b) 'Generating Power Without Politics', unpublished address to a Conference of the Muslim Institute, London.

Simmel G. (1959) 'Pure Sociability', in K. Wolff (ed.), *Georg Simmel 1858–1918,* Ohio State University Press, Columbus.

Smith, A. (1986) *The Ethnic Origins of Nationalism,* Blackwell, Oxford.

Smith, D. (1977) *Racial Disadvantage in Britain,* Penguin, Harmondsworth.

Smith, M. G. (1965) *The Plural Society in the British West Indies*, University of California Press, Berkeley.

Smith, M. G. (1974) *Corporations and Society*, Duckworth, London.

Smith, M. G. and Kuper, L. (eds) (1969) *Pluralism in Africa*, University of California Press, Berkeley.

Steinberg, S. (1981) *The Ethnic Myth*, Beacon Press, New York.

Steinberg, S. (1990) 'The Underclass: A Case of Colour Blindness', *New Politics*, vol. 2, no. 3, New York.

Steinberg, S. (1994) 'The Liberal Retreat from Race', *New Politics*, vol. 5, no. 1, New York.

Stone, M. (1981) *The Education of Black Children in Britain: The Myth of Multi-cultural Education*, Fontana, London.

Tonnies, F. (1955) *Community and Association*, translated by C. P. Loomis, Routledge & Kegan Paul, London.

Touraine, A. (1971) *The Post-Industrial Society: Tomorrow's Social History: Classes, Conflict and Culture*, Fontana, London.

Touraine, A. (1977) *The Self-Production of Society*, Chicago University Press, Chicago.

Touraine, A. (1990) 'Pour un Societé Multiculturelle', in *Liberation* 15/10, Paris.

Troeltsch, E. (1931) *The Social Teachings of the Christian Churches*, 2 volumes, translated by Olive Wyon, Allen & Unwin, London.

Troyna, B. (ed.) (1987) *Racial Inequality in Education*, Tavistock, London.

Verma, G. (ed.) (1989) *Education for All – A Landmark in Pluralism*, Falmer, Brighton.

Warner, W. Lloyd and Lunt, P. (1947) *The Social System of a Modern Community*, Yale University Press, New Haven, Connecticut.

Weber, M. (1930) *The Protestant Ethic and the Spirit of Capitalism*, Allen & Unwin, London.

Weber, M. (1968) *Economy and Society*, 3 volumes, Bedminster Press, New York.

Werbner, P. (1991) 'Stamping the Earth with the Name of Allah: Zikr and the Sacralising of Space Amongst British Muslims', unpublished paper.

Werbner, P. (1989) 'The Fiction of Unity in Ethnic Politics: Aspects of Representation and the State amongst British Pakistanis', in Pnina Werbner and Muhammad Anwar (eds), *Black and Ethnic Leaderships*, Routledge, London.

Wieviorka, M. (1994) 'Ethnicity as Action', in Rex and Drury, (1994).

Williams, R. (1961) *The Long Revolution*, Chatto & Windus, London.

Williams, R. (1963) *Culture and Society*, Penguin, Harmondsworth.

Wilson, W. (1978) *The Declining Significance of Race*, University of Chicago Press, Chicago.

Wilson, W. (1987) *The Truly Disadvantaged*, University of Chicago Press, Chicago.

Index

246